enough is enuf

enough is enuf

OUR FAILED ATTEMPTS TO
MAKE ENGLISH EASIER TO SPELL

Gabe Henry

DEYST.

An Imprint of WILLIAM MORROW

DEYST.

FIRST EDITION

Designed by Jennifer Chung
Squiggle line space break ornament © Icons-Studio/stock.adobe.com
Hand and eye emojis © Cali6ro/stock.adobe.com

Library of Congress Cataloging-in-Publication Data

Names: Henry, Gabe, author.
Title: Enough is enuf : our failed attempts to make English easier to spell / Gabe Henry.
Description: First edition. | New York : Dey Street, 2025. | Includes bibliographical references and index.
Identifiers: LCCN 2024025117 (print) | LCCN 2024025118 (ebook) | ISBN 9780063360211 (hardcover) | ISBN 9780063360235 (ebook)
Classification: LCC PE1148 .H46 2025 (print) | LCC PE1148 (ebook) | DDC 428.1/3—dc23/eng/20241217
LC record available at https://lccn.loc.gov/2024025117
LC ebook record available at https://lccn.loc.gov/2024025118

ISBN 978-0-06-336021-1

25 26 27 28 29 LBC 5 4 3 2 1

To Roothee

Those people spell best who do not know how to spell.

—Benjamin Franklin

Real *G*s move in silence like lasagna.

—Lil Wayne

Contents

Introduction *xi*

Part I: Washington, D.C., 2010 1

1. A Man of Letters *5*
2. English: A Simplified History *11*
3. The Faýer, Sun, and Holi Ghoost *22*
4. O Spare, We Beseech You, Our Mother-Tongue! *32*
5. A Nue Merrykin Dikshunary *47*

Part II: Illinois, 1859 61

6. The Phunny Phellows *63*
7. The Deseret Alphabet *70*
8. The Charge of Suffragist Shorthanders *79*
9. Frĕdum Speling *88*
10. The Sentenial Ekspozishun *97*

Part III: Washington, D.C., 1906 109

11. Ruzevelt Speling *111*
12. Ye Olde or the Nu? *126*
13. Our Drunken Alphabet *134*
14. Hi Soesiety *141*

Part IV: Washington, D.C., 1962   151

15. Mad Men   *155*
16. Cn U Rd Ths?   *164*
17. Shaw(t)hand   *176*
18. Kool Kidz   *186*
19. Εεzy Rεεding   *197*
20. Nothing Compares 2 U   *204*
21. Txtspk   *221*

An (Abbreviated) Dictionary of Simplified Spelling   *235*
Muzik and Liriks   *242*
Acknowledgments   *248*
Notes   *250*
Index   *277*

Introduction

Why does the *G* in *wage* sound different from the *G* in *wag*? Why does *C* begin both *crease* and *cease*? And why is it funny when a phonologist falls, but not polight to laf about it?

Anyone who has the misfortune to write in English will, every now and then, struggle with its spelling. In our woeful orthography, *choir* and *liar* rhyme, *daughter* and *laughter* don't, and God help you if you encounter a *pterodactyl* out in the wild. There's an old British joke, first told around 1855, about a nervous schoolboy who is called upon to spell the word *fish*. He understands *just* enough about English spelling to be utterly confused by it. He knows that *GH* makes the sound of an *F* in *tough*, *O* sounds like an *I* in *women*, and *TI* is pronounced *SH* in *station*. And so he recites this combination:

G-H-O-T-I

There's a reason spelling bees are only common in English-speaking countries: English spelling is absurd.

So why do we continue to use it? If our system of writing words is so tragically inconsistent—from the unpronounced *B* in *doubt* to the ghostly whisper of an *R* in *colonel*—why haven't we standardized it, phoneticized it, brought it into line? How many brave linguists have ever had the courage to state, in a declaration of phonetic revolt, "Enough is *enuf*"?

The answer: *many.* In the comic annals of linguistic history, legions of rebel wordsmiths have died on the hill of spelling reform, risking their reputations to bring English into the realm of the rational. This book is about them: Mark Twain, Eliza Burnz, Benjamin Franklin, George Bernard Shaw, Noah Webster, and the innumerable others who, for a time in their lives, became fanatically occupied with writing *laf* instead of *laugh, tung* for *tongue, fyzics* for *physics,* and *dawter* for *daughter* (and tried futilely to get everyone around them to do it too).

For most of these "simplified spellers," the passion was intense but short-lived—a temporary project abandoned for lack of support and abundance of ridicule. For others, simplified spelling became a lifelong obsession.

~~~~~

Learning to spell in English can be a harrowing experience. According to a study in the *British Journal of Psychology,* children take two to three times longer to grasp English spelling, compared to more phonetic orthographies like German or Spanish. And what do we do with our extra schooling? We memorize little rhymed sayings like "*i* before *e* except after *c,*" a rule that has so many exceptions that it's not even worth calling a rule. We study the eight pronunciations—yes, *eight*—of the letter quartet *ough.* We learn that *row* rows your boat and *roe* goes on your plate, and that a *rose* is not *arose* despite what the poets say. (Interestingly, this is also what makes our language good for punning.)

The heart of our problem, linguists tell us, is this: English has 44 sounds but only 26 letters. To make up for those missing 18 phonemes, some letters are forced to work multiple jobs. *C* performs three roles in *cup, lace,* and *charge. H* helps out in *honor, thicket,* and *laugh.* If 26 employees had to cover 44 positions, the work would suffer, and so would those employees.

Another problem is this: Every sound in English has, on average, four ways of spelling it. Ask a toddler to spell *cat*. Then ask them to spell *kid, chrome,* and *queen*. Watch their face as they develop a hatred for English in real time—then ask them to spell *face*. Our spelling is so vexing, in fact, that even William Shakespeare misspelled his name—repeatedly. Of the six signatures he left behind, no two are spelled alike, and his surname appears on official documents variously as Sakspere, Shakespeer, and Shaxpyere. If even our best English writers couldn't spell, what chance do the young spellers of today have?

Questions like this have plagued us since, well, the Plague, and we've been trying to find solutions for nearly as long. Ormin, a medieval monk, sought to bring order to English orthography by addinng morre letterrs to worrds. Auguste Thibaudin, a London professor, tried 9dding n3mbers. Our ideas for simplifying spelling have ranged from the rashonal to the redikulus to the döunnryt ubsërrd, and with each whimsical solution we seem to get further away from cognitive stability.

I first encountered one of these "solutions" in college. One day, a Wednesday—I remember because I'd had to spell it—a college professor of mine projected an old Revolutionary War–era text on a large screen in front of the class. It looked entirely typical of the times, all sepia toned and faded, but the spelling seemed strangely modern, even childlike: *ruf, laf, thru, tho, hav, pleez, beleev*.

This was called "simplified spelling," Professor Palencsar explained, and despite its somewhat silly appearance it was an earnest movement, led by some very earnest adults, to reform the way we spell. It had roots stretching back centuries and advocates from every field of learning. It once had the backing of the world's richest man, America's highest-selling author, and the president of the

United States, all at the same time. And yet, for all that star-studded support, the public never took simplified spelling even remotely seriously. One look at some of its literature and it's easy to see why:

THE PIONEER
OV SIMPLIFIED SPELING.

VOL. III, No. 6.	JUUN 1914.

OUR PETISHON.

WE ar nou raizing a Petishon bi meenz ov which we hoep tu obtain a Roial Komishon on the kwestion ov Speling Reform. With the ko-operaishon ov our reederz we shal obtain a larj number ov signatyurz and thus maik a sukses ov an enterpriez in which numberz tel.

Simplified spelling is a curio, a fascinating "What If" in the annals of language and history. What if Noah Webster, author of the definitive American dictionary, succeeded in removing all silent letters from his pages instead of the occasional *U* (*colour*), *K* (*publick*), and *O* (*diarrhoea*)? What if Parliament passed its 1953 bill to rid Inglish uv al speling iregyularitiz? What if the Victorian fad for "rebus" poetry inspired every1 in England 2 start spelling like twenty-first-century teens? These questions still hang in the air as texting and social media carry the movement into the digital age, where the swift pace of online exchanges pushes us all 2ward simplification, and abridgments like *thru* and *tho* are more common than Noah Webster ever imagined when he proposed them in 1789.

As you turn these pages, I invite you to ponder the What Ifs, the Why Nots, the What the Hells, and the curious cast of pedantic obsessives who comprise this unsung movement to reform our language. You're welcome to sneer. You're welcome to scoff. But every so often, take a moment to cheer on these intrepid reformers as they toil, quills poised over parchment (and now fingers over touchscreens), attempting to solve the grand conundrum of English spelling. Who knows? They might have the last laf yet.

Part I

Washington, D.C., 2010

The flash of cameras and buzz of anticipation fill the ballroom of the Grand Hyatt Hotel as the Scripps National Spelling Bee begins. In their last quiet moments before the telecast goes live, America's prodigy spellers peer into their dog-eared dictionaries and color-coded note cards, chanting through their practiced mnemonics and quietly mouthing their problem words:

P-S-A-M-M-O-P-H-I-L-E, noun, Greek: a plant or animal that thrives in sandy areas.

P-L-U-M-B-I-F-E-R-O-U-S, adjective, Latin: containing or yielding lead.

B-O-U-I-L-L-A-B-A-I-S-S-E, noun, French: a type of fish stew.

A young contestant steps up to the microphone. The moderator announces the word, defines it, and then the room plunges into silence. The contestant leafs through pages in her mind. She writes the word in the air with her fingers. The ticking seconds seem to stretch into infinity, etching the tension deeper, deeper, until finally she starts to spell.

E-N-O-U...

The first Scripps champion was an 11-year-old boy from Kentucky. His winning word was *gladiolus*, a flower genus meaning "little sword," a Latin cousin of the word *gladiator*. For this, he won $500 and a visit with Calvin Coolidge. Since then, gladiolus flowers have been part of the iconography of the bee, encircling the Scripps trophy with their bright petal blades. And as these little gladiators duel for the national prize, they demonstrate their understanding or misunderstanding of a linguistic universe that has been millennia in the making—a universe that continues to evolve and expand even as they stand onstage, spellbound by the gravity of the task before them.

And then the contest is over. A winner is announced, confetti flutters from the ceiling, and the audience files out.

As they exit the building, winners or losers, they are confronted by a strange group of protestors. One is dressed like Benjamin Franklin. Others are dressed like bumblebees. They are holding up signs. One reads, "Spelling shuud be lojical!" Another says, "All you need is L-U-V!"

These are the last of the simplified spellers—relics of a fanatical and (mostly) fruitless movement that tried to change the way we write our language. At its peak, the simplified spelling movement boasted hundreds of thousands of energized supporters. Today, only a few hundred are left. They run a smattering of websites and Facebook pages. They hold quarterly video calls and post their discussions to YouTube. And every few years, when the energy is there, a few of them make their way to the nation's capital to picket the bee.

A bumblebee drops his sign for a moment to fix his antennae. Ben Franklin chats with a passerby about the Founding Father's advocacy for simplified spelling. A woman steps forward carrying a tray of brightly colored buttons. Written across each is the same message, a rallying cry. It is more than just a piece of metal; this button is a badge of protest. It embodies the fading spirit of the movement and imagines a future in which English spelling is truly as simple as sounding it out. It's a future she believes in, one she has condensed into a wearable statement, a modest accessory, a sartorial contrast to her friend over there in the powdered wig.

"Enuf is enuf," reads the button. "But enough is too much."

1

A Man of Letters

orthografi (*n*) • The art ov riting wurdz with the korekt letterz, akording tu kommon usaj

Benjamin Franklin never cared much for "good" spelling—that is, spelling as it appears in this sentence and in most English books since the eighteenth century. A man of reason and science, he viewed traditional English orthography as pure irrational nonsense, with its fickle silent *E*'s, erratic *ough*s, and stubborn allegiance to the forms of the past. Franklin lived his life by a set of principles, and English spelling seemed to go against many of them:

- It impedes education, requiring nearly three times longer to learn than French or Spanish spelling. (Franklin did not like wasting time.)
- It is economically inefficient, with its superfluous silent letters stretching the page counts of books and running up printers' costs. (Franklin did not like wasting money.)
- And it is painfully inconsistent, with *G* doing triple duty in *wage, wag,* and *weigh* and *T* spread thin between *throne, table, natural, nation,* and *them*—all while poor *Q*, the wallflower of Roman letters, just stands around, waiting for its *U*. (Franklin did not like waiting.)

So, in 1768, armed with nothing but his wits and a quill (and a revolutionary zeal he would later bring to America's War of Independence), Franklin embarked on a campaign to transform the alphabet.

He began by eliminating the letter *C*; all *C* sounds, according to Franklin's new system, would now be the domain of *K* and *S*, as in *kup* (*cup*) and *sity* (*city*). Next, he nixed *Q* and *X*, those low-frequency, high-value Scrabble favorites, and again passed their duties to *K* and *S*, as in *kuestion* (*question*) and *ekstrakt* (*extract*). *W*, too, got the boot—it is quite literally a redundant *U*—and likewise *Y*, which can be replaced in most instances by *I*. The last letter to go was *J*: frankly, before *J* joined the alphabet in 1524, we had been getting along gust fine.

After purging these unnecessary letters, that dead weight that kept English in the Dark Ages, Franklin invented six new ones and assigned them the following sounds:

Letter	Name	Sound
ɑ	Aw	*O*, as in *folly*
ʮ	Uh	*UM*, as in *umbrage*
ħ	Ish	*SH*, as in *ship*
ŋ	Ing	*ING*, as in *writing*
ħ	Eth	soft *TH*, as in *think*
ħ	Edh	hard *TH*, as in *that*

As a final phoneticizing measure, Franklin developed a technique for conveying long vowels. The *A* sound in words like *remain* and *late* would be written as a double *E*. The long *E*, naturally, would be written as a double *I*. *Remain* and *late* were now *remeen* and *leet*. *Seized* and *teased* were *siized* and *tiised*. *Pleased* was *pliised*, and so was Franklin.

Since his early childhood, Franklin had been driven to *invent*. In the summer of his eleventh year, he took two oval wooden planks, fashioned them to fit over his palms, and used them to paddle through the Charles River in Boston, thereby inventing the modern swim fins. By the time America broke away from Britain in 1776, Franklin had given the world the Franklin stove (a metal-lined fireplace designed for better heating and less smoke); the flexible catheter; the glass armonica; and an early version of an odometer that counted the revolutions of his carriage wheels and outputted a rough mileage estimate. In the last few years of his life, as his body weakened but his mind still hungered for knowledge, Franklin would invent an extendable arm that allowed him to reach books off high shelves in his study.

But *this* wasn't like his other inventions. It wasn't a physical object; it was a linguistic tool, an efficient new system of communication that would touch every stratum of English-speaking society. It was also America's first foray into phonetic science—proof of what can be achieved when rational analysis is applied to language. Eager to share his design with a world gasping for linguistic clarity, Franklin sent his proposal, "A Scheme for a New Alphabet and Reformed Mode of Spelling," to his closest confidante, the one person who could be counted on to champion his wildest ideas: Mary "Polly" Stevenson, the 29-year-old daughter of his landlady. In his accompanying letter, dated "Dƕulɥi" (July) 1768, Franklin makes his plea (translated in the footnotes on the next page):

Diir Pɑli,

ɥi intended to hev sent iu ħiz Pepers sunɥr, bɥt biiŋ bizi fɑrgɑt it . . .

ɥi uiħ iu to kɑnsider ħis Alfabet, and giv mi
Instanses ɑf syħ Iŋlis Uɥrds and Sɑunds az iu mee
ħink kannɑt perfektlɥi bi eksprest bɥi it. ɥi am
persueeded it mee bi kɑmplited bɥi iur help . . .
    ɥi am, mɥi diir Frend, Iurz afekħɥnetli,

                                              B. Franklin*

For a moment, Polly might have dismissed this as another one
of Franklin's jokes. He was a consummate prankster, after all. (His
1781 "Letter to a Royal Academy," which proposed scientific im-
provements for the odor of flatulence, is legendary.) The idea that
he might craft a comically unreadable system of writing and tout it
as "scientific advancement" was certainly his brand of humor. But
Franklin's gags typically ran in newspapers, not in personal cor-
respondences, and Polly soon realized that this gloriously incom-
prehensible spelling was, in fact, a serious proposal. She decided to
master Franklin's new writing system—and two months later, in a
letter dated "Septembɥr" 1768, Polly sent back her phonetic two
cents:

    Diir Sɥr,

    ɥi have transkrɥib'd iur Alfabet &c. huitħ ɥi ħink
    mɥit bi ɑv sɥrvis tu ħoz hu uiħ tu akuɥir an
    akiuret pronɥnsieħɥn if ħat kuld bi fiks'd, bɥt ɥi si
    meni inkɑnvinienses az uel az difikultis ħat uuld

---

*   Tr: "Dear Polly, I intended to have sent you these Papers sooner, but being busy forgot
it . . . I wish you to consider this Alphabet, and give me Instances of such English Words
and Sounds as you may think cannot perfectly be expressed by it. I am persuaded it may
be completed by your help . . . I am, my dear Friend, Yours affectionately, B. Franklin."

atend ḥi briŋiŋ iur letʏrs & ɑrḥagrafi intu kɑmʏn
ius.*

Polly then proceeds to list all the "difikultis" she sees in Franklin's alphabet:

It would erase all the "etimɑlodḥis" ("etymologies") that language enthusiasts like her love, as in the Greek root *logia* in *etymology*;

It would muddle "ḥi distinkʃʏn . . . bituiin uʏrds ɑv difʏrent miiniŋ & similar sɑund" ("the distinction . . . between words of different meaning & similar sound"), as in the homophonic pairs *meet/meat* and *sun/son*;

And it would render obsolete "ɑɑl ḥi buks ɑlredi riten" ("all the books already written"), as their current library of English literature—every scroll, folio, and manuscript—would eventually become unintelligible to future generations of Franklinian spellers.

Polly Stevenson, depicted here in 1770, casts what might be a disapproving eye over Benjamin Franklin's new alphabet.

In short, she says, "ui mʏst let pipil spel ɑn in ḥeer old ue"—"We must let people spell on in their old way"—and do the same ourselves.

Polly might've gone on criticizing Franklin's proposal, but one paragraph in his spelling is all she can muster. As she loses orthographic steam, she resorts to standard Eng-

---

* Tr: "Dear Sir, I have transcribed your Alphabet &c. which I think might be of Service to those who wish to acquire an accurate pronunciation if that could be fix'd, but I see many inconveniences as well as difficulties that would attend the bringing your letters and orthography into common use."

lish. "With ease & with sincerity," she signs off her letter, "I can in the old way subscribe myself . . ." The sigh of relief is almost audible.

And with that, Franklin's short-lived campaign was effectively over. He thanked Polly for her "well-spelt" feedback, slipped his "Scheme for a New Alphabet" into a drawer, and moved on like it never happened.

$$\sim\!\sim\!\sim\!\sim$$

Franklin's experience is typical. Wherever history finds a simplified speller, the story follows a similar arc. It begins with a burst of enthusiasm. The reformer, believing they've discovered the cure for English's centuries-long woes, announces their plan to simplify conventional spelling. The design is comprehensive—here they've removed the silent *I* in *friend,* there they've turned *chaos* into *kaos.* But as they present their ideas to the unsuspecting public, they find that *change,* especially in language, faces stiff resistance from a society rooted in tradition. In the best case, the world will respond to their proposal with a collective shrug of indifference. In the worst case, it'll unleash upon the reformer a sustained barrage of mockery and scorn that forever will tarnish their name and reduce their legacy to a punch line.

Their conviction withers. Embarrassment takes hold. At this point, some reformers will simply let their idea fade into silent oblivion, never to be spoken of again. Others, overcome with shame, will publicly disavow their linguistic treasons in an attempt to claw back some dignity. And then there are the indomitable few, unswayed by the pushback, who will press forward in the face of ridicule, thru hel and hi water, driven by a clear and unwavering vision of linguistic utopia.

English: A Simplified History

> Our language is a rich verbal tapestry woven together
> from the tongues of the Greeks, the Latins, the Angles, the
> Klaxtons, the Celtics, the 76ers and many other ancient
> peoples, all of whom had severe drinking problems.
>
> —Dave Barry

Benjamin Franklin wasn't the first simplified speller, nor among the first dozen. By the time he came along in 1768 with his "Scheme for a New Alphabet," the language had already fought off many zealous simplifiers bent on reshaping English in their ideal image.

The first English spelling reformer was a twelfth-century monk known as Ormin—a name that once meant "dragon man" in Old Norse but which translates, less flatteringly, into Modern English as "worm man." Ormin lived during the era of Middle English, a time when the concept of standardized spelling didn't exist. To write a simple word like *though*, you could either (a) make up your own spelling; or (b) choose from the seemingly infinite variations in use in England at the time, such as, but not limited to, *thowh, thowgh, thoagh, thoughe, thow, thowe, thauth, thoff, thauh, thaugh, thagh, thaghe, thaw, thoghe, thogh, thouh, thou,* and *tho*.

There was no manual, no dictionary, no uniform approach to spelling that could guide a scribe or reader. It was orthographic anarchy.

Of all the problems plaguing English, Ormin was bothered most by its inability to distinguish short and long vowels. Today, of course, we have a nifty solution for this—the silent *E*—which we place after a short vowel to turn *win* into *wine* and *fin* into *fine*. But the silent *E* wouldn't fully take root until around the sixteenth century. Instead, Ormin had to devise his own nifty technique. In every case where a short vowel occurs, Ormin proposed doubling the consonant that follows it. Instead of *cat*, write *catt*. Instead of *dog*, write *dogg*. Write *furr* for *fur* and *sirr* for *sir*. And where there's a digraph—like the *th* in *with*—well, you can just go ahead and double both letters: *withth*.

Emboldened by his ingenuity, Ormin published a book of biblical homilies titled the *Ormulum* (he named it after himself), written entirely in his reduplicate spelling. In this eye-straining tome, *after* becomes *affterr*, *living* becomes *livvinng*, *kinsman* becomes *kinnessmann*, *alderman* becomes *allderrmann*, and all multisyllabic words swell to a Mississippi level of superfluous consonant doubling.

Simpler? No. Practical? Not particularly. Extra letters meant extra time, extra labor, extra parchment, and extra ink—and for those poor scribes already working morning to night hand-copying biblical texts,* Ormin's "helpful" new spelling proved no help at all. "Ormography," as some have playfully called it, translates to "worm writing," and in the end it was just that: slow as a worm.

~~~~~

Ormin was first in a long lineage of visionaries seeking to bring simplicity (or their version of it) to English spelling. But before

---

* The average medieval scribe copied three to four pages a day. If they were good, they could churn out a Bible every 18 months. If they were great, they could do it in 15 months.

we meet his descendants—before Ruzevelt, Karnegi, and the Phunny Phellows come barreling onto the stage—we should address a question that, if it isn't on your mind already, probably will be soon: *How did English spelling become so complicated in the first place?*

To understand the drive of the simplifiers, we need to understand the tangled roots of the language itself—the historical forces, linguistic traumas, and curious twists of fate that turned English into the sad, jumbled orthography it is today. In the spirit of Ormin, we'll keep this simple.

The Celts

The earliest documented language in England was Celtic, named after the Celts who brought it from Central Europe around 600 B.C.E. (give or take a few hundred years—the records are notoriously poor). Celtic wasn't a single cohesive language like we think of today—it was a *family* of related but distinct languages—and the Celts weren't one unified group but a collection of different tribes. Their influence is all over the British Isles (Welsh, Irish, Scottish Gaelic, and Breton derive from branches of Celtic), and several dozen Celtic words remain in English today, notably in the names of waterways (*Thames* and *Avon*), grassy terrains (*bog* and *glen*), and mythical creatures (*banshee* and *leprechaun*).

Because of its location off mainland Europe, the Celtic land was both desirable and vulnerable to seafaring invaders. And because the Celts had no central government or language, they seemed like easy pickings. Enter the Romans.

The Romans

Julius Caesar had tried to conquer England *twice* before Emperor Claudius finally succeeded in 43 C.E. As the Roman Empire expanded across England, the Celts fled into the outer rural areas (eventually giving Wales, Ireland, and Scotland their distinctive tongues), and Latin became England's new dominant language.

For the next four hundred years, Latin was the language of law and literature, of military and government, and it's here that we get words like *castle* (from the Latin *castrum,* also in Lan*caster* and Win*chester*) and *port* (from the Latin *portus*). Relatively speaking, though, Latin's impact on English during the Roman Empire was minimal. (Most Latin-derived words we use today arrived after the sixth century, when St. Augustine brought Christianity to England.) In 410 C.E., Rome was sacked by the Visigoths, the vast empire began to crumble, and the Romans pulled abruptly out of England, taking their Latin language with them. England returned to a state of limbo—not quite Celtic, not quite Roman, not quite anything—and the door was wide open for new groups to move in.

The Anglo-Saxons

Into this linguistic void rushed four Germanic tribes: the Angles, Saxons, Jutes, and Frisians. They came, they saw, they liked the rain, and they decided to stay in England.

Over the next generations, as these tribes mixed and mingled, their Germanic dialects merged into a single, semi-cohesive language. If you look closely at this language today—if you really squint, and blur your eyes, and maybe tilt your head—you might recognize something resembling English. In fact, this is Old English—a.k.a. Anglo-Saxon—and it's where our language officially begins.

Compared to Ormin's Middle English, the orthography of Old English was surprisingly simple. Words were spelled as they sounded, free of silent letters and irregular pronunciations. And though spellings often varied from dialect to dialect (again, standardization didn't exist), their phonetic structure allowed for wide comprehension across regions. It was a paradise of phonetic simplicity, a golden age of orthographic bliss. Many hope to experience it again one day.

The Norse

The downfall of Old English can be summed up in a single ominous line—words that throughout history have marked the death of civilizations, the end to peaceful and prosperous eras, and the beginning of many a TV miniseries: then the Vikings came.

They came from Denmark on longboats in 865, landing in East Anglia (in modern-day Suffolk, on England's eastern coast) and igniting a series of territorial wars. The Norse invaders wove their linguistic peculiarities into the fabric of Old English, and English and Danish mingled into an Anglo-Norse dialect. In northern England, where the Norse eventually settled,* their preference for *SK* sounds turned *shirt* into *skirt*. *Ship* became *skip*. And some Anglo-Saxon words, like *dic* (meaning "to dig"), split into distinct versions with similar meanings and sounds: the Norse called it *dyke*; the Anglo-Saxons called it *ditch*. Over time, English also adopted hundreds of

---

* This is partly why, today, Britons in the north have distinct accents from those in the south. It's also the reason northern England is peppered with placenames ending in *-kirk, -wick, -by,* and *-thorpe* (all of them Norse-derived).

Scandinavian loanwords, including *skull, scream, ransack, heathen, slaughter, leg, skin, anger, hit, die, knife,* and *snare* (many of which, incidentally, seem to describe a particularly vivid Viking battle). Pronunciations changed. Syntax shifted. The era of simplicity was over.

The Normans

In 1066, the Vikings came again. (Sort of.) These invaders hailed from Normandy, a former Viking stronghold in France named after the Northmen, or Normans, who first conquered the region in the tenth century. The Normans (who boasted Viking blood but considered themselves French) spoke a dialect known as Norman-French, which trickled down through the noble and scholarly classes of Britain. The English courts adopted French words like *judge, justice, attorney, felony,* and *perjury. Cows, pigs,* and *sheep* became *boeuf, porc,* and *mouton.* Traditional Old English names like Harold and Edward fell out of favor, and whole generations of Williams, Henrys, Roberts, and Richards, all French, grew up in England never speaking a word of the mother tongue. In fact, for the next three centuries, no English monarch spoke English.

Had this sudden frenchification touched all of England equally, it's possible we would all be speaking French today. But the Franco influence reached only England's upper classes; the lower classes, meanwhile—the peasants, bakers, craftsmen, laborers—continued speaking English as if nothing had changed. England thus became bilingual along class lines. As scribes struggled to pin down the chaos, the mixture of Anglo-Norse and Norman-French scrambled the linguistic landscape. In the resulting mélange, English evolved five major English dialects—Northern, Southern, East Midlands, West Midlands, and Kentish—each boasting its own regional accents and its own regional spellings.* We call this hodgepodge Middle English.

A story from the period illustrates how unintelligible English had become even among Englishmen. A group of London sailors are traveling to Holland. On their way, they dock in Kent and approach a local house for food:

> [He] axed for mete; and specially he axyd after eggys. And the goode wyf answered, that she coude speke no frenshe. And the merchant was angry, for he also coude speke no frenshe. But wolde have hadde egges, and she understode him not. And thenne at laste a nother sayd that he wolde have eyren. Then the good wyf sayd that she understood hym wel. Loo, what sholde a man in thyse days now wryte, egges or eyren?

Ormin was the first to articulate what, by the twelfth century, many already knew: English was spiraling fast and in desperate need of saving. Rock bottom, however, was still a long way down.

The Great Vowel Shift

In the late fourteenth century, English entered a period of transformation known as the Great Vowel Shift.† Over the next three cen-

---

* For reasons historians don't fully understand, regional accents and regional spellings sometimes became mismatched during this period. The word *bury*, for instance, began life as the Old English word *byrgan*. But after centuries of Viking marauding, *byrgan* split into four distinct regional spellings: *burgen, burien, berien,* and *birien.* Today, we use the spelling favored in the West Midlands—*bury*—but most English speakers pronounce it as they did 100 miles away in Kent—*berry.* The word *busy* underwent a similar process. *Busy* is also a West Midlands spelling; by all orthographic logic, then, it should rhyme with *bury.* And yet, it acquired the *East* Midlands pronunciation, and today we pronounce it *bizzy.*
† Otto Jespersen, the Danish linguist, coined the term in 1909.

turies, we gradually shifted our pronunciations, forming our long vowels higher up and closer to the fronts of our mouths. Feel the vowel move as you utter the following words: *Nom. Nem. Name.* The sound migrates from the lower back of the mouth (*nom*) to midway along the soft palate on the roof of the mouth (*nem*) and then into its modern location on the front roof (*name*). This is the general path many (but not all) of our vowels took between 1400 and 1700. But our spellings—this is key—didn't evolve with our speech. Thus, a rift formed between the way we *spoke* and the way we *wrote*. *Meat* and *great*, which once rhymed, drifted apart. So did *foot* and *boot*. Everywhere we look today, mismatched vowels laugh at us from the Middle Ages. The great rift remains. It keeps linguists up at night.

The Printer

In the fifteenth century, a glimmer of hope emerged in the form of William Caxton, a middle-class textile merchant from Kent. On a trading trip to Cologne in 1471, Caxton encountered Germany's thriving printing industry. He saw his first printing press—a revolutionary device invented by Johannes Gutenberg in that country less than 20 years earlier—and when he returned to England two years later, he leased a room in Westminster Abbey Church, cobbled together a winepress and movable block type, and set up a printing press of his own. With mass printing came the promise of language standardization, and as England's first printer it became Caxton's duty to select a standard English dialect. The future of English hinged on Caxton's printing press. *Egges* or *eyren,* it was up to him.

Caxton considered his home dialect of Kentish to be too "broad and rude," fit for the lower classes he had grown away from. He chose instead a variety of East Midlands called Chancery Standard, the dialect of London's universities and courts. Chancery was associated with nobility, in part because it contained scores of French loanwords. (*Mots de France* still carried the elegance they had when the Normans ruled the English aristocracy.) It was the speech of "a clerke and a noble gentylman," Caxton wrote—and it was now Standard English.

As Caxton's books reached the far corners of England, so did Chancery Standard, and for the first time in its history England had a universal model for its written language. Today, Chancery remains the foundation upon which all English literature and communication are built. This sentence is descended from Chancery Standard. So is this one.

But while the printing press brought much-needed order to English, it also brought fresh complications. By standardizing English in 1476, Caxton froze our orthography during a time of linguistic flux. Our spellings today are therefore anchored to a pronunciation spoken sometime between Chaucer and Shakespeare, back when we voiced the *S* in *aisle*, the *G* in *gnarl,* and the *K* in *knife*. Over the next 600 years, we gradually silenced these letters in our speech, and yet there they remain on the page—echoes of an old pronunciation, fixed in time by Caxton's press, confounding kindergarteners into the twenty-first century.

Further confusion arose inside Caxton's print shop. With the future of English in Caxton's hands, any decision, no matter how small, had potentially catastrophic implications for the language. Caxton, ever the perfectionist, liked the look of justified margins and square-block text (like you see on this page). Modern publishers, when faced with an awkwardly long word approaching the right margin, will split it with a hyphen and carry one half down to the next line. The margin therefore remains neat and even, all straight lines to the scanning eye. These "marginal hyphens," as they're called, were popularized by Gutenberg. Many printers followed Gutenberg's example, but not Caxton. Instead, Caxton preferred to fiddle with his spellings, adding or subtracting letters to keep his lines flush with the margins. If a line ended one space shy of the right edge, Caxton might squeeze in one extra letter. It's the reason Caxton's works contain such variants of *pity* as *pitty* and *pittye,* and why *music* appears in one place as *musik* and in another as *musycque.* At times, Caxton would append an *E* to the ends of *booke, goode, gete,* and *acte,* a spelling convention that fortunately never caught on—but he's also responsible for the *E* in *done, come, have,* and *give,* which did.

The Typesetter

To help run his print shop, Caxton hired a typesetter named Wynkyn de Worde. Wynkyn spoke fluent Flemish but broken English. Wherever he encountered an English word that reminded him of a Flemish one, he deferred to the Flemish spelling. That's where we get the silent *H* in *ghost*; in Flemish, it's *gheest.** Once established, the Flemish *H* migrated into *ghoul, aghast,* and other spectral conjugations. Wynkyn also had a habit of confusing the lowercase letters *f* and *s.* (In his defense, they do appear similar in Caxton's typeface.) In 1493, after Caxton died and Wynkyn inherited his Westminster press, he reprinted a manuscript that included the English word *fnese,* a term of Norse origin meaning to "puff" or

---

* In Caxton's works, we also find *goose* spelled *ghoos, goat* spelled *ghoot,* and *girl* spelled *gherle*—each in deference to a Flemish standard.

"snort" (pronounced *fuh-NEEZE*). But Wynkyn printed it *snese*—thereby coining our modern word *sneeze*.

William Caxton shows his printing press to King Edward IV and his wife, Queen Elizabeth Woodville, of England. The man turning the spindle is likely Caxton's assistant, Wynkyn de Worde. (Published in *The Graphic* in June 1877 for the Caxton Quadricentennial Celebration in London.)

~~~~~~

This is a simplified history, of course—a compact answer to the complex question *What went wrong?* With each foreign conquest, with every fateful sneeze, the weight of linguistic baggage had grown heavier until, by around the sixteenth century, it had reached the state of complication that we call Early Modern English. And so, as the pages of history turned, teachers, preachers, journalists, and politicians embarked on a journey to restore reason, to simplify spelling, and to salvage English from the clutches of chaos, as we moved steadfastly into the aj of simplifyd speling.

3

The Faýer, Sun, and Holi Ghoost

An intelligent child who is bidden to spell debt, and very
properly spells it d-e-t, is caned for not spelling it with a b
because Julius Caesar spelled it with a b.
—George Bernard Shaw, 1948

The year is 1550. Copernicus's heliocentric theory is shaking the
foundations of science. Europeans are tasting chocolate for the
first time. And John Cheke, a tutor to the twelve-year-old King of
England, is developing his seven-point plan for simplifying English
spelling:

1. Remove the silent *E* at the ends of words: e.g., *prais*
   (*praise*), *giv* (*give*), *excus* (*excuse*).
2. Remove all unpronounced consonants within a word:
   e.g., *dout* (*doubt*), *det* (*debt*), *receit* (*receipt*).
3. Where a long *A, E,* or *I* vowel sound appears, replace
   with duplicate letters: e.g., (*made*), *eet* (*eat*), *desiir*
   (*desire*).
4. Where a long *U* appears, add a long stroke above: e.g.,
   presūm (*presume*), *assūm* (*assume*).
5. Replace the letter *Y* with *I* or duplicate *E*: e.g., *awai*
   (*away*), *sai* (*say*), *personalitee* (*personality*).

6. Where a *TH* appears within a word, replace with an accented *ý*: e.g., *faýer* (*father*), *ýe* (*the*), *ýees* (*these*).

7. Otherwise respell all words to better express their sounds: e.g., (*good*), *britil* (*brittle*), *sufferabil* (*sufferable*).

As a royal tutor, instructing young Edward VI (and occasionally his older sister Elizabeth, the future queen) in the study "of toungues, of the scripture, of philosophie and all liberal sciences," Cheke grew to despise one particular quirk of English: silent Latin letters. These quiet pests—the superfluous *B*'s and *C*'s in words like *doubt* and *indict*—served no phonetic purpose and needlessly befuddled children at the start of their linguistic journeys. Plus, until recently, these letters didn't even *exist* in English. As the print revolution exploded at the turn of the sixteenth century and English spelling slid inexorably toward anarchy, some British scholars had proposed a solution: to fix English spelling, they would make it look more like Latin. Latin was solid, sturdy, anchored in the bedrock of antiquity. Just the word alone—*Latin*—evoked a sense of historical grandeur and lexical precision, a world of marble columns and concrete syntax. It was the language of philosophers and emperors, of Cicero and Caesar, and it was a language that every educated schoolboy in Britain grew up learning. And so, as the linguist David Crystal explains it: "If English spelling was a mess, and all literate people knew Latin, why not put Latin to work to help reduce some of the uncertainties in English?"

Thus, scribes began peppering letters throughout English to align it with Latin. Consider the word *doubt*. Before the sixteenth century, it showed up variously as *doute*, *dout*, and *dute*. It comes to us from the French *doute*, and the French got it from the Latin *dubitare* (pronounced *doo-bee-TAH-ray*, with every letter voiced), the root shared with *dubious* and *indubitably*. During the Renaissance, as scholars looked with renewed interest to the classical world, they decided to trace *doute* back to its original Latin *dubitare* and restore the *B* to its "rightful" place in the word. Now whenever a scribe grappled with its spelling, he could call back to his childhood Latin studies. The *B* was a mnemonic of sorts—a silent reminder of how to spell certain words.

This same Latinizing effort also gave us the silent *B* in *debt* and *subtle,* the *L* in *balm* and *salmon,* and the *P* in *receipt.* (From Latin's *debitum, subtilis, balsamum, salmo,* and *recepta,* respectively.) For these Renaissance scholars, it made more sense to conform English to its etymological *past* than to its phonetic *present.* Spelling, they believed, shouldn't just be a guide to pronunciation; it should also be a record of the word's origins.

Cheke found these silent letters both pointless and confusing. But that wasn't the only reason he wanted them gone. Cheke was a linguistic patriot; he hated the *B* in *doubt* simply for the fact that it came from Latin—and Latin *wasn't English.* "Our own tung should be written cleane and pure," he argued, "unmixt and unmangled with borrowing of other tunges . . . For then doth our tung naturallie and praisablie utter her

> Attempts to Latinize the English language sometimes missed the mark entirely. The word *sissors* received a silent *C* based on the misconception that it derives from the Latin *scindere,* meaning "to split." But the term actually has its roots in the Latin *cisorium,* meaning "cutting implement." Elsewhere, *iland* became *island* by a mistaken derivation from the Latin *insula,* rather than from the Germanic *iegland,* saddling us with five centuries and counting of an erroneous *S.* And *sovereign* comes from the Latin *superanus* ("highest one"), not the Latin *regnare* ("to reign") as one scribe apparently assumed, and therefore has no etymological reason for its *G.*

meaning, when she bouroweth no conterfeitness of other tunges."
His new spelling would be pure, phonetic, "unmangled" by foreign
influence. He began work on an "English" edition of the New Testament, translated into his simplified anti-Latinate style. In 1550,
he published the first installment, the Gospel of Matthew:

> Enter in bi a narrow gaat, for ŷe gaat is wiid and ŷe
> way brood, ŷt leadeth to destruction, and maní goeth
> in theerbí. And ŷe gaat is narrow, and ŷe waí streight ŷt
> ledeth to life, and few ŷeer be ŷt find it. Taak heed of fals
> propheets which cõm to yow in scheeps garments, and in-
> wardli ŷei be ravening wolfes. (Matthew 7:13)

Cheke would only get as far as the second Gospel. In 1553, he
landed behind bars on a treason charge for backing Lady Jane
Grey's ill-fated claim to the throne—a disastrous miscalculation,
especially with Mary I already sitting on it—and in the damp stone
walls of the Tower of London, Cheke's spelling reform died a silent
death. Four years later, he did too.

John Cheke wasn't the only simplified speller in Tudor England,
nor the only simplifier in the Tudor court. A decade later, John Hart,
a high-ranking officer of arms under Queen Elizabeth, would offer
his own prescription for our spelling ills: "To use as many letters in
our writing as we doe voyces or breathes in speaking," he vowed, "and
no more." To this end, Hart cut *C, J, W,* and *Y* from the alphabet and
removed silent letters with gusto. *Heaven* became *hevn, bread* became
bred, and *words,* with the loss of its *W,* became *urds.* He placed a dot
beneath long vowels (*A, E, I, O, U*) to let the reader know when to
stretch their pronunciation (a less dizzying approach than Ormin's
excessssivve redoublinng) and he introduced five new letters, ᴳ, ᶘ, ᶁ,

6, ʤ for the sounds of *CH, SH, TH* (as in *this*), and *TH* (as in *thin*), and the soft *G* of *gentle.* "Hierbei iu mẹ persẹv," Hart wrote in his spelling in 1569, "ðat our singl sounding and ius of letters, mẹ in proses ov teim, bring our họl nasion tu ọn serten, perfet and ʒeneral spẹking."*

Despite his proximity to the throne, Hart, like Cheke, was powerless against the relentless

In his pursuit to keep English pure, John Cheke took great pains to avoid using words rooted in Latin. Instead of *lunacy,* which comes from the Latin *luna,* he wrote *moond.* Instead of *founded,* he wrote *groundwrought.* And instead of *exiled*—as in, the Jewish people were "exiled to Babylon" (Matthew 1:11)—he wrote *out-peopled.*

descent of English. Instead of lobbying for a sweeping, language-wide ban on silent letters,[†] Hart quietly circulated his ideas in a trio of reform books, for the eyes of a learned few and the practical use of no one. His final book—the egregiously titled *A Methode, or comfortable beginning for all vnlearned, whereby they may bee taught to read English, in a very short time, vvith pleasure* (1570)—presented his new translation of the Lord's Prayer (opposite).

For all their talk of concision

From *A Methode* by John Hart, 1570.

---

* Tr: "Hereby you may perceive, that our single sounding and use of letters, may in process of time, bring our whole nation to one certain, perfect and general speaking." (Due to typographical limitations, Hart's new characters are rendered in International Phonetic Alphabet, or IPA, letters.)

† If any monarch might've been receptive to spelling reform, it was the broad-minded linguaphile Elizabeth I. An avid reader and writer, Elizabeth was deeply fascinated by the English language (and many others) throughout her life.

and simplicity, sixteenth-century reformers could be a verbose and long-winded bunch, particularly in their elaborate book titles. William Bullokar, a London schoolteacher, took subtitling to the extreme in his 1580 *Booke at large:*

Bullokars Booke at large, for the *Amendment* of *Orthographie* for English ſpeech: wherein, a moſt perfeſt ſupplie is made, for the wantes and double ſounde *of letters in the olde Orthographie, with Examples for the* ſame, with the eaſie conference and vſe of both Orthographies, *to ſaue expences in Bookes for a time, vntill this amendment grow to a generall vſe, for* the eaſie, ſpeedie, and perfeſt reading and writing of Engliſh, (the ſpeech not changed, as ſome vntruly and maliciouſly, or at the leaſt ignorantlie blowe abroade) by the which amendement the ſame Authour hath alſo framed a ruled Grammar, to be imprinted heereafter, for the ſame ſpeech, to no ſmall commoditie of the Engliſh Nation, not only to come to eaſie, ſpeedie, and perfeſt vſe of our owne language, but alſo to their eaſie, ſpeedie, and readie entrance into the ſecretes of other Languages, and eaſie and ſpeedie pathway to all Straungers, to vſe our Language, heeretofore very hard vnto them, to no ſmall profite and credite to this our Nation, and ſtay therevnto in the weightieſt cauſes. There is alſo imprinted with this Orthographie a ſhort Pamphlet for all Learners, and a Primer agreeing to the ſame, and as learners ſhall go forward therein, other neceſſarie Bookes ſhall ſpedily be proui- ded with the ſame Orthographie.

Bullokar was a maximalist: He believed orthographic clarity lay not in the reduction of letters but in the addition of accent marks. Where Cheke had cut out *B*'s and *C*'s, Bullokar would add in dots and carets. In Aesop's Fables, where others saw moral lessons, Bullokar saw an opportunity to bedazzle the language back to coherence:*

---

* In addition to his orthographic changes, Bullokar proposed changing the names of *Z* and *W* to "zee" and "wee" to rhyme with *B, C, D, E, G, P, T,* and *V.* America has since adopted "zee" to replace the British "zed." But no one, not even the Scottish, uses "wee."

> Æſopꝛ Fáblż
> in tru Ortögraphy with Gram
> mar-nótꝛ.
> He'r-yntoo ąr alſo jooined the ſhort ſentenc'eꝛ
> of the wÿȝ Cato im-printed with lýk
> form and order : bóth of which
> Aųtorż ar tranſláted
> oųt-of Latin in-
> too E'ngliſh
> By William Bųllokar.

Otto Jespersen, the great twentieth-century linguist, would later deride Bullokar's system as "nothing but the traditional spelling with a host of mystical and inconsistently employed dots and accents over and under the letters," and Bullokar himself was a "muddle-headed spelling-reformer" for proposing it. Jespersen preferred the simplified spelling of Alexander Gil the Elder, the ruthless and often vicious headmaster of St. Paul's School in London. In 1621, Gil published his 40-letter alphabet that introduced, among other characters, an *NG* combo letter to replace all *-ng* word endings and a *WH* combo to replace all *wh-* beginnings. "Etymology should never make us write letters which are not actually heard and which neither can nor ought to be heard," Gil wrote in *Logonomia Anglica* (1619). "Thus I object strongly to writing *houer, honor, honest* instead of *ouer, onor, onest*, because we say an *ouer*, not a *houer*, etc . . . educated people who have learnt etymology, should write *divjn, skolar, onor, kungurer . . .*"

Gil's passion for language occasionally reached a violent degree. At St. Paul's, he was given to "whipping fits" as punishment for student infractions (his student John Milton may have received a flogging or two), and nothing boiled his blood so much as linguistic errors. He once suggested crucifying anyone who purveyed "cant speech," for it contributed to that "poisonous and most stinking ulcer of our state" (a.k.a. the English language). Until such linguistic abuses could be answered with penalty of death, whipping would have to do.

Of all the zealous simplifiers slicing and dicing the language during the Renaissance, only Charls Butler had the courage to turn the pruning knife upon himself. In an act of personal rebranding, Butler cut the silent *E* from *Charles* to become a living, breathing embodiment of simplified spelling. He walked the walk, and he typd the typ.

Butler was intrigued by the sounds and rhythms of nature. A trained musicologist and professional beekeeper, Butler had once transcribed the buzz of a beehive into a musical score, and it emboldened him with a sense of possibility: If he could capture all those hums and drones on the written page, how hard could it be to transcribe spoken English into a phonetically consistent spelling? In 1633, the 62-year-old apiarist began picking at the alphabet. He turned all silent vowels into backward apostrophes (strang', hiv', medicin') and crafted eight new letters (Đ, Ѡ, Ǥ, Ⱡ, to nam' a few). A year later, he combined his dual passions, spelling reform (which promised order and efficiency) and bees (who had already achieved it), into a singular work that aimed to make language as harmonious and functional as the hive itself: *Đe Feminin' Monarḳi', or Đe Histori of Bee's.*

The backlash to Butler's book had nothing to do with spelling and everything to do with bees. Bee science (apiology) was in its infancy then—many still believed that honeybees grew spontaneously out of rotting meat—and readers of *Đe Feminin' Monarḳi'**

---

* Full title: *Đe Feminin' Monarḳi', or Đe histori of bee's. Shewing đeir admirable natur', and propertis; đeir generation and colonis; đeir government, loyalti, art, industri; enemi's, vvars, magnanimiti, &c. Togeder with de riht ordering of dem from tim' to tim': and de sweet' profit arising der'of. Written out of experienc'.*

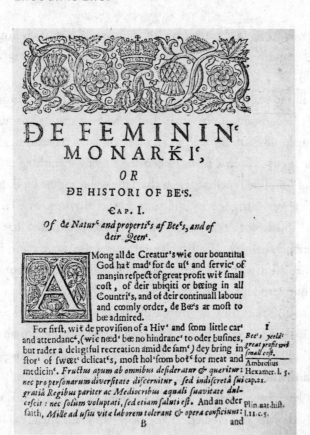

were shocked by Butler's theory that beehives are governed by *female* bees, not male bees.* Until then, bee colonies were thought to have a patriarchal structure, with the king bee ruling over all. If Butler was right, it meant that Aristotle (and everyone since Aristotle) had been wrong about nature's hardest-working creature. Butler *was* right, of course—all hail the queen bee—but in this primitive era of natural science, his book caused a small uproar in

---

* The idea of a feminine monarchy shouldn't have surprised a sixteenth-century Englishman. Between 1553 and 1603, three women held the British throne. Elizabeth's reign, at 44 years, was the longest. Lady Jane Grey's, at nine days, was the shortest.

the apiary community. And in the noise and furor of the debates that followed, his ideas for simplified spelling were forgotten.[*]

~~~~~

In the mid-1600s, calls for spelling reform declined as England discovered a new target for its linguistic concerns: America. The Colonial Age was underway, and with British citizens dispersed around the world, the language had begun to morph and diffuse with the local tongues. In America's Jamestown and Plymouth colonies, settlers evolved new accents and vocabulary, acquiring Indigenous words like *canoe* and *maize* and crude colloquialisms like *pissburnt* ("stained with urine"). Within a few generations, American colonists would be speaking a fully distinct *American English* dialect, with slangs and twangs that the British didn't understand (or just didn't want to). American English became a lightning rod for British cultural resentment—and over the next century, it stirred linguists to a level of rage that silent letters never could.

---

[*] Butler originally published his work under a different title in 1609, but it's this expanded 1634 edition, written in simplified spelling, that became the age's definitive study of honeybee science. To this day, it continues to be read by linguists and beekeepers alike, albeit in Modern English.

O Spare, We Beseech You, Our Mother-Tongue!

I am willing to love all mankind, except an American.
—Samuel Johnson, 1778

In 1787, a London magazine condemned Thomas Jefferson, that most florid Independence-declarer, for using what was then considered an unforgivable mark of American vulgarity—the word *belittle*:

> Belittle! What an expression! It may be an elegant one in Virginia, and even perfectly intelligible; but for our part, all we can do is to guess at its meaning. For shame, Mr. Jefferson! Why, after trampling upon the honour of our country, and representing it as little better than a land of barbarism—why, we say, perpetually trample also upon the very grammar of our language . . . O spare, we beseech you, our mother-tongue!

As *belittle* and other American-born words reached England's shores, they were denounced as "vulgarisms," "barbarisms," or—worst of all—"Americanisms." And what *were* Americanisms exactly? Americanisms were indigenous terms like *moccasin* and *tobacco*. They were compound words like *eggnog* (formed from the English slang *grog*, meaning "rum," and *noggin*, meaning "a wooden cup"). And they were culinary treats like *cookies*, from the Dutch *koeckjes*, a substitute for the English *biscuits* and a blatant affront to English culture if there ever was one.

In short, Americanisms were evolutions in language that emerged to meet the needs of a new land and new people. They were signifiers of a new national identity—and to Britain, they were a worrying indication that the English language, much like the Americans using it, was separating from its British roots.

The most vehemently opposed to the new American dialect (and the most in any position to do something about it) was Samuel Johnson, a 37-year-old British writer living in London. Johnson was the quintessential linguistic conservative: he loved his language as much as he hated its transatlantic cousin, and he took it as his patriotic duty to preserve English before Americans eroded it any further. The plan: to compile a dictionary—the first that most Englishmen would ever know—and, in doing so, to help strengthen English's superiority over the burgeoning American English. This was about more than language. It was about national pride.

Samuel Johnson's disdain for Americans went beyond their "barbaric" language. He seemed to hate these New Worlders just for existing. "I am willing to love all mankind," he once wrote, "except an American." He also called them "a race of convicts, [who] ought to be thankful for anything we allow them short of hanging."

On a June morning in 1746, in a rented townhouse overlooking Gough Square in London, Johnson got to work. He pulled a book from his shelf, underlined all the words and quotations he deemed worthy of inclusion, and passed the book to an assistant to transcribe his selections onto paper cards for alphabetization. Then he continued to another book, and another, and so on. "The books he used for this purpose were what he had in his own collection," described Johnson's friend John Hawkins, "a copious but a miserably ragged one, and all such as he could borrow; which latter, if ever they came back to those that lent them, were so defaced as to be scarce worth owning."

With the precision of a scientist (and the gall of a man who underlines books that don't belong to him), Johnson classified the language into an accessible framework, organizing and defining as he went. His project paralleled that of Carl Linnaeus in Sweden. While Johnson was in London cataloging English, Linnaeus, a Swedish botanist, was in Uppsala writing *Species Plantarum* (1753), the first major work to catalog plants according to binomial nomenclature.* The timing of their projects was no coincidence. "Both men were smack in the middle of the Enlightenment," explains Peter Sokolowski, a lexicographer at Merriam-Webster and historian of English. "It was an era of classification, of absolute fascination with scientific order. So here we have one man who's classifying plants, and another man who's classifying words, born only 20 months apart, working at their desks during the exact same years." To many Enlightenment thinkers, *classification* was the key to scientific understanding. Linnaeus was bringing this understanding to the natural world. Johnson was bringing it to language.

Despite Johnson's scientific rigor, his spellings could be, at times, puzzlingly inconsistent. He doubled the *L* in *uphill* but not in *downhil*, in *muckhill* but not *dunghil*, in *instill* but not *distil*, in *pitfall* but not *downfal*. He included the *P* in *receipt* but not in *deceit* (a hasty oversight that we're still living with today). And in

---

* Most scientific plant names, from *Coffea arabica* to *Cannabis sativa* to *Aloe vera*, come from this seminal 1753 book.

In addition to his often-erratic spellings, Johnson was given to often-bizarre definitions. Some of these border on the whimsical, others on the downright insane. The following are a few famous head-scratchers:

to worm: To deprive a dog of something, nobody knows what, under his tongue, which is said to prevent him, nobody knows why, from running mad.

tarantula: An insect whose bite is said to be only cured by musick.

etch: A country word, of which I know not the meaning.

lunch: As much food as one's hand can hold.

And last but clearly the best:

bellygod: A glutton; one who makes a god of his belly.

---

cases where Johnson couldn't parse the variant spellings of a word, he simply included them all. Thus, he retained both *soap* and *sope*, *choke* and *choak*, *choir* and *quire*, *tailor* and *taylor*, *fuel* and *fewel*, and *jelly* and *gelly*.

Johnson also took dogmatic stances on spelling that now appear laughably archaic. He declared that a word should never, ever, end in the letter *C*. This explains his antiquated spellings of *critick*, *musick*, *lyrick*, and *publick* (which had existed long before Johnson, but never with such ironclad enforcement). Johnson's fondness for *-ck* endings would linger in England well into the 1800s, and today we find mismatched remnants in words like *frolicked* and *picnicked*, which retain their Johnsonian *-ck* even while *frolic* and *picnic* discard it.

In the spring of 1755, after nearly a decade of daily, solitary work,*
Johnson completed *A Dictionary of the English Language*. It was, to
use his own spelling, *gigantick*. His book included 42,733 entries.
It spanned more than 2,300 pages. (Not our modern six-by-nine-
inch trade pages, but those old ten-by-eighteen-inch folio ones.†)
Stacked atop each other, the two volumes of Johnson's dictionary
measured seven inches thick, and carried together, they weighed
about as much as a car tire. For the first time in history, the en-
tirety of English—or the closest thing to it at the time—had been
captured in book form. For the first time, a wall had been built
between English and American English.

As Johnson hoped, his dictionary became a symbol of nationalis-
tic pride, a tribute to his native English and a bulwark against the
"barbarisms" of the New World. But just as Johnson pushed back
against the American tongue, so did America start pushing back
against the British. Across the Atlantic, a cadre of American scholars and intellectuals, chafing under the yoke of their mother orthography, were already preparing to declare—in their own langwij
and their own spelings—their lingwistic independens frum Britain.

〰〰〰

Polly Stevenson's response had been harsh, but Franklin took it
humbly. "We must let people spell on in their old way," she had
written him, and so he did. By the end of 1768, Benjamin Frank-

---

* Such tedious, solitary work might destroy most men, but it was exactly what Johnson
needed. Many historians now believe that Samuel Johnson suffered from Tourette's syndrome, which precluded him from public-facing roles like teaching. Instead, he found
solace in writing—"the invisible occupation of authorship," as his biographer Robert
DeMaria put it—and thus was well suited for the lexicography life.
† Five pages alone—or about six square feet—were devoted to defining the word *take*.

> **Language, as well as government, should be national. America should have her own distinct from all the world.**
>
> **—Noah Webster**

lin had abandoned his new and improved alphabet and reverted to old and irrational English, readopting the *throughs* and *thoughs* that so thoroughly bugged him. It would take 18 long years (8 of which were spent in revolution for American independence, one of which was spent inventing bifocal glasses) before Franklin could bring himself to revisit the cause of simplified spelling.

It was now 1786, and Franklin, 80 years old, found himself in the audience of a lecture hall in Philadelphia. The speaker was a young man of 27, well dressed though not particularly charismatic, with red hair and a high-pitched voice that some would later describe as "squeaky." From a pile of papers, which he read without lifting his head, he shared his thoughts on language: If America hoped to rebuild as an independent nation, he argued, shouldn't it also have an independent language? If the English spoke English, shouldn't Americans speak . . . *American*? Three years after the Revolution, America hadn't yet found its identity; in custom, in habit, and especially in language, it was still largely English. "Language, as well as government, should be national," he would later write. "America should have her own distinct from all the world."

As the crux of his platform, the speaker made his case for a simpler spelling—a modern spelling, an *American* spelling—based on the omission of silent and superfluous letters. Franklin beamed; it was the first sincere argument he'd heard on the subject in nearly two decades.

The man was Noah Webster, a former reserve militiaman in the Revolutionary War and the author of a recent trilogy of textbooks titled *A Grammatical Institute of the English Language*. His first volume, *The American Spelling Book*—nicknamed the *Blue-Backed Speller** for its bright cerulean cover—would go on to sell nearly 25 million copies in his lifetime, and, at a penny royalty on each, was the closest Webster would ever get to a steady income. As Franklin listened to this young man challenge the foundations of English, he realized that he already had a copy of Webster's spelling book sitting at home; Franklin had been using it lately to teach his granddaughter how to read.

Webster's *Blue-Backed Speller*, published two years earlier, had made no attempts to challenge traditional English. It followed the common Samuel Johnson spellings of the day—preserving the *-re* in *centre* and *theatre*, the final *K* in *musick* and *publick*, the *U* in *favourite* and *colour*—and rebuked any troublemaking wordsmiths who would dare stray from the norm. "There seems to be an inclination in some writers to alter the spelling of words, by expunging the superfluous letters," Webster had written in the book's introduction. ". . . Into these and many other absurdities are people led by a rage for singularity."

He cautioned his readers against following these "new fashions"—only extravagant rogues spelled *musick* without a *K*—and urged them to wait out the craze.

---

* After the Bible, the *Blue-Backed Speller* was the most popular English-language book of the nineteenth century. Most Americans born in this period, from Mark Twain to Louisa May Alcott, would have learned to read and write using Webster's 168-page spelling primer.

But in 1783, shortly after the release of his *Speller*, Webster's views unexpectedly shifted. As the Revolutionary War drew to a close, the new American republic began rejecting anything and everything British, including the mother tongue. For a brief period during this anti-British wave, America considered swapping out English entirely for a non-Anglo language. A few influential voices nominated Greek as a replacement. Others floated French. Marquis de Chastellux, a French major general in the Revolution and companion to George Washington, even wrote of a campaign to have "Hebrew substituted to the English, taught in the schools, and used in all public acts," as a rallying measure to unite Americans as a chosen people. Webster had a different idea.

In pursuit of an all-American linguistic identity, Webster developed a plan for simple, no-nonsense spelling. He cut out unpronounced vowels—the *U* in *favourite* and *colour,* the final *E* in *determine* and *give,* the *I* in *friend.* Then he dropped redundant consonants—the second *G* in *waggon,* the second *L* in *traveller,* and the *K* in *musick, publick,* and *knight.* He converted Old Latin ligatures into simple letters, turning *æon* and *œconomics* into *eon* and *economics,* and removed the frivolous *ough* clumping that diverges three ways into *enough, plough,* and *thorough*—now to be respelled, more naturally, as *enuf, plow,* and *thoro.*

An America with its own spelling would help shake off the last vestiges of British influence, Webster believed. At the same time, it would boost American solidarity around a shared system of communication. As he gradually pulled away from his blue-backed spellings, paring down words to only their fundamental sounds, Webster saw a vision for America's future: one day, Websterian orthography might be hailed as an exemplar of linguistic innovation, a testament to American exceptionalism—a simple, shining language upon a hill.

Following the Philadelphia lecture, Webster and Franklin began corresponding about a potential American spelling project. Eager to collaborate on a joint proposal, Franklin mailed Webster his aborted 1768 alphabet along with a set of metal typeface for the six new letters he had created. "Our ideas are so nearly similar," Franklin enthused, "that I make no doubt of our easily agreeing on the plan." Webster wasn't as enthusiastic. He wanted to change *spelling*, not the alphabet (ideally, he would have "as few new characters and alterations of the old ones as possible"), and the more he studied Franklin's proposed reform, the less practical it seemed. "Webster soon realized that he didn't see eye to eye with the Doctor," writes Joshua Kendall in his biography of Webster, *The Forgotten Founding Father.* ". . . After careful consideration, Webster politely informed Franklin that he wasn't willing to dust off his types in order to create a new alphabet." For the second time in 18 years, Franklin's spelling proposal was rejected.

Webster did like the idea of collaboration—as long as the collaborator obediently agreed with Webster—so in early 1788 he cofounded a small organization devoted to the purpose. The New York Philological Society started convening on Monday evenings with the goal of "ascertaining and improving the American tongue." They drafted a constitution, a flag, and a coat of arms that prominently featured, as a nod to the Society's obsession with all things lingual, three mouths sticking out their tongues. Webster, ever the self-admirer, gave himself the title of Society "Monarch."

Over the next six months, Webster would use the Society as a sounding board. At a meeting in April 1788, he read from his early draft of an essay on spelling reform:

It has been observed by all writers on the English language, that the orthography or spelling of words is very irregular; the same letters often representing different sounds, and the same sounds often expressed by different letters . . . The question now occurs; ought the Americans to retain these faults which produce innumerable inconveniences in the acquisition and use of the language, or ought they at once to reform these abuses, and introduce order and regularity into the orthography of the AMERICAN TONGUE?

The Philological Society struggled to attract members, but it did catch the wary eye of a nearby lawyers' society, which viewed its new neighbors as an intrusion. A modest rivalry formed—two societies of pedantic, overeducated young men, each vying for intellectual supremacy over Lower Manhattan. To defuse tensions, the New York Philological Society rebranded that fall as the Friendly Club. But without the name to center its mission, it drifted from

---

During meetings of the New York Philological Society, Webster's lectures could be both painfully boring and brutally antagonistic. William Dunlap, a member of the Society, parodied Webster as "Noah Cobweb" in a theater play about the Society's creation. Dunlap writes, in the voice of Cobweb:

> When first I join'd them how oft did I hammer
> Night after Night, to teach the dunces Grammer
> My Rules, my lectures, ev'ry night repeated
> Began to talk sometimes ere they were seated
> To shew my zeal I ev'ry night held forth
> And deep imprest th' Idea of my worth.

"What a curst boring fellow now that is," a character later says of Cobweb, "you may read Pedant in his very phiz."

spelling reform. By December, it had become little more than a men's book club. At the end of the year, it quietly disbanded.

Webster, buzzing with orthographic energy and in need of a new outlet, resolved now to write. That winter, he returned to his "Essay on a Reformed Mode of Spelling," the long-standing project born of his lectures, which had been percolating in his mind for years. This essay, he decided, would serve as his definitive statement on simplified spelling. It would be his manifesto, his grand dream for an American utopia, a phonetic republic in which *through* is spelled *thru, women* is *wimmin,* and *enough* is *enuf.* It would be his legacy.

So, as the winter winds howled outside his window, Webster hunkered down with pen in hand and unleashed his ideas upon the page:

> Thus *greef* should be substituted for *grief*; *kee* for *key*; *beleev* for *believe*; *laf* for *laugh*; *dawter* for *daughter*; *plow* for *plough*; *tuf* for *tough*; *proov* for *prove*; *blud* for *blood*; and *draft* for *draught.* In this manner *ch* in Greek derivatives, should be changed into *k* . . . Therefore *character, chorus, cholic, architecture,* should be written *karacter, korus, kolic, arkitecture*; and were they thus written, no person could mistake their true pronunciation.

In clear and simple prose, Webster outlined the benefits of simplified spelling for childhood education:

> A child would learn to spell, without trouble, in a very short time, and the orthography being very regular, he would ever afterwards find it difficult to make a mistake.

And foreigners:

> . . . foreigners would be able to acquire the pronunciation of English, which is now so difficult and embarrassing, that they are either wholly discouraged on the first attempt, or obliged, after many years labor, to rest contented with an imperfect knowledge of the subject.

And printers:

> Such a reform would . . . save a page in eighteen; and a saving of an eighteenth in the expense of books, is an advantage that should not be overlooked.

That spring, Webster spent four hundred of his own dollars (more than $14,000 today) to self-publish *Dissertations on the English Language,* a 410-page essay collection adapted from his lectures. "Essay on a Reformed Mode of Spelling" comprised the final section of the book. He released his *laf*s and *masheen*s into the world with high hopes—what reason was there to think otherwise?—then, settling back, waited for the accolades he believed were due. Webster, alas, is still waiting.

The backlash was swift and brutal. To his face, Webster's friends expressed their judgments gently ("I suspect," cautioned the president of Yale, "you have put in the pruning Knife too freely"), but behind his back, his fellow intelligentsia bristled with sarcasm and mockery. "I join with you in reprobating the . . . new mode of spelling . . ." quipped Jeremy Belknap, in faux-phonetics, in a letter to Ebenezer Hazard, "*ov No-ur Webstur eskwier junier*." In London, one critic wrote cheekily that Webster's "proposal for reformation of spelling may rather be called a scheme for the corruption of it," and another called Webster's spelling just plain "peculiar and unsightly."

Instead of pulling back, Webster doubled down. He followed *Dissertations* with *A Collection of Essays and Fugitiv Writings* in 1790. This time, he committed to writing entirely in his simplified spelling. "There iz no alternativ," Webster declared. "Every possible reezon that could ever be offered for altering the spelling of words, stil exists in full force; and if a gradual reform should not be made in our language, it wil proov that we are less under the influence of reezon than our ancestors."

Unlike Franklin, who abandoned his alphabet before it reached the public eye, Webster would be dogged for decades by guardians of style and convention. In 1810, one particularly irate reviewer declared that Webster's simplified spelling "must strike every reflecting mind with a sense of the mildness of the municipal regulations of this land of *liberty,* which permitted the writer to roam abroad, unrestrained by a strait waistcoat . . ." Even Webster's brother-in-law admitted in a letter, "I ain't yet quite ripe for your orthography."

To this linguistic wunderkind who had been celebrated since the age of 25—whose first spelling book had nearly outsold the Bible—the feeling of rejection was new. He hadn't prepared for it. Webster had risked most of his finances and all of his reputation on the project; now the literary laughingstock of colonial America was reduced to begging his in-laws for loans and local schoolmasters for jobs. *Dissertations* and *Fugitiv Writings* sold so poorly that in 1791, as boxes of unpurchased books piled up, Webster confessed in a letter to Timothy Pickering that his surplus stock—those proud tomes he'd hoped would change the world—might soon have to "be sold for wrapping paper."

〜〜〜

Change is hard to accept—especially when the source of that change is a pompous and self-obsessed pedagogue. Indeed, the near-total opposition to Webster's spelling may be due to the simple fact that most of his peers couldn't stand him. Webster was unremorsefully condescending, unable to prove his worth without undercutting someone else's, and many openly expressed their distaste for him. A list of invectives hurled at Webster during his life reads like a colonial insult dictionary:

- a pusillanimous, half-begotten, self-dubbed patriot
- a toad in the service of sans-culottism
- a great fool, and a barefaced liar
- a spiteful viper
- a prostitute wretch
- a maniacal pedant
- a dunghill cock of faction
- an incurable lunatic
- a deceitful newsmonger

Great swaths of early America were excited to criticize Webster. In particular, he rankled one Dr. William Thornton, a rival spelling reformer, who emerged shortly after the publication of *Dissertations*. A British American physician, architect, and abolitionist, Thornton* entered his spelling proposal into a 1792 essay competition held by the American Philosophical Society, an organization in Philadelphia founded 50 years earlier by Benjamin Franklin. Ad-

---

* Among Thornton's greater achievements, he drafted the architectural plans for the United States Capitol building. Among his greater embarrassments, he once proposed to resurrect George Washington's corpse, which had "remained in a frozen state" in the cold winter weather when Washington died, by thawing it in cold water and infusing it with lamb's blood.

dressed to "Ð] Sitiznz ov Norθ Am]rika" ("The Citizens of North America"), Thornton proposed an overstuffed 30-letter alphabet with new symbols such as Θ, ⊙,], and ⊡.

On page 10 of his winning submission, Thornton appears to aim a subtle barb at Webster. While listing his acknowledgments, Thornton cites Benjamin Franklin and "the dissertations of the ingenious Noah Webster" as particular inspirations for his reform work. Then, with a callous stroke—knowing that the paper would land before Webster and the whole of the American Philosophical Society—Thornton strikes a clear and conspicuous line through the words "the ingenious."

> Tu ᴆꞁ Sitiznz ov Norᴇ Amꞁriка,
>
> Mai diir ᴋuntrimen,
>
> Iꞑ prizentiꞑ tu iu ᴆis smᴔᴔl uꞁrk ai süк leꙅ ᴆꞁ gratifiкeerꞁn óv obteeniꞑ iur feevꞁr, ᴆan ᴄv rendꞁriꞑ maiself iusfꞁl; and if ᴆꞁ benifits ai ᴋontempleet ɾud bi diraivd from mai leebꞁr, ai ɾal endꞁoi a satisfaᴌɾꞁn ᴇitɾ deᴇ onli ᴋan tꞁrmineet;

Introduction to Thornton's simplified spelling proposal. Tr: "To the Citizens of North America, My dear countrymen, In presenting to you this small work I seek less the gratification of obtaining your favour, than of rendering myself useful; and if the benefits I contemplate should be derived from my labour, I shall enjoy a satisfaction which death only can terminate."

A Nue Merrykin Dikshunary

Avoid the fashionable impropriety of leaving out the u
in many words, as honor, vigor, etc. This is mere childish
affectation.

—John Wesley, founder of Methodism, 1791

Lexicographers (*plural noun*: people who compile dictionaries) tend to be a compulsive bunch. As a teenager, Peter Mark Roget would count his steps to school every day. While writing his 1755 dictionary, Samuel Johnson would count lines of Latin poetry. Noah Webster liked to count houses.* During his spelling lecture tour across America in 1785 and 1786, he spent his leisure time walking the streets of each new city he visited, tallying the residences. Salem had 730 houses, he noted. New York had 3,340. Philadelphia, with its suburbs, had 4,500.

By 1800, with his lecture and reform days behind him, Webster craved a new enterprise, a new immersion, a new set of items to compile and organize. His new project would consume the next 25 years of his life.

That June, Webster announced that he would write an American dictionary. It wouldn't be the first American dictionary (that honor belongs, by sheer coincidence, to a New England school-

---

* Some historians believe that Noah Webster suffered from obsessive-compulsive disorder and likely took on methodical, monotonous projects as a form of self-therapy. Individuals with OCD sometimes find that counting and listing alleviate anxiety.

teacher named Samuel Johnson Jr.), but with Webster at the helm, it promised to be the most thorough compilation of English terms and definitions that any lexicographer, American or otherwise, had ever undertaken. It would embrace all the *chowders, tomahawks,* and other Yankee barbarisms that Samuel Johnson railed against. It would include new scientific words like *planetarium.* And Webster would try, as slyly as he could, to scatter some of the spelling simplifications he had pushed for in *Dissertations* throughout its pages.

Both sides of the Atlantic reacted to Webster's announcement with gleeful disdain. The *Gazette of the United States,* still giggling over his simplified spelling debacle from ten years earlier, published fake letters mocking Webster's attempt to legitimize America's low-class lexicon. "Plese put sum HOMMANY," read one letter, written in stereotyped pidgin, "and sum GOOD POSSUM fat and sum two tree good BANJOE in your new what-you-call-um Book for your fello Cytzen." A letter from a "Brother Jonathan" read, "Instead of *I keant keatch the keow,* an English man or *a town bred american* would say, *I cannot Catch the Cow,* but you being a brother Yankey will be sure to spell right in your new Yankey dictionary." A "Pat O'Dogerty" wrote, in exaggerated brogue:

To Mr. noab Wabstur,

Sur,

by rading all ovur the nusspaper I find you are after meaking a nue Merrykin Dikshunary; your rite, Sir; for ofter looking all over the anglish Books, you wont

find a bit Shillaly* big enuf to beat a dog wid. so I
hope you'll take a hint, a put enuff of rem in yours,
for Och 'tis a nate little bit of furniture for any Man's
house so it 'tis.

This time, Webster wouldn't run from the ridicule. He would face
it with every *possum*, *skunk*, and *canoe* he could muster. Slowly and
methodically, with the obsessive focus of his house-counting days,
Webster defined his way through the language. Working alphabeti-
cally, Webster spent the first six years of his project on the letters *A*
and *B*. Seven years later, he reached *H*. Another two years brought
him to *R*. And at last, in 1825, with a final flourish on *zygomatic*, he
was done. "When I had come to the last word, I was seized with a
trembling which made it somewhat difficult to hold my pen steady
for the writing . . ." he wrote. "But I summoned strength to finish
the last word, and then walking about the room a few minutes I
recovered."

Webster published *An American Dictionary of the English Lan-*
guage† shortly after his seventieth birthday, and for the first time
since his twenties, he felt the literary world smile upon him. Even
those who hated Webster (and there were still plenty) couldn't
deny the scope of his accomplishment. He had added some
30,000 words to Samuel Johnson's already impressive 40,000. He
introduced thousands of scientific terms (*psychology*, *phosphores-*
cent) as well as some trendy new hyphenations (*savings-bank*, *re-*

---

* A *shillelagh* is a wooden club often used as a weapon to settle disputes.
† Under pressure to publish, Webster had rushed out an early abridged edition, *A Com-*
pendious Dictionary of the English Language, in 1806. The slim volume, which included
only 356 pages of definitions and cost $1.50, sold poorly. A year later, Webster shortened
it further and listed it for a dollar. It sold even worse. Clearly, there was no market for
concision here; when it came to dictionaries, the public wanted comprehensive, meticu-
lous, exhaustive, substantial. They wanted *big*.

organize). But as inclusive as it was, Webster's dictionary was also noted for what it *didn't* include. It didn't include the *U* in *colour* or *favourite*. It didn't include the *K* in *publick*. In fact, Webster had quietly smuggled in dozens of simplifications from his reform days, dispersing his new one-*L travelers* (formerly *travellers*) and *O*-less *maneuvers* (formerly *manoeuvres*) throughout his book's 70,000 entries. We're all familiar with at least a few of these Websterian spellings:

Traditional English*	Webster's English
honour	honor
colour	color
favourite	favorite
neighbour	neighbor
waggon	wagon
publick	public
programme	program
theatre	theater
centre	center
cheque	check
diarrhoea	diarrhea
gynaecologist	gynecologist
plough	plow
draught	draft

These are the relics of simplified spelling, enduring remnants of Webster's vision to streamline and Americanize the language.

---

* Canada, Australia, New Zealand, South Africa, and most former British colonies (with the exception of the U.S.) also have the honour of using these pre-Webster spellings.

Today, it's merely American English—so seamlessly blended into everyday language that it's easy to forget its radical roots and the radical mind behind it.*

Britain rallied to defend its *U* from Noah Webster's ax (formerly *axe*). Julius Hare, the Archdeacon of Lewes, derided Webster's *honor* and *favor* as orthographic "abominations," and Henry Alford, the Dean of Canterbury, cautioned his peers to avoid the Websterian fad "of leaving out the 'u' in the termination 'our' . . . [I]t is part of a movement to reduce our spelling to uniform rule as opposed to usage, and to help forward the obliteration of all trace of the derivation and history of words." In a satirical article for the *United States Telegraph*, "To the Last of the Vowels," an anonymous writer made light of England's precious attachment to its twenty-first letter:

> I have not heard from U lately so often as I used to, before U was dismissed from many of your employments by Noah Webster. Though *u* are not in *favor* at present, with your superiors or your neighbors, yet *u* are always in sec*u*rity, and have still a respectable share in the p*u*blic p*u*rse, without any thing to do with *labor*—by which it would seem that *u* must be concerned in a sinec*u*re.

With his project now complete, Webster faced idleness for the first time in decades. Adrift and directionless, Webster continued to pick at his dictionary, abridging definitions, expanding etymologies, and refining his book to an impossible ideal of perfection. He exhausted himself and his savings, and in 1838 was forced to

---

* Webster's dictionary also included *tung* (*tongue*) and *ake* (*ache*), but these spellings didn't catch on.

mortgage his home to finance a new edition. "I desire . . . to be relieved from the toil of study and business," he wrote three years later, ". . . [but] I am so accustomed to action that I presume inaction would be tedious and perhaps not salutary." Webster would go on revising his dictionary until his death in 1843.

~~~~~

Webster's *American Dictionary* was both a personal and cultural milestone, cementing the author's own name in the language— *Webster* is practically synonymous with *dictionary* now—and ushering in what the linguist David Crystal calls "the age of dictionaries,"* a decades-long craze for encyclopedias, thesauruses, dictionaries, and reference books of all kinds among the English-speaking public. It also sparked, for an underground fringe of orthographic meddlers, fresh enthusiasm for simplified spelling. Webster's *color*s and *honor*s, though only mild reforms, had proven that the movement could indeed effect real change. So, as the lexicographer stepped off the stage, a new generation of simplifiers stepped on, bringing along new ideas, new letters, and Webster-size egos for world-changing reform.

---

* During "the age of dictionaries," Webster's former copying assistant became embroiled in a plagiarism scandal. Inspired by Webster's success, Joseph Worcester decided to publish a dictionary of his own. When his *Comprehensive Pronouncing and Explanatory Dictionary of the English Language* came out in 1830, sharp-eyed critics accused him of stealing from his former employer. Webster wrote to Worcester, directly asking if he had plagiarized his entries. "No," Worcester wrote back, "not many."

Something New

In 1829, James Ruggles, a 34-year-old schoolteacher from Ohio, put out a slim treatise proposing a "Universal Language"* designed to phoneticize spelling as well as regularize all plurals and verb tenses. He shortened *could* to *cood*, as most simplified spellers would, but he also changed the past tense of *know* to *noed*, as nobody but Ruggles would. "I hav noed meni mans hoo cood rite a gooder hand than miself," he wrote in defense of his system, "but fu can skribed swiftlier." A year later, a Quaker named Michael Barton crafted a 40-letter alphabet to capture a broad range of English's unique sounds. It captured them all right, but it did so with such complexity that something like the Lord's Prayer becomes entirely unrecognizable:

Barton may also have overextended himself with the project, for when it finally came time to *name* his alphabet, he clearly had nothing left in the tank: "Something New," he called it, and he spent the next several years trumpeting the virtues of the Something New alphabet.

---

* In 1887, a different "Universal Language" was proposed by a Polish doctor calling himself "Doktoro Esperanto." The doctor—real name: L. L. Zamenhoff—took aspects of Russian, Polish, Hebrew, German, English, Latin, Greek, French, and Italian and fused them into a new international language, with unique grammar rules, vocabulary, orthography, and pronunciation. "Were there but an international language," Zamenhoff wrote, ". . . all nations would be united in a common brotherhood." He initially called his system "Lingwe uniwersala"—"Universal Language"—but most users referred to it as *Esperanto*, meaning "one who hopes." Esperanto remains the most widely used constructed language today, with more than 100,000 fluent speakers worldwide.

A Radical, Universal and Philosophical Reform

The first truly inspired proposal from the post-Webster era came from, of all people, a French scholar. Like Benjamin Franklin and Michael Barton, Auguste Thibaudin understood the inefficiency of using 26 letters to cover English's 44 sounds. But where other reformers might have crafted new letters to fill in the alphabetical gaps, Thibaudin used numbers. First, he removed *C, Q, J,* and *X* from the alphabet and redistributed their roles among *S, K, G,* and *Z*. Next, he drew up a three-by-three grid, numbered 1 to 9, to represent our range of vowels—with 1 representing the *U* in *debut,* 9 being the *A* in *arms,* and 2–8 covering the gradation of sounds in between.

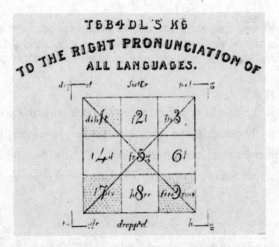

The faded words behind each number in the grid denote the vowel that the number represents. They are as follows: 1. Debut 2. Fool 3. Dieu 4. Toad 5. Frog 6. Eel 7. Lady 8. Hare 9. Firearms. From *A. Thibaudin's Proposed Original System For A Radical, Universal And Philosophical Reform In The Spelling Of Languages,* 1842.

To capture even finer vowel nuances, Thibaudin mirrored some of his numbers. (3 flips into a Ɛ to indicate the vowel in *earth*.) Thus, without introducing new characters or purchasing pricy metal fonts, Thibaudin added 18 letters to the alphabet.

Like Barton's before him, Thibaudin's version of the Lord's Prayer, featured here in all its alphanumeric glory, pushes the limits of legibility:

92R F9THƐR H26TSH 9RT 6N H8VN
H9L58D B6 TH96 N7M.
TH96 K6NGDƐM KƐM,
TH96 26L B6 DƐN 6N ƐRTH,
9Z 6T 6Z 6N H8VN.
G6V ƐS TH6S D76 92R D76L7 BR8D.
9MN.

The Anti-Absurd Alphabet

Many decades later, the world would embrace the fusion of numbers and letters (looking at you, future texters), but in the conservative early Victorian era, Thibaudin's radical reform went nowhere. His technique of flipping letters on their axis, however, resurfaced in the work of Major Bartłomiej Beniowski, a Polish-Lithuanian military officer living in London. Beniowski is best remembered, if he's remembered at all, for developing a memory mnemonic in 1842 called "phrenotypics," which some professional memory athletes[*] still use today to memorize long series of numbers for the World Memory Championships.[†] Beniowski was obsessed with

---

[*] Yes, that's a thing.
[†] Yes, that's a thing too.

systems of logic. Polish, his primary language, has a highly phonetic and logical orthography. English, which has eight ways of pronouncing *ough*, does not. Beniowski used one word to describe English, and he used it so often that it became his refrain: *absurd.* English spelling is an "ABOMINABLE ABSURDITY," he wrote (his caps, not mine), and within it are contained smaller "glaring absurdities," "monomaniacal absurdities," "stupefying absurdities," and "oppressing, incubus-like absurdities" that suck out the souls of their users. Hoping to thwart these orthographic incubi, Beniowski proposed the "Anti-Absurd Alphabet."*

Instead of flipping his letters horizontally, as Thibaudin had, Beniowski flipped his vertically, assigning new upside-down sounds to his new upside-down letters. By inverting two lowercase vowels (*A* and *E*) and seven consonants (*V, Y, C, G, H, T,* and *L*), Beniowski could bring the alphabet nine letters closer to perfection, and nine letters further from absurdity. In 1844, he put his 35-letter alphabet to work on the Lord's Prayer—now apparently the customary sample text for spelling reformers:

> Ɜr fʃɟer, whiʃ ʌrt in hevn, hʌləed bɐ ɟy
> nam : ɟy kingdɥm kɥm : ɟy wil bɐ dɥn in
> erɹ ʌz it iz in hevn; giv ɥs ɟis da Ɜr dalɐ
> bred : ʌnd fɔrgiv ɥs Ɜr trespʌsez ʌz wɐ forgiv
> ɟem ɟʌt trespʌs agenst ɥs : ʌnd lɐd ɥs not
> intu temtashon : bɥt dɐliver ɥs from ɐvl : fɔr
> ɟyn iz ɟe kingdɥm, ɟe pɜer, ʌnd ɟc glərɐ, fɔr
> ever ʌnd ever.   amen.

---

* When asked where the name came from, Beniowski explained that doctors often "manufacture names for their remedies, by simply prefixing the little word 'anti'" to the illness, as in *anti*-spasmodics, *anti*-epileptics, or *anti*-narcotics. We have a fever, and the only prescription is *anti*-absurdics.

Just how absurd is English spelling anyway? To help explain, Bartłomiej Beniowski came up with an analogy.

Imagine that the names of our everyday objects—lamps, desks, spoons, socks—fluctuated as wildly and arbitrarily as our spelling. For instance: The object you have in your hands is called a *book*—but only on the first day of the month. The rest of the month it's called a *pasta strainer*—unless it's raining or windy, in which case it's a *garden gnome*.

Now imagine codifying such absurdity into a language guidebook. Beniowski shows what that might look like:

> The piece of furniture usually called table you should continue to call "*table*," with the following few restrictions:

1. You shall call it "*broom*" on Sundays, Tuesdays, Wednesdays, and Fridays. N.B. The *m* to be silent.
2. On Mondays, Thursdays, and Saturdays, you shall name it "*window*" (except the first Saturdays of January, April, June, September, and November, when it must be called, according to Statute 1, "*broom*.") N.B. The *oo* to be sounded *i*.

> The same piece of furniture you shall name "candle," according to the following exact philosophical rules:

1. On Sundays, from 35' 49" after twelve till sun-set, call it clearly "*candle*," sounding the *c* as *sh* and the *a* as *o* [except on cloudy days, to be defined hereafter].
2. You will occasionally call the four-legged furniture not exactly *candle*, but candle with the prefix "kabooo," and sometimes with the trifling addition of a few mute liquido-hard diphthongal consonants: for instance, thus—"Kaboo candle-shwyoukrt" (bearing always in mind the regulations above-mentioned).

Sometimes, though, you will call it simply "table," but this must be left to your tact and taste, which we hope and trust are very great . . .

Beniowski dubbed his converts "anti-absurdists" and urged all books to be printed "anti-absurdly." "Every man short of an idiot," he declared, "or a broken-hearted, enthralled, and obfuscated A B C teacher's assistant, ought to have the courage and judgment to call [our present spelling] a 'most ridiculously despotic nonsense.'"

To further illustrate the nonsense of English, Beniowski offered a personal anecdote. Years earlier, on his first trip to England, Beniowski dined at a hotel overlooking the harbor where his ship had just docked. At the time, he had a working understanding of English, but he had never spoken the language aloud. When he tried ordering a salad from the menu, the waiter couldn't understand him. "Sailaid," Beniowski repeated, sounding out the word with the elongated *A* of *say* and *lay*. "Sailaid, sailaid, SAILAID!" Eventually, his repeated alarms caused his fellow diners to rush to the window in panic. They thought their ship had *sailed* off without them.

"What is to be done?" Beniowski asks rhetorically. "Little things," he answers himself, "very little things, very easy little things." He lists his new very easy little rules for anti-absurd spelling:

- Reject the double final consonants.
- Reject the letters representing sounds not in existence in the English language.
- Agree upon each of your letters representing one sound, and one sound only—one and the same sound on all occasions without any exceptions, restrictions, or provisos.
- Stick to your agreements, and let nobody, not even Madam Etymology, divert you from sticking to your agreements.
- Form no entirely new symbols.
- Borrow from nobody.

THE PRIMER.

THE ANTI-ABSURD OR PHRENOTYPIC
ALPHABET.

a ʌ ʎ b ch d
ʋ e f g h y i
j k l m n o
ə ɔ ʒ p r s
sh t th ꞁ u
ꞁ v w z ɪ

		Absurdly			*Anti-absurdly*
a	ape	.	.	ap
ʌ	apple	.	ʌpl
ʎ	arm	.	.	ʎrm
b	babe	.	.	bab

(L) The 35 letters of Beniowski's Anti-Absurd Alphabet. (R) Four
common words spelled "absurdly" versus "anti-absurdly." (1844)

When Beniowski published the *Anti-Absurd Alphabet* in 1844,
it landed with predictably little fanfare. The problem, he decided,
was that his alphabet wasn't anti-absurd *enough*. There were still
too many vowels in it—and not enough *numbers*. He realized
that if he could integrate his Anti-Absurd Alphabet with phrenotypics, his number-based mnemonic system, he could create a single unified scheme that would translate any word into numbers. What's more logical than that? So, Beniowski drew up a 0–9 grid, and to each number he assigned a series of consonants. Number 8 contained *F, V,* and *W.* Number 9 contained *P* and *B.* Vowels were nowhere to be found. It

NUMBERS.

THE Arabic figures 0, 1, 2, 3, 4, 5, 6, 7, 8, 9,
we shall represent by consonants according
to the following diagrams

was a numeric lingua franca, a digital Rosetta stone; simply by consulting the grid, any word could be written numerically.

To write *paper*, one would first reduce the word to its consonants: P-P-R. The letter *P* falls on the number 9 and *R* on the 4, so *paper* thus becomes the number 994. *Knowledge*, spelled anti-absurdly as "nolej" and further reduced to *N-L-J*, becomes 256.

"Any given word may be translated into numbers," Beniowski promised. "Thus: the word *man* contains the consonants *m n*, and is therefore 32." In theory, any work of prose or poetry could be memorized by first translating it into a string of numbers and then using phrenotypics to commit the numbers to memory. The World Memory Championships record for "most pi places memorized" is 70,000 digits. That's the length of *Animal Farm*.

On that note, I present the Lord's Prayer, translated to the best of my own abilities, in Beniowski numerals:

4 814 86 41 2 682
6581 9 1 23
1 72713 73
1 85 9 12 2 41 0 1 0 2 682
78 0 10 1 4 15 941
21 8478 0 4 640900
0 8 8478 13 11 64090 7201 0
21 51 0 21 21 139162
91 1584 0 843 85
84 12 0 1 72713, 1 984, 21 1 754, 4 84 21 84.
32.

At last, simplicity had arrived.

Part II

Illinois, 1859

Abraham Lincoln has just suffered the fifth electoral loss of his career, a dramatic Senate defeat to the incumbent Stephen Douglas. Returning to his law practice in Springfield, Illinois, he begins preparing for his next electoral challenge: a long-shot campaign for the U.S. presidency in 1860.

As his platform takes shape, Lincoln receives a peculiar envelope in the mail. The sender is a man named A. B. Pikard—and the recipient is "A. Linkon Esq."

Lincoln unfolds the papers inside and begins to read:

> I trust u wil hav no difikulti in redin dis. U se it is ritn in de
> Fonetik Alfabet, and if u deturmin a letr in eni plas u deturmin
> it in evri plas.

Lincoln has seen spelling like this before. He's an avid reader of Artemus Ward, the American humorist who spins tales in a style known as "phunny phonetics." ("Utica is a trooly grate sitty," reads one of Ward's sketches. ". . . The people gave me a cordyal recepshun.") But this letter is neither funny nor phunny. In fact, as Abe reads on, he finds himself being criticized for not denouncing the 1850 Fugitive

Slave Act, a series of laws requiring states to return runaway slaves (an issue upon which Lincoln will dally until 1862):

> Yr Fadrz mad a deklarashn undr hwich owr batls wer fot—and owr konstitooshn Guvernment inogarated—That ol men are kreated ekwal iz Selfevident . . . I undrstand dat de wurd Slav woz purpusli & Stoodiusli left owt ov de konstitooshn; if so I tak it dat it woz nevr dezind tu be put in, and hens hwil de konstitooshn providz for return ov personz hoo o Survis, it sez nutin ov returnin persons hoo hav eskapt from infurnal pirasi.*

Pikard's words—or the few that Lincoln can make out—don't have an immediate effect on Lincoln's platform. But in three short years, President Lincoln will sign legislation repealing the Fugitive Slave Act. Eventually, he'll abolish the "infurnal pirasi" of slavery altogether.

On September 22, 1862, Lincoln calls his Cabinet together for the first reading of his Emancipation Proclamation. It's the most important executive order in American history and the defining moment of Lincoln's career. Before he begins, however, he has some crude comedy he wants to share with his Cabinet. "'You egrejus ass, that air's a wax figger,'" Lincoln reads aloud from the latest Artemus Ward essay, undercutting this historic occasion with the low humor of phunny phonetics. "'That Judas Iscariot can't show hisself in Utiky with impunerty by a darn site!'" "The President," one observer writes, "seemed to enjoy it very much."

---

* Tr: "Your Fathers made a declaration under which our battles were fought—and our constitution Government inaugurated—That all men are created equal is Self-evident . . . I understand that the word Slave was purposely and studiously left out of the constitution; if so I take it that it was never designed to be put in, and hence while the constitution provides for return of persons who owe Service, it says nothing of returning persons who have escaped from infernal piracy."

6

The Phunny Phellows

I attrybute my suksess in life to mi devoshun to spelyng.

—Josh Billings

Simplified spelling looks silly. There's no getting around that.
For most readers today, the mere appearance of *nolej* or *edukayshun*
instantly sets the funny bone a-tingling, and no matter how
many Webster dissertations or Victorian number schemes they
read, they'll never see simplified spelling as anything but a source
of amyuzmint. In that sense, not much has changed since the
1800s.

As the simplified spelling movement gained ground in the nineteenth century, America's humorists couldn't resist poking fun at
the pedantic craze. Wits like Artemus Ward ("Toosday nite I peared
be4 a C of upturned faces in the Red Skool House") and Petroleum
Vesuvius Nasby ("I hev bin in the Apossel biznis more extensively
than any man sence the time uv Paul") capitalized on the growing
appeal of simplified spelling by turning it into an irreverent form
of wordplay (letterplay?) and eventually into its own micro literary
genre. In 1864, when Josh Billings failed to find an audience for
his "Essay on the Mule," he rewrote it as "Essa on the Muel bi
Josh Billings" and it launched his literary career. Suddenly, Billings
was the comedic superstar of misspelled literature. "I attrybute my
suksess in life to mi devoshun to spelyng," he once wrote, and he
wasn't kidding: spelyng, or rather "misspelyng," became his brand.

He found his calling in 1870 with his "Farmer's Allminax," an annual parody publication that offered phonetic advice to young men ("Dont be diskouraged if yure mustash dont gro") and monthly "horoskopes" ("The yung female born during this month will show grate judgement in sorting her lovers, and will finally marry a real estate agent").

JOSH BILLINGS'
Farmer's Allminax

FOR THE YEAR
1870

Being tew years since leap year, and ninety-four years since the Amerikan people left Grate Brittain tew take care ov herself, and started a snug little bizziness ov their own, which I am instrukted tew state, iz payin well.

CONTAINING
all that iz necessary for an Allminax, and a good deal besides.

Billings, Nasby, and Ward were known collectively as the "Phunny Phellows"—humorists who cashed in on the inherent silliness of simplified spelling. In the 1880s, critics began grouping another author with them: Mark Twain. Twain had been toying with quasi-phonetic spelling for years, but it was his 1884 *Adventures of Huckleberry Finn* that earned his induction into this merry band of misspellers. "The Widow Douglas, she took me for her son," says the ruffian Huck Finn, "and allowed she would sivilize me." For Billings and his ilk, simplified spelling was not only an easy laugh but a mark of socioeconomic class. Simply by simplifying the spelling of a character's speech, they could indicate their humble background. The simpler they spelled, the less sivilized they were.

Simplified spelling humor is a close cousin of "dialect writing," a literary device that uses distorted spelling in the vernacular of a (usually low-class) character. Eliza Doolittle might be the eternal archetype: "Ow, eez ye-ooa san, is e?" she warbles in her signature cockney, dutifully transcribed by her author George Bernard Shaw. "Wal, fewd dan y' de-ooty bawmz a mather should, eed now bettern to spawl a pore gel's flahrzn than ran away atbaht pyin. Will ye-oo py me f'them?"* The techniques of the simplified spellers are there, if subtle: *flowers* rewritten as *flahrz*, *girl* rendered as *gel*. But while dialect writing serves to bring depth or authenticity to a character, simplified spelling humor aimed merely to entertain. It was primarily a visual gag, not an expression of dialect. It was more for the eye than for the ear.

Jokey misspellings had been on the rise since the 1830s, when a brief orthographic fad captured New England's journalists. Certain writers would amuse themselves with an inside joke: First, they would deliberately misspell a short phrase. "No go," for instance, would be

---

* Don't worry, I can't understand it either.

#66

> ### "Affurisms" by Josh Billings (a selection)
>
> - "Laffing iz the sensashun ov pheeling good all over, and showing it principally in one spot."
> - "There iz only one good substitute for the endearments ov a sister, and that iz the endearments ov sum other pheller's sister."
> - "A good reliable sett ov bowels, iz wurth more tu a man, than enny quantity ov brains."
> - "There iz 2 things in this life for which we are never fully prepared, and that iz twins."
> - "Suckcess iz az hard tew define az falling oph from a log, a man kant alwuss tell exackly how he did it."
> - "Flattery iz like Colone water, tew be smelt ov, not swallowed."
> - "Most ov the happiness in this world konsists in possessing what others kant git."
> - "I don't know ov a better kure for sorrow than tew pity sum boddy else."
> - "He who wears tite boots will hav too acknowledge the corn."

"know go." Then they would abbreviate that misspelling, as though communicating with each other in insider shorthand. "Know go" thus becomes KG. "No use," respelled as "know yuse," was abbreviated as KY. OW meant "all right" ("oll wright") and OR meant "all wrong" ("oll rong"). NC was "enough said" ("nuff ced"). And OK—the lone vestige of this lingo—meant "all correct"—that is, "oll korrect."

"OK" debuted in a Boston newspaper on March 23, 1839 ("OK Day," to those who observe) and quickly caught on. A year later, the *Boston Daily Times* printed a poem on the trendy sensation sweeping New England:

> What is't that ails the people, Joe?
> They're in a kurious way,
> For every where I chance to go,

There's nothing but o.k.
They do not use the alphabet,
What e'er they wish to say,
And all the letters they forget,
Except the o. and k.

I've seen them on the Atlas's page,
And also in the Post,
When both were boiling o'er with rage,
To see which fibbed the most.
The Major has kome off the best;
The Kurnel is surprised!
The one it seems meant Oll Korrect,
The other, Oll kapsized!

Processions have been all the go,
And illuminations tall;
Hand bills were headed with k. o.,
Which means, they say, kome oll!
The way the people sallied out,
Was a kaution to the lazy;
And when o. k. I heard them shout,
I thought it meant oll krazy.

. . . This theme has on Pegasus' way
Most wantonly obtruded,
And now, with joy, I have to say
It's o. k. oll konkluded.
Yet four more lines I needs must write,
From which there's no retreat,

O. k. again I must endite,
And—lo! It's oll komplete!

Newspapers played a pivotal role in relaxing the spelling norms of nineteenth-century America. Confronted with the dual demands of capturing reader attention and navigating narrow column space, editors began adopting abbreviated, catchy headlines. Words were shortened, and alternative spellings like *thru* and *nite* became common practice. The Phunny Phellows were all former newspapermen themselves, and they used the tricks of their journalistic trade in their comical storytelling.

Eventually, the Phunny Phellows found they could make more money taking their humor writings on the road and "performing" them for audiences. Their rough-speaking, semiliterate, jargon-heavy characters made for great one-man comedy (even if the phonetic spellings didn't translate to the stage), and humor-lovers around the country paid top dollar to watch the Phellows present their works in colorful vernacular.

Dave Chappelle and George Carlin owe a great debt to the Phunny Phellows. They were the first comic monologists, the first literary funnymen to earn a living as live entertainers, and as a result are often considered the first stand-up comedians. Artemus Ward, the first of the Phellows, is hailed by many as the original king of comedy.

The phonetic antics of the Phunny Phellows would cast a long shadow over the simplified spelling movement. With their laffably low-class, comically uncouth spellings, the Phellows turned phonetic orthography into a marker of indignity, a style of writing closer to Huck Finn than to Ben Franklin. The Phunny Phellows would forever taint simplified spelling in the eyes of the world.

Shood it be my fate 2 perish on the battle-feeld, amid the rore uv battle and the horrors uv missellaneous carnage, my last thot, ez life ebbs slowly away shel be uv her, and ask her ef she can't send me half or three-quarters uv the money she gits fer washin, ez whisky costs fritefully here.

—Petroleum Vesuvius Nasby,
The Nasby Papers, 1864

The Deseret Alphabet

The incarnations of the Hindoo gods are very numerous,
but the inconsistencies of English orthography are infinite.

—George Watt

Until the 1850s, simplified spelling in America remained a phenomenon of the East, tending to gather around universities, printing houses, and other sites of language and learning. But as America expanded west, this peculiar, pedantic pursuit jumped the Mississippi and the Rockies and leaked into the wild red-rock desert plains of Utah.

In 1847, a small Christian sect arrived in the Salt Lake Valley, led by a charismatic young preacher named Brigham Young. Like so many westward pioneers before and since, Young saw in the open expanse a vision of Zion—the Promised Land. He furnished it with all the rudiments of a working paradise, digging irrigation ditches, planting potato farms, and pacing out a series of interconnecting roads. He formed a legislature and a militia. And then he turned to spelling.

"The English language," Young told a congregation in 1852, "in its written and printed form, is one of the most prominent now in use for absurdity." He provided the example of *P*: we force this poor letter into wildly different roles in *apple* (the sound of a *P*), *physic* (the sound of an *F*), and *phthisic* (no sound at all). "I say," he said, "let it have one sound all the time."

One of the more comical looks at spelling absurdity is Alexander J. Ellis's *Plea for Phonotypy and Phonography*. In this 1845 pamphlet advocating for English spelling reform, Ellis presents a list of common words: *favorite, servant, orthography*, etc. He then deconstructs each to its distinct sound components and respells it to farcical excess. *Favorite* transforms into *phaighpheawraibt* through a fusion of *PHysic, strAIGHt, nePHew, EArth, WRite, captAIn*, and *deBT*. By the same demon alchemy, *servant* becomes *psourrphuakntw* and *orthography* becomes *eolotthowghrhoighuay*.

Ellis, an expert mathematician, then extends his scrutiny to the word *scissors*. He reduces it to its phonemes—*S-I-Z-R-Z*—and counts all the possible letter combinations for each. *S*, for instance, can be spelled in 17 different ways (*S, SC, SS, PS, C, TS*, and so on). *I* has 36 possible spellings. Multiplying all these variations together, Ellis gets a staggering figure: in our wonderful English language, we have 58.4 million ways to spell *scissors*.

When a group finds itself on the fringes of society, language can be a powerful way to define its identity and solidarity. To Young, the leader of the Church of Jesus Christ of Latter-day Saints, better known as the Mormon Church, the identity marker for his community would be a rational spelling system, one that wouldn't overload letters with multiple roles and wouldn't overload children with wasted years of schooling. According to Young, children squander precious time learning English spelling—and as the parent of 54 children by 15 wives,[*] he knew this better than anyone. "The child is perplexed," Young once complained of one or another of his brood, "that the sign 'A' should have one sound in *mate*, a second sound in *father*, a third sound in *fall*, a fourth sound in *man*, and a fifth sound in *many*."

Benjamin Franklin had come to the same conclusion. So had

---

[*] A prolific polygamist, Young would eventually have 56 wives and 57 children.

Noah Webster. But unlike his reformist forebears, Brigham Young didn't need the blessing of a literary establishment or the vote of a political body to construct his linguistic utopia. He had in front of him a new society, a virgin land, a blank page. He could write upon it any language he chose.

~~~~~

Young saw spelling reform as he saw the steam engine: a symbol of progress, industry, and the growing speed of the modern world. If the Mormon Church hoped to thrive in America, it would need to embrace certain innovations in written language. So, in 1850, Young tasked his secretary, George Darling Watt, to construct an alphabet.

It should be a large alphabet, Young instructed—close to 40 letters to capture our spoken nuances—with a one-to-one correspondence of characters and sounds. It should also comprise a "new and original set of characters"—none of those English letters, Greek letters, Franklin letters, upside-down letters, or other failed alphabets attempted by previous simplified spellers. And, most certainly, no numbers.

Watt, who had little to qualify him for this linguistic undertaking, spent the next four years sketching out an alphabet to meet Young's criteria. After a succession of bad drafts,* he unveiled a 38-letter phonetic scheme in January 1854. The *Deseret News,* the official Mormon newspaper, sang its praises:

---

* When Watt submitted his first draft in 1853, one Mormon leader reproached him, in front of the whole Board of Regents, for copying the alphabets of previous reformers: "We want a new kind of alphabet, differing from the compound mess of stuff upon that sheet . . . What have you gained by the alphabet on that card I ask you? Show me one item, can you point out the first advantage that you have gained over the old one? . . . You have the same old alphabet over again, only a few additional marks, and they only mystify it more, and more."

These characters are much more simple in their structure than the usual alphabetical characters . . . We may derive a hint of the advantage to orthography, from spelling the word *eight*, which in the new alphabet only requires two letters instead of five to spell it, viz: AT. There will be a great saving of time and paper by the use of the new characters . . . an ordinary writer can probably write one hundred words a minute with ease . . .

Early Mormon flyer explaining the 38 letters of the Deseret Alphabet and their usage. (Utah State Historical Society)

Deseret is a word from the Book of Mormon meaning "honeybee." Young had christened his territory Deseret to signify the Mormons' industriousness and unity, and he petitioned, unsuccessfully, to make Deseret the 31st state in the Union. Young named Utah's first college the University of Deseret (now the University of Utah) and his newspaper the *Deseret News*. Naturally, when it came to his new orthography, he called it the "Deseret Alphabet."*

That spring, the Mormon Board of Regents sent orders to start peppering Deseret letters into schoolbooks, road signs, shop signs, headstones, coins, and municipal notices. "It will be the means of introducing uniformity in our orthography," said Young, "and the years that are now required to learn to read and spell can be devoted to other studies." The Board also arranged to print a section of the *Deseret News* in the Deseret Alphabet, and authorized a new Deseret edition of the Book of Mormon, two Deseret readers for elementary school instruction, and a Deseret dictionary.

Offshoot Christian sects flared and fizzled in the 1800s the way tech start-ups do today, but Young believed that he had found the key to his

The *Deseret First Book*, a school primer published in the Deseret Alphabet, 1868.

---

* The word *bee* in *spelling bee* has nothing to do with the buzzing insect. It likely originates from the Old English word *bēn* or *bene*, meaning "prayer" or "service," both of which were often performed in a community social gathering. A *spelling bee*, etymologically speaking, is a communal spelling gathering.

George D. Watt, the inventor of the Deseret Alphabet, had long been the darling of the Mormon Church. He was the first official British convert to Mormonism—the first Englander to take the plunge—and thus was celebrated across Deseret as a symbol of international expansion.

His claim to this title, however, was all due to some quick footwork. Just after sunrise on July 30, 1837, Watt and eight other British men arrived at the River Ribble in Lancashire to be baptized. As the would-be converts changed out of their clothes at a nearby clearing, Watt and another man sprinted to the riverbank, hoping to steal the title for themselves. Watt got there first. He plunged into the Ribble waters and emerged a reborn man, and the Mormons' first English convert.

community's survival. By using a spelling that only Mormons understood, the Church could control what its members read (and, by extension, what they thought). It would also build unity within the early Church, gathering its members around a shared project—the mass implementation of a new written language—while limiting communication with those outside the Church. And in times of war, secrets could be kept safe: All communication would be automatically encoded in the Mormon language. The Deseret Alphabet was therefore a fortress, a way to keep outsiders *out* and insiders *in,* a symbol of unity and a barrier to assimilation. For this community of nontrinitarian Christians, which had been chased by pitchfork mobs from New York to Missouri to Illinois to Nebraska, any kind of barricade was welcome.

Constructing the Deseret Alphabet was the easy part. The real challenge lay in persuading the community to use it. When the new Deseret primers landed on their desks in 1854, Mormon schoolteachers, eyeing Watt's funky new alphabet and bracing for the inevitable headache of teaching it, left the books to collect dust.

Pressured by Young, the *Deseret News* agreed to reserve one section in each edition for Deseret-language articles—but refused his request to cast the whole newspaper in the new type.

Of course, any kind of abrupt change in language will have resisters. (Does anyone actually *want* to learn to read all over again?) In the case of Deseret, much of the pushback centered on its visual appeal. It is a uniquely unattractive alphabet. To save money, the Board had directed Watt to lop off all "ascenders" and "descenders," those lacy garnishes that extend above and below the main body of a letter. (All the consonants in *alphabet*, for instance.) During the life of a metal typeface, ascenders and descenders are the first to wear out. And yet—as it becomes clear looking at the Deseret Alphabet—they are aesthetically critical, and the result of losing them is a boxy, stilted design. The Board's goal was function, not fashion, and it showed.

Finances strained the Deseret Alphabet throughout the decade. After spending $20,000 on its first sets of metal letters (which had to be custom ordered from St. Louis—and then, when Young rejected the St. Louis design, from a different foundry in New York), the Church estimated that continuing to print materials in Deseret would cost $5 million over the next several years. It was a mighty figure for a fledgling church trying to survive in the middle of an unforgiving desert. Already in a precarious financial state, the Deseret Alphabet lost the balance of its budget to war. Ten years after the Mormons arrived in the Salt Lake Valley, federal troops came to oust Young as Utah governor on suspicion of plotting against the United States. Young answered with a militia, and over the next fourteen months the Mormons faced off with the U.S. Army in what came to be known as the Utah War.

This could have been a shining moment for Deseret—an opportunity to foster patriotism, loyalty, and unity in the community, rallying the faithful around a common linguistic banner. Instead, Deseret faded into the background, as the funds once earmarked for typeface and schoolbooks now went to fortifications and supplies.* Ultimately, the war remained (mostly) cold, and a year later resolved without a single large-scale battle. But with the Mormon budget nearly depleted, Deseret sputtered.

Ironically, it was the steam engine—the very symbol of industry that helped inspire Young's reform in the first place—that marked Deseret's downfall. In 1869, the Union Pacific railroad track reached the Utah border, bringing with it new settlers, new cultures, and new religions from far and wide, none of which had patience for Young's orthographic fantasies. The Board of Regents had lost patience by now, too, and after fifteen years, it officially stopped promoting the Deseret Alphabet. In all, only four complete books were ever printed in Deseret.

Following the fall of his alphabet, George Watt began straying from the Mormon Church to follow the teachings of William S. Godbe, a Mormon dissident. Watt joined Godbe's sectarian offshoot, the Godbeites, and in 1874 was officially excommunicated from the Church of Jesus Christ of Latter-day Saints.

The Deseret Alphabet faded from shop windows and coins, but its blocky letters lingered for years in Utah as familiar, if meaningless, symbols of the Mormon community. In 1876, seven years after the death of Deseret, a businessman named Feramorz Little† ran for mayor of Salt Lake City. A campaign ticket lists Feramorz's name

---

* Vastly outnumbered by U.S. troops, the Mormons employed a strategy of calculated pestering. "On ascertaining the locality or route of the troops," Mormon general Daniel H. Wells instructed his men, "proceed at once to annoy them in every possible way." This included setting midnight grass fires to prevent the U.S. Army from sleeping, and making loud noises to rouse the army's animals to stampede.

† By polygamous entanglement, Feramorz Little was both nephew and brother-in-law to Brigham Young.

above candidates for councilor, treasurer, and marshal. The text is written in traditional English spelling, using the familiar English alphabet, except in one key place: the flyer's border. There, flanking both sides of the ticket, are Watt's unmistakable Deseret letters, relics of a once-promising reformed spelling.

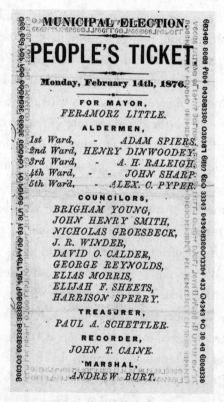

An 1876 campaign ticket for the People's Party
of Utah, with Deseret type around the border.

And what do the letters spell? Is it a Mormon tenet? A line of scripture? A political motto? No. They spell nothing. The letters are pure gibberish.

8

The Charge of Suffragist Shorthanders

> I attribiut mei helth and pouer ov endiurans tu abstinens
> from flesh meat and alkoholik drinks.
>
> —Isaac Pitman

In England in the mid-1800s, if someone self-identified as a simplified speller, there was a good chance they also belonged to one (or more) of the following countercultural movements of the time: alcohol temperance, vegetarianism, mysticism, homeopathy, and anti-vaccination.

Isaac Pitman—vice president of Britain's Vegetarian Society and inventor of the most popular simplified writing system of the nineteenth century—checked every one of these boxes. After quitting alcohol and meat at the age of 24, Pitman found he could work harder and longer hours—hours that he devoted to reforming language, practicing Swedenborgian mysticism,* and campaigning against mainstream medicine. "I attribiut mei helth and pouer ov endiurans tu abstinens from flesh meat and alkoholik drinks," he wrote in his invented spelling in 1859. "I kan kum tu no uther konkluzhon when I see the efekt ov such eks-

---

* Emanuel Swedenborg (1688–1772) was a Swedish scientist, theologian, and mystic. His teachings formed the basis of Swedenborgianism, a Restorationist Christian sect that preached simple, ethical living and regular communion with angels and spirits. His book *Heaven and Hell* (1758) is a first-person account of his visions of the afterlife.

tended ourz ov labor on uther men who eat meat and drink wein or beer."*

Temperance, a word usually reserved for alcohol, was a catchall for restraint and moderation in all endeavors, including language. *Simplicity* equalcd *wholesomeness* equaled *godliness*. And though they differed on the surface, these virtue movements were all bound underneath by a desire to return humanity to a state of purity and innocence. To Isaac Pitman, the irrationality of English spelling was a societal impurity like any other. Through spelling reform, he would bring language back to its primeval simplicity.

〜〜〜

Born in 1813 in Wiltshire, England, to an amateur astrologist and cloth manufacturer, Pitman quit school at 13 and joined a library, where he consumed anything and everything he laid hands on. He developed a large vocabulary. But because he only knew these words by their visual forms, rather than by their vocalized sounds, Pitman became embarrassingly prone to mispronunciation. He accented the wrong syllables, sounded out silent letters, and otherwise fell into every trap laid by tricky English spelling.

At 17, Pitman borrowed a copy of John Walker's *Critical Pronouncing Dictionary* and wrote out all the terms he had trouble pronouncing. He made a careful study of their sounds and spellings. At night, walking home from his 12-hour clerking shift, he practiced the lilts and inflections of the English tongue. He became obsessed with the *sounds* of words.

---

*   Tr: "I attribute my health and power of endurance to abstinence from flesh meat and alcoholic drinks. I can come to no other conclusion when I see the effect of such extended hours of labor on other men who eat meat and drink wine and beer."

From the start, words and music were inextricably linked in young Isaac's head. His childhood music teacher was also his town's only bookseller, and he referred to music and books as the "two loves" of his early life. As a teenager, he took a job transcribing songs into sheet music, and he temporarily gigged as the house organist in the Conigree Chapel in Trowbridge. As Pitman's musical and literary studies entwined, he became aware of the exquisite efficiency of musical notation as a sound guide. Using just a handful of symbols, positioned on the lines or spaces of a staff and often accompanied by tiny "articulation marks," Western musical notation can communicate a broad and nuanced vocabulary of sound.

Three different articulation marks in traditional
musical notation, modifying an E note underneath.
(From left to right, staccato, tenuto, and accent.)

If musical notation can capture all those good vibrations with just a few dots, arrows, and lines, thought Pitman—why not spelling?

In 1837, the year of his avowed temperance, Pitman printed *Stenographic Sound-Hand,* a pamphlet proposing a new writing system—"sound-hand"—modeled after musical notation. "By means of the principle of writing words in position," Pitman explained, words can be "readily distinguished, as are musical notes by means of the difference of place assigned to them on the staff."

In sound-hand, words are written precisely as they are pronounced. Every vocal articulation, or *phoneme,* in the English language has a single mark, and every mark represents only one unit of sound.

Sound-hand divides all the consonants of English into lines,

Three different vowel articulations in Pitman
shorthand, modifying the consonant *P*. (From
left to right, the vowels are *AH*, *AW*, and *I*,
which create the words *pa*, *paw*, and *pie*.)

hooks, and circles. (Sylvia Plath called them "scribbled little curli-
cues.") Their sounds are determined in part by their position on the
written line, which acts as a staff. Vowels are represented by dots,
dashes, and arrows adjoined to the consonant. "To the untrained
eye," wrote the humorist Bill Bryson, "Pitman's phonographic alphabet looks rather like a cross between Arabic and the trail of a
sidewinder snake."

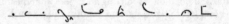

"The quick brown fox jumps over the lazy dog,"
as rendered in Pitman shorthand. (Courtesy of
the Encarta online encyclopedia.)

Pitman later changed the name of his system to "phonography,"
from the Greek *phōnē* ("sound") and *graphē* ("writing"). Today we
know it as "Pitman shorthand."*

Pitman hoped that, in time, his writing system would replace

---

*   Pitman's was not the first shorthand. Marcus Tullius Tiro, the slave-secretary (there's
a profession you don't hear about anymore) of Cicero, developed "Tironian shorthand"
in the first century B.C. to capture his master's speedy dictation. Both Charles Dickens
and his fictional character David Copperfield were adherents of "Gurney shorthand," an
eighteenth-century system devised by British clockmaker Thomas Gurney. In the early
1900s, the all-cursive "Gregg shorthand" became the go-to system for secretaries and
reporters in the United States, while Pitman continued to be favored in the U.K. into the
mid–twentieth century.

the old English orthography. Until then, it would serve merely as a shortcut for the old spelling, designed to capture thoughts and dictation quickly for later transcription into traditional long-hand.

The first professionals to utilize Pitman shorthand were stenographers—clerks and secretaries transcribing legal proceedings, business meetings, and other workplace communiqués. Until the 1860s, most stenographers were male. But when men vacated their secretarial jobs to fight in the Civil War, women began to infiltrate the field. Gradually, stenography transformed from a majority male occupation to an almost exclusively female one, aided by a flourishing of women's shorthand schools in the U.S. and U.K. and a changing attitude toward women joining the workforce.

Isaac Pitman's brothers, Benjamin and Jacob, also got into the shorthand game. Benjamin helped to popularize Pitman shorthand in the United States, while Jacob did the same in Australia. Jacob's epitaph, on a grave in Sydney, utilizes "phonotype," a form of simplified spelling using English letters, created by his brother Isaac:

IN LUVING MEMORI OV JACOB PITMAN

. . . INTRODIUST FONETIK SHORT HAND AND WOZ THE FERST MINISTER IN THEEZ KOLONIZ OV THE DOKTRINZ OV THE SEKOND OR NIU KRISTIAN CHURCH WHICH AKNOLEJEZ THE LORD JESUS CHRIST IN HIZ DEVEIN HIUMANITI AZ THE KREATER OV THE YUNIVERS, THE REDEEMER AND REJENERATER OV MEN. GOD OVER AUL, BLESED FOR EVER.

Some of these women's schools, such as Maud Slater's Short-hand and Typing School in Scotland, doubled as meeting spots for suffragists, who gathered after hours to recruit supporters, hold fundraisers, and print suffrage literature. Naturally, the groups commingled: suffragists learned the art of shorthand, stenographers joined the feminist fight, and suffrage and shorthand thus became linked in the struggle for women's rights.

Pitman shorthand, like the Bloomer dress, came to be a symbol of female empowerment. If the Bloomer liberated women from their sartorial constraints—long skirts, tight waists, organ-squeezing corsets—then shorthand unshackled their orthographic cuffs, quickening their transcription rates and increasing their job efficiency. Women often referred to the Bloomer as their "freedom dress." They might rightly have called shorthand their "freedom spelling."

The charge of suffragist shorthanders was led by Eliza Burnz, a Pitman acolyte and women's rights activist best known today as "the Mother of Women Stenographers." Born Eliza Boardman Burns (note the final *S*) in Essex in 1823, Eliza discovered Pitman shorthand in an 1845 article in the pseudoscientific *Phrenological Journal.* "As I read, the whole plan in its wonderful simplicity and beauty unfolded before my mental vision," she recalled. ". . . I perceived the numerous and still greater blessings which would come to all future generations, when the truth, as it is in phonetic science, should be made the basis of language teaching."

From that moment, Burns committed herself body and soul to phonetic spelling. She began styling her name *Burnz,* with a *Z* instead of an *S,* to make it known—loud, clear, and phonetic—what she stood for. In 1850, she gave birth to a daughter. She named her Foneta.

As a schoolteacher in Tennessee, where Eliza had moved with her family as a teenager, she struggled to teach children the irrational orthography of English. When she introduced them to the simple

Vegetarians, homeopaths, teetotalers, and simplified spellers all fell under the general term "cranks"—activists attracted to the health and wellness fads of the day. Their critics noted, with amusement, that the narrower the social cause, the wordier the name of the organization. "The Dominion Alliance for the Total Suppression of the Liquor Traffic," "The London Society for the Abolition of Compulsory Vaccination," and "The International Convention for the Amendment of English Orthografy" were among the worst offenders. "The Association for the Total Suppression of White Hats!" parodied a journalist in 1883. "The Anti-Flower-in-the-Button-Hole League! The Society for the Abolition of Green-Tea Drinking! The Association for the Restriction of Glove-Fastenings to One Button! The Local Option Snuff Confederation!"

wonders of Pitman shorthand, however, they were supposedly so glad to finally be spelling sensibly that, according to Burnz, they went on a genuine spelling rampage, joyfully practicing Pitman outside of school and at all hours of the night (to the apparent exasperation of their parents). Following a stern reprimand from the school for unleashing anarchy, Burnz packed a bag and fled for a place "where greater intelligence reigned." She settled in New York and opened the Burnz School of Shorthand for women, teaching her own brand of Pitmanesque stenography called "Burnz' Fonic Shorthand."

As the century wore on, Eliza Burnz became a loud and disruptive voice for both spelling reform and suffrage. In 1888, she managed to wrap her dual passions into one memorable publicity stunt. Amid a tight campaign for New York City mayor, Burnz arrived at a Manhattan polling station and asked to be registered to vote.

When the polling officer denied her entry, Burnz replied sharply:

"But the Constitution does not make any mention of women. It speaks only of persons. Am I not a person?"

A commotion ensued, and as officers escorted her out, and the press readied their pens, Burnz took the opportunity to promote her other cause. "When you write down my name," she announced to all scribes within earshot, "be sure to write it *Burnz*. You should know that 'Burns' does not sound like 'Burnz.'"

~~~~

As railroads began stitching together the American landscape, reformers and educators started referring to Pitman shorthand by a new nickname: "Railroad Writing." The implication was clear: shorthand was as swift and efficient as a train. Just as American steam came to epitomize industry in the nineteenth century, shorthand became synonymous with the modern, fast-paced demands of the professional world. You could almost hear the engines chugging in the furrowed brows of stenographers as, hands skipping over notepads, they captured human speech at a velocity once thought impossible. Shorthand wasn't just a tool—it was an ideology, a tacit endorsement of an accelerating world—a shorthand, if you will, for society's broader obsession with progress and efficiency.

And shall not we the railroad-writing scheme
From Ignorance and Bigotry redeem,
And leave the horse-power system to the sages,
Who stick to oldness in their words and pages,
And cling to a decrepit system's form,
Lest something new might trouble them with storm,
Dry up the ocean, hurl down all the mountains,

And start volcanoes from their glowing fountains?—
All this will happen surely, you're afraid,
Because, forsooth, an Alphabet is made!

—Attributed to "M.D." (1846)

Frĕdum Speling

In their quests to live pure and ethical lives, many simplified spellers, including Isaac Pitman and Eliza Burnz, practiced a form of
sexual abstinence known as "Dianism." Named for Diana, goddess
of chastity in Roman mythology, Dianism was the immaculate
brainchild of Henry M. Parkhurst, a radical spelling reformer and
Chief Court Reporter for the U.S. Senate. In his 1882 pamphlet
*Diana: A Psycho-Fyziological Essay on Sexual Relations, for Married
Men and Women,* Parkhurst introduces the basic principles of his
philosophy of non-indulgence—all rendered, of course, in simplified spelling:

> [The idea] that man needs fyzical relief from a continūus
> secretion, is anserd by the . . . fact that men, not deficient
> in sexual vigor, liv for munths . . . with no such fyzical in-
> convenience as is often complaind of by men who happen
> to be deprived of their acustomd indulgence for a week or
> two at a time . . . The fyzical manifestations which do not
> invite ultimation, ar the best and surest evidence of sexual
> affection, and the hihest posibl manifestation of sexual luv.

When it came to sexual luv, some simplified spellers took the
opposite view. Stephen Pearl Andrews, the publisher of the *Anglo-
Sacsun*—the "ferst fonetik pêper publisht in America," as one
writer succinctly noted—was New York's biggest free-love advo-

cate. In 1853, he founded a private club on Broadway called the New York Free Love League, secretly referred to as "The Club" in the presence of non-Club members. The Club practiced a philosophy of "freedom of the affections"—a euphemistic phrase defined by one visitor as "the implicit following of every freak of fancy or libidinous curiosity in the sexual relations." If you were lucky enough to receive an invitation, you would head over to Taylor's Saloon, one of New York's ritziest restaurants (in what is now Soho), and take a side door into a small hallway and up three flights of stairs. At the top floor, a bouncer would ask your purpose for coming. "Passional Attraction?" he'd ask. "Passional Attraction," you'd reply. "Twenty-five cents admission, Sir!" (This actual interaction was reported in *The New-York Daily Times* on October 10, 1855.) After paying the fee, you would proceed into a large, carpeted room filled with sofas and crimson curtains. Here, in the private sanctum of high society, ladies and gentlemen would indulge in all manner of carnal exploration, the details of which are much too lurid to print here.

The New York Free Love League, however, was about more than promiscuity. At its core, the Club stood for individual freedom— freedom of choice, freedom of autonomy, freedom of sexual expression. At a time when women were confined to rigid and often oppressive gender roles, Andrews created a space to explore new partners and pleasures outside society's prying eyes. He emphasized consent in all "free love" activities and hired floor managers to eject anyone who made unwanted physical advances. He believed in "the right to one's own premises and to the choice of companionship" as well as in the radical concept of "free divorce"—the idea that either party (not just the husband) can dissolve a marriage. To Andrews, the Club epitomized his ideal world, one grounded in sexual agency and equality of the sexes. It wasn't just a place of pleasure. It was a road map for society.

As membership swelled into the thousands, the Club began to self-select for a particular type of high-society New Yorker: the Social Reformer. There were vegetarians and teetotalers, suffragists and shorthanders, pacifists and socialists, all united by a common vision of social progress. Andrews embraced the intellectualist strain running through his sensualist community. He organized a series of educational classes, elevating the Club into a sanctuary for both the body and the mind, for both knowledge and pleasure. By night, the New York Free Love League was a safe place for sexual exploration. By day, it offered classes in French, dance, and, yes, Pitman shorthand.

Within the New York Free Love League, one social cause rose above the rest: abolition. The Club boasted a large anti-slavery contingent, led by none other than Stephen Pearl Andrews himself. Years earlier, while working as a lawyer in the Republic of Texas, Andrews had devised a plan to liberate Texas's slaves: He would sell Texas to Britain. Britain would then, as part of the deal, free all 11,000 slaves in the state and pay out slaveowners for their lost income. Several British politicians actually liked the idea. Texas slave owners did not. When they heard Andrews's pitch for a slave-free Texas, they dubbed him a "negrophilist" and chased him with guns and nooses into Louisiana. Andrews eventually made his way to the Northeast, where he would establish himself as a leader in the abolitionist movement.

Two years after his Texas debacle, Andrews was invited to speak at the World Anti-Slavery Convention in London. As he finished his speech, an unknown man approached him and shoved a stack of books into his hand. "Examine them," said the mysterious man, "and use [your] influence to get the subject . . . introduced to the American public." Looking down, Andrews saw for the first time the name Isaac Pitman. After a long steamship journey poring over the material, he arrived in New York a devoted Pitmanite. "I resolved to become a propagandist of the Pitmanian project in this country," he would write, ". . . [and] crowd on the public the most enthusiastic accounts of Mr. Pitman's great discovery."

Andrews, already one of New York's most prominent abolitionists, would now become its most prominent Pitman evangelist, spreading the gospel of shorthand and publishing America's first phonetic journal, the *Anglo-Sacsun*. It marked the start of a long alliance between abolitionists and spelling reformers—two strains of reformist zeal united under the banner of social progress, fighting for freedom in their own distinct ways.

Like Isaac Pitman, Eliza Burnz was obsessed with "pure" living, subsisting mostly on vegetables, fruits, and grains, and rejecting intoxicants like alcohol. Also like Pitman, Burnz saw slavery as a profound stain on humanity. Her state of Tennessee, just south of the Mason-Dixon Line, was the last to join the Confederacy and the first to fall to the Union. After the Civil War, it contained one of the largest freed Black populations in the South, and Burnz would spend her postbellum years teaching former Tennessee slaves how to read and write. Naturally, she found that the quickest path to literacy was through simplified spelling.

In the Venn overlap between abolitionists and spelling reformers, the word **LITERACY** is writ big and bold. Literacy was a slave's key to survival. The power to form and decipher text meant not only intellectual independence—the ability to *mentally* escape chains while confined to the plantation—but also *physical* independence, as freed and runaway slaves relied on road signs and maps

Wherever a zealous reformer was working towards the light— working for the material, moral and intellectual advancement of the race, whether in national education, removal of the "taxes on knowledge," abolition of slavery, or whatever the field of reform, if its end was the removal of obstacles to human progress, the reformer found a point of contact with Isaac Pitman's effort for the quickening of the means of communication between one mind and another, and found in Isaac Pitman himself a sympathetic friend.

—*Pitman Journal*,
Volume 8, 1912

to navigate their environments. After the fall of the Confederacy, many southern states would employ literacy tests to prevent former slaves from voting. (One of numerous disenfranchisement tactics used during Reconstruction and beyond.) Black voices were thus silenced in elections, and segregationist lawmakers remained in power to enact more policies of suppression, restriction, and control. Reading meant freedom. Literacy was life.*

So, beginning in the mid-1800s, the cause of spelling reform joined with the movement for Black education, as spelling reformers took up the mantle of educating freed slaves in the basics of simplified spelling and phonetic shorthand.

One such reformer was Joseph B. Towe, a former slave himself from Norfolk, Virginia. Like Pitman, Towe had a background in music.† Following his liberation in 1865, Towe traveled the South collecting and preserving spirituals, plantation songs, and other musical relics of slavery, which he would later perform for northern audiences. Exactly how and where Towe first encountered simplified spelling is unclear—perhaps in the pages of the *Wecli Fonetic Advocat* (the local phonetic journal of "Sinsinati") or in the *American Fonografur* (printed in "Nu-Yorc")—but upon returning south to Norfolk, he founded a primary school and began teaching former slaves the phonetic basics of the new orthography.

Towe made a quick name for himself in the spelling reform underground. In 1876, he was an honored speaker at a convention of simplified spellers in Philadelphia. "Mr. Towe spoke for his rase,"

---

* Even on the battlefield, Black soldiers understood the value of literacy for a life beyond bondage. "The spelling book was always carried with the rifle," wrote the *Southern Workman,* reporting on Black soldiers in the Union Army, "[and was] often studied under fire."

† As a student at Hampton University in the 1870s, Joseph Towe helped to build a renowned music department that would one day host concerts by Duke Ellington and Marian Anderson and performances by the Alvin Ailey Dance Theater.

read the proceedings of the convention, phonetically recorded in the official log, "and ov the great work to be dun in educating the colord pceple of the South. They spel naturally in the simplest manner, and cannot be persuaded that silent letterz hav eny use."

English has long been a tool for social gatekeeping, and during Reconstruction, the barrier of orthography prevented untold intelligent but illiterate freed persons from entering the higher ranks of society. To Towe, the only solution was a large-scale adoption of simple, reliable, phonetic orthography. The only way through the gate was with simplified spelling.

While Towe was teaching simplified spelling to the freed slaves of Virginia, Joseph Medill was editorializing for racial equality in the pages of the *Chicago Tribune,* the national newspaper that he ran from 1855 to 1899. Medill, a fervent spelling reformer and anti-slavery advocate, transformed the *Tribune* into the leading pro-Lincoln newspaper in the country, and in the years following the Civil War it was common to find Medill's two targets of reform—slavery and spelling—woven together in op-eds, hailing "Linkin" and all that he had done for the great cause of "ablishun."

The two causes also came together in abolitionist literature. Angelina and Thomas Grimké, siblings from South Carolina, peppered their anti-slavery essays with simplifications like *thro, tho, lov, pleas, believ, prais, deserv, purifyd,* and *qualifyd,* and Cornelius Larison incorporated phonetic spelling into the fabric of the "slave narrative," a popular genre of storytelling by and about African slaves that emerged in the late eighteenth century. Larison's famous work is his 1883 biography *Silvia Dubois (Now 116 Yers Old): A Biografy of the Slav who Whipt Her Mistres and Gand Her Fredom,* about a six-foot-tall, 200-pound supercentenarian from New Jersey who attained her freedom with a sharp right hook. Larison's small-press publishing house, located in his Jersey backyard, published all its books in Larison's invented spelling. In Larison's biography of Dubois, he recounts her years of "bŏndaġ" and deep, intrinsic impulse for a life of "frĕdum":

> Hĕr lŭv ŏv tredŭm ĭs̱ boundlĕs. To̱ be tre ĭs̱ the al-ĭmportánt thĭng wĭth Sĭlvĭá. Bŏndaġ, or evĕn restrant, ĭs̱ to̱ ner ákĭn to̱ dĕth for Sĭlvĭá. Fredŭm ĭs̱ the gol; fredŭm ŏv speeh, fredŭm ŏv labŭr, fredŭm ŏv thĕ pāshŭng, fredŭm ŏv the ăpetit—ŭnrestrand ĭn aḻ thĭngs. To̱ ĕnjoy thĭs, she wu̱d go to̱ ĕnȳ ĕxtrems— evĕn to̱ the ĕxtrems̱ ŏv lĭvĭng ŭpŏn the ehārĭtȳ ŏv hĕr aqwantánçĕs̱, ĭn the hŭt ĭn hwĭeh we found hĕr,—áwa frŏm çĭvĭlizashŭn ănd cŭltur, wĭth bŭt lĭtl to̱ et, wĭth lĕs to̱ war, ănd the po̱rĕst kind ŏv shĕltĕr. Thŭs she gang̱ the ŏbjĕct ŏv hĕr desĭr. And, she ĭs̱ ĭnded fre—ĕvĕrȳ pāshŭn ĭs̱ fre, ĕvĕrȳ desĭr ĭs̱ grātĭfĭd. Lĕs re-stránt I nĕvĕr sa̱ ĭn ĕnȳ pĕrsŭn—nor ĭnded cu̱d thĕr be.

If simplified spelling could (in the right hands) become a tool for social change, it could also (in the wrong hands) become a weapon against it.

In the latter half of the nineteenth century, as simplified spelling began to infiltrate commercial advertising, it became suddenly

---

* Tr: "Her love of freedom is boundless. To be free is the all-important thing with Silvia. Bondage, or even restraint, is too near akin to death for Silvia. Freedom is the goal; freedom of speech, freedom of labor, freedom of the passions, freedom of the appetite—unrestrained in all things. To enjoy this, she would go to any extremes—even to the extremes of living upon the charity of her acquaintances, in the hut in which we found her,—away from civilization and culture, with but little to eat, with less to wear, and the poorest kind of shelter. Thus she gains the object of her desire. And, she is indeed free—every passion is free, every desire is gratified. Less restraint I never saw in any person—nor indeed could there be."

trendy to respell words with a *K* instead of a hard *C* as a gimmick to catch the eyes of shoppers. Brands such as Klenzo (toothpaste), Kant-Leek (water bottles), Nuklene Shoe Whitener, Flistikon (sticky fly-catchers), and Keen Kutter (cutlery) found their way into the American general store. Local businesses rebranded themselves as purveyors of "klean klothes," "kreem kake," and the like. But it was a small society, founded by Confederate veterans in Eliza Burnz's state of Tennessee in 1865, that made a sad legacy of the whimsical *K*. Its members wore white robes, adopted mock-mythical titles, and organized themselves into hierarchies of Dragons, Wizards, Goblins, and Magi. For their name, they adopted the Greek word for "circle"—*kuklos*—and, with a phonetic flourish, turned the word *clan* into *klan*.

The Sentenial Ekspozishun

The greatest obstacl to reform is the want of agreement
among scolars as to the best mode of effecting it.
—James Hammond Trumbull, 1875

In the spring of 1876, America's first World's Fair—the "Centennial Exposition"—opened in Fairmount Park, Philadelphia, to commemorate the hundredth anniversary of American independence.

For fifty cents, a fairgoer could marvel at all the latest in gadgetry and innovation: an early dishwasher and typewriter, Alexander Graham Bell's newly patented telephone, a 6-inch-diameter slice of cable from the half-finished Brooklyn Bridge, and exotic foods like popcorn and ketchup. One of the more popular attractions was a severed arm, 40 feet long and copper brown, fingers clenched around a flaming torch. It was the first delivered section of the Statue of Liberty.

Meanwhile, a hundred yards outside the Exposition gates, in a large room at the Atlas Hotel, several dozen simplified spellers rang in the centennial in their own way. In a display of transcontinental unity, leading reformers from America and England gathered for an "International Convention for the Amendment of English Orthografy," a four-day summit to build consensus in the fight for reform. Its goal: to draft a single cohesive plan that the entire movement could embrace, that every reformer could endorse, and that all English speakers might eventually adopt. One proposal to unite the world. A simplified spelling for all.

By some measures, it had been a good century for the simplified spellers. In the years since Noah Webster declared linguistic independence from Britain, droves of orthographic converts had come to the light of phonetic simplification. It had been adopted by scientific journals and national newspapers, peppered into dictionaries, and had even been, briefly, the lifeblood of America's newest religion. But the successes were dispersed, pooling mostly in disconnected urban enclaves. It caused the movement to fragment, and factions to form instead of alliances. By 1876, nearly every major city in America and Britain had sprouted its own community of eager simplifiers, each diagnosing the same problem areas (silent letters, inconsistent pronunciations) but prescribing their own slightly different solutions (more letters, fewer letters, new letters, Greek letters). If a reform society in Boston, say, backed an expanded 30-letter alphabet with new characters for *TH, SH, PH,* and *CH,* a London group might counter with a slimmer alphabet, with 22 letters instead of 26. One city's traθ was another city's trezher. "The greatest obstacl to reform," the philologist James Hammond Trumbull observed in 1875, "is the want of agreement among scolars as to the best mode of effecting it."

So, in August 1876, as the nation celebrated its first hundred years and millions descended upon Philadelphia to experience the transcendent delight that is ketchup, the two nations, once divided, came together in partnership to show a united front in the battle against traditional orthography.

~~~~~

The Atlas Hotel bustled as linguists, professors, scientists, zoologists, archaeologists, schoolteachers, and vegetarians crammed in, each armed with their own pet project, their own cure for spelling, and ready to defend it. There was David Lindsley, a Chicago linguist, who had invented a shorthand rival to Pitman's called "Takigrafy" (Greek for "speed writing"). There was Samuel Haldeman, author of the "Analytic Orthography" system of spelling, who taught zoology at the University of Pennsylvania and whose theories on species distribution had influenced Charles Darwin's *On the Origin of Species*. And there was Eliza Burnz—the mother of Women Stenographers, inventor of Burnz' Fonic Shorthand, and president of the Burnz School of Shorthand in New York—who had recently founded the Burnz & Company publishing house, which would go on to print books about spelling reform for the next four decades.

"The questions which the Convention is called to discuss, are of great importance," began Samuel Haldeman,* chairman of the Convention. His long white beard flapped as he talked. ". . . Upon what basis shall we build our system of spelling? Shall we find out the original powers of the letters so far as we can, and endeavor to bring the spelling in harmony with those powers? The question is not so much, 'How shall we spell this word?' as 'What shall these combinations spell?'"

"I should have some fear," worried one reformer, whose concerns were mailed ahead and read aloud by the assembly secretary, "that some imprudence at the convention might bring ridicule or opposition upon our cause . . . It is far less important that we should

---

* Haldeman also studied geology, conchology, entomology, and chemistry. He once said, "I never pursue one branch of science more than ten years, but lay it aside and go into new fields."

inaugurate our reform speedily, than that we should make it as thorough as possible."

"There are none who have greater need of patience," concurred a third reformer, ". . . than spelling reformers . . . [It] is the long laborious task to which the spelling reformer must set himself."

Following a series of motions, mission statements, calls to order, and other procedural formalities, the Convention turned to the subject of phonetics in Indigenous and minority populations. Reverend William S. Robertson shared his experiences living with the Creek Indians of Florida, who used a 16-letter phonetic alphabet and became functionally literate after only a day of instruction. Joseph B. Towe, the celebrated musician and former Virginian slave, spoke of his work teaching simplified spelling to his fellow freedmen, who organically spelled in a rational, phonetic way "and [would] not use the irregular forms of our present spelling." After the morning speeches, eight official spelling proposals were taken up and the room divided into two committees: those in favor of *adding* letters to the alphabet, and those against. Debates were held—some in calm reason, others in fiery passion—and over the next three humid days in Philadelphia, as rain poured and temperatures approached 90 degrees, the delegates sweated out their differences. On the fourth day, they emerged with a single, hard-won compromise: the 29-letter "Anglo-American Alphabet." The name was meant to highlight the binational nature of the resolution—America and Britain, together again—but it would soon be replaced by a more colorful nickname: the "Alfabet ov Least Rezistanç."

A century of reform attempts now boiled down to 10 spelling commandments. According to the Alfabet ov Least Rezistanç, thou shalt:

1. Omit the *a* from the digraph *ea* when pronounced as a short vowel, as in *hed, heven, helth,* and *welth.*

2. Omit the silent *e* after a short vowel, as in *hav, giv,* and *motiv.*

3. Omit the final *ue* in *catalog, colleag, tong,* etc.

4. Omit *gh* when silent, and replace it with *f* when not silent, as in *dauter, slauter, tho,* and *enuf.*

5. Replace *ph* with *f* in *alfabet, fantom, filosofy,* etc.

6. Write *k* or *c* for *ch* in words in which *ch* is pronounced as *k,* as in *arkitect, monark,* and *kemistry.*

7. Omit *b, c, d, f, g, h, k, l, m, n, o, p, r, s, t, w, z, ch, rh,* and *th* when silent, as in *det, lam, bluf, flem, vinyet, gost, nife, caam, tauk, autum, iland, brunet, glisen, sord,* and *buz.*

8. Omit *a, e, i, o,* and *u* when silent, as in *frend, lepard, biskit,* and *garantee.*

9. Change *eau* to *o,* as in *buro* and *shato.*

10. Change *ed* to *t* or *d,* as in *imprest, approacht, compeld,* and *livd.*

Burnz, Haldeman, Lindsley, and their fellow reformers had, in four days, achieved something thought impossible: they had mended the linguistic rift between America and Britain, nations that had been drifting apart in speech and spelling since the 1500s. The delegates pledged to nurture this newfound solidarity, and on the final day of the Convention they voted to unite into the "Spelling Reform Association" and continue their reformist work as a single global body. Francis March, a linguistics professor at Lafayette College, would head the organization as SRA president. Burnz and Haldeman were named vice presidents. Lindsley became treasurer. The first international society of spelling reformers was born.

The SRA wasted no time in spreading the word. Its first order of business was distributing leaflets, bulletins, and other printed materials to advertise its new Anglo-American alphabet. This work was tasked to the recording secretary, a somewhat eccentric 25-year-old Bostonian named Melvil Dewey. Dewey launched a quarterly series called the "Bulletin of the Spelling Reform Association" to keep members abreast of the latest happenings in the cause. "Never before in the history of the language has there been so much promise of a reform in our orthography as at the present time," began the SRA's first bulletin the following spring. ". . . The time has finally come for an international organization to take in hand and guide to a successful completion, the reform so happily begun."

Dewey was the right man for the job. Before the launch of the SRA, he was known across New England for his systematic organization and scrupulous recordkeeping. In 1873, as a 21-year-old undergraduate at Amherst College in Massachusetts, Dewey invented the book classification method that bears his name. The "Dewey Decimal System," as most Americans born before 1995 have learned and probably forgotten, works on a metric number scheme: all books fall into ten main classes (religion, language, history, etc.), each marked by a three-digit number between 000 and 900; each class then subdivides into ten divisions, and each division into ten sections represented by fractional decimals. In 1876, the same year he cofounded the Spelling Reform Association, Dewey cofounded the American Library Association (ALA), the oldest library association in the world, still around today.*

It's said that Dewey became a simplified speller at age 12 when,

---

* Dewey also created the Library Bureau, a now-defunct organization that supplied libraries with index cards and filing cabinets. As a secondary function, the Bureau tracked down delinquent borrowers for overdue books.

having scrounged together a few coins, he hiked into the nearest town and picked up an unabridged *Webster's Dictionary* to improve his spelling. He read it, studied it, devoured it, but his immersion into the irrational mess of our orthography only confused him more. So, he started spelling his own way.

"Speling Skolars agree," Dewey would write, "that we hav the most unsyentifik, unskolarli, illojikal & wasteful speling ani languaj ever ataind." He later shortened his name from Melville Dewey to Melvil Dui, vowing to make himself a living example of simplified spelling. The Dui never stuck—he was already too well known by his surname at that point—but the Melvil did, and we still refer to him by it today.

At first, the Spelling Reform Association adopted a straightforward approach: 10 simple rules for one simple spelling. The list was deliberately brief, easy on the eye and mind, designed to incite only mild annoyance among the general populace.

> In 1876, upon leaving Amherst for Boston, Melvil Dewey wrote a simplified love letter to his beloved city:
>
> Sum day, dear Amherst, may it be my happy lot tu pruv how great iz the love I bear yu. Proud, always, everwher to be counted among yur sonz, I am Very truly, Melvil Dui.

But despite its initial restraint, the Association soon followed the typical path of reformers and slipped into overzealous styling. To fill the SRA's quarterly meetings, members continually sought new topics for discussion. To fill its bulletins, they determined to show continual progress. So, every three months the SRA added new rules, new letters, new diacritic marks, in their pursuit to capture every nuanced shade of sound, forever chasing that dream of the perfect alphabet.

Everyone likes a round number 10—perhaps none more than Melvil Dewey, who worshipped it as a cosmic unit of measurement. In his tireless quest to instill order in the world, Dewey tried to do everything in tens. He based his library classification on 10 and wrote 10-page letters. He was proud to share a birthday with the metric system (he was born on December 10, the day the first country adopted metric measurements, in 1799) and after college founded the American Metric Bureau, a short-lived effort to draw Americans into his numerical fixation. The craze even extended to Dewey's sleep routine: he made sure to sleep 10 hours every night, or, as he put it, "to sleep decimally."

As the years passed, even the SRA's name devolved into ever more phonetic versions.

The Spelling Reform Association (1876)
The Speling Reform Asoshiashun (1877)
Dhi Speling Reform Asoshiashun (1881)
Dhi Speling Reform Asoshiĕshun (1882)

"The air is ful of hope," declared an early SRA bulletin, full of sunny optimism and clarity. Within a year, the message had already taken a turn toward the illegible: "Last yīr wī tōct ov hop. Dhis yīr it iz a sīrius cweschun hwedher imīdiet diūti duz not pres hārd upon us . . . Ot wī not tu atempt mor . . . ?" *

The Spelling Reform Association set up offices on Boston's Hawley Street, and for the next three decades led the simplified spelling scene on both sides of the Atlantic. In 1879, a sister organization launched in Britain—the English Spelling Reform Association—with a vice presidency shared by Charles Darwin and Alfred, Lord

---

* Tr: "Last year we talked of hope. This year it is a serious question whether immediate duty does not press hard upon us . . . Ought we not to attempt more . . . ?"

BULLETIN
OF THE
SPELLING REFORM ASSOCIATION,
General Offices 32 Hawley Street, Boston.

No. 14.   **SEPTEMBER.**   **1879.**

THE PRESENT STATE OF THE SPELING REFORM IN AMERICA.

BY PROFESOR FRANCIS A. MARCH, LL. D.,
President of the Speling Reform Asociation.

RED BEFORE THE SPELING REFORM DEPART-
MENT OF THE NATIONAL EDUCATIONAL ASO-
CIATION AT ITS ANUAL MEETING IN PHIL-
ADELPHIA, JULY 29, 1879.

The movement for the reform of English
speling is a product of the spirit of the age,
a tru *birth of time*, as Bacon likes to cal his
filosofy. The great curents of thought and
action set towards reform. We ar for reforming everything that can help us in the
discovery of truth and the improvement of
man's estate.

Givn a spoken language, the easy com-
unication of it by riting and printing is
a problem in labor-saving mashinery. But
ther is so much that is complex and super-
fluus in our present speling that hundreds
of milions of dolars ar wasted by it in our
printing ofices every year.

Our teachers see that two or three years of
the scool-life of every child ar worse than
wasted in trying to lern to spel.

BULETIN
EV DHI
SPELING REFORM ASOSHIĒSHUN.

No. 16.   **1880.**

[From dhi Prosidings ev dhi Nashunal Ejucashunal Asoshieshun.]

DHI SPELING REFORM ACOMPLISHT.

Opening Adres deliverd at dhi Anyual Miting, Julai 15, 1880, bai
F. A. MARCH, LL.D.

Wi congratyulat ich udher tu-da upen anudher hapi yir.

At aur last aniverseri dhi sumeri ev events hwich wez
mad in dhi opening adres, wez much ecyupaid widh dis-
cushunz, rezolushunz, petishunz, memorialz and udher pre-
limineri wurc. Opinyunz in favor ev reform wor red from
ẽtheritiz in fileloji, ejucashun and soshal saiens, Max Mueller,
Dr. Morris, Bishop Thirlwall, Profesorz Hadley, Whitney,
and Trumbull, Charles Sumner, W. E. Gladstone, and udherz.
An acaunt wez givn ev acshun in favor ev dhi reform bai
dhi Nashunal Yūnyun ev Elementeri Ticherz, reprezenting
10,000 ticherz in Ingland and Walz ; and ev dhi acshun ev dhi
American Fllolejical Asoshieshun, dhi American Institūt ev
Instrucshun, dhi Nashunal Ejucashunal Asoshieshun, dhi
Depārtment ev Public Instrucshun at Shicãgo, dhi Stat
Ticherz' Asoshieshunz ev Masachusets, Niū York. Pensilva-
nia, Ohaio, Niū Jūrzi, Ilinõi, Aiowa, Mishigan, Wisconsin,
Misūri, Virjinia. Acshun ev dhi Stat lejislachurz wez de-
scraibd, ãlso dhi reports ev dhãr Comitiz.

Two bulletins of the Spelling Reform Association,
showing how its spelling evolved over its early
years.

Tennyson. They were perfect stewards of this new spelling: Darwin with his rigorous, scientific approach and Tennyson with his elegance of expression, championing reform through the lenses of science and language. The American and English associations, working in harmony, seemed to finally be making headway in the simplified spelling movement. It would only take 22 years before they started seeing results.

~~~~

Over the final quarter of the century, the Spelling Reform Association subjected the world to thousands of its new and peculiar spellings. (*Peciŭlyar* was a uniquely peculiar one.) Of the many offerings, the National Education Association liked precisely twelve.

Since its founding in 1857, the NEA had driven much of the educational policy of the United States.* Its endorsement was the holy grail for any simplified speller, and two decades into its campaign, the Spelling Reform Association finally obtained it. In 1898, the NEA picked out a dozen of the SRA's more moderate simplifications to begin weaving into its official publications. The chosen twelve—*tho, altho, thru, thruout, thoro, thoroly, thorofare, program, prolog, catalog, pedagog,* and *decalog,* otherwise known as the "Apostolic Twelve" or the "Twelv Words"—represented a small step toward linguistic modernization, a manageable start for a wider reform. It was a "feeler," as one reformer put it, "to familiarize a part of the public, especially teachers," with the idea that a new spelling was out there, biding its time, waiting to strike.

With the NEA's endorsement, state teachers' associations across

---

* In the 1970s, the NEA relaunched as a teachers' union representing educators and administrators. Today, it's the largest labor union in the United States.

the U.S. adopted the Twelv Words, and educational journals, like *The Educational Review* and *The Intelligence*, accepted them into their house style. Three years later, Edwin Vaile, the editor of *The Intelligence,* lobbied the NEA to fund a permanent national Simplified Spelling Commission, which would have the power to enforce the Twelv Words in U.S. schools. The NEA put Vaile's motion to a vote. A debate was held in Chicago, and Vaile came to make his case.

Slosson Thompson, the editor of the *Chicago Times-Herald*, began the debate arguing against simplified spelling. "How do you explain the phenomenon that you cannot find a master of the English language in the ranks of the spelling reformers?" he asked his audience (which comprised many more traditionalists than reformers). "Scores of philologists rail against it, [yet] not one writer complains. The good workman seldom finds fault with his tools."

Vaile, who had heard similar arguments before, then delivered his rebuttal. The following exchange was recorded in the debate transcript:[*]

> **Vaile:** Do you admit that Alfred Tennyson was a master of the English language or contributed anything of value to English literature?
>
> **Thompson:** Why, yes.
>
> **Vaile:** Mr. Tennyson was a vice-president of an English spelling-reform association. Do you admit that Charles Darwin was a master of English or contributed anything of value to literature?
>
> **Thompson:** He is a great scientist.

---

[*] This exchange between Vaile and Thompson is pieced together from two separate transcripts, differing slightly from each other, both printed shortly after the debate.

Vaile: Is he a great writer of English?

Thompson: No.

Vaile: Very well. Mr. Darwin was also a vice-president of an English spelling-reform association. Do you admit that William Dean Howells ever contributed anything of value to English literature?

Thompson: I should like to discuss Howells with you.

Vaile: Of course you would, you would like to discuss a great many people who do not agree with you . . . Well, I guess I am done with you.

With that, the NEA voted. Those in favor of funding a Simplified Spelling Commission: 77. Those against: 105. The loss illuminated a stark reality for Vaile and the reformers: that even with the endorsement of teachers, principals, journals, and labor unions, the simplified spelling movement still struggled to find financial support. Shortly after the vote, the Spelling Reform Association drained the last of its meager funds. Without money, the SRA couldn't print bulletins or finance meetings. Without money, the SRA disintegrated.

Henry G. Paine, an early historian of spelling reform, wrote the last word on the short-lived SRA: "The Spelling Reform Association had in its ranks the best scolarship in the country, [but] it had in its tresury only such funds as the scolars themselvs could contribute." In the end, not even the pooled coffers of Dewey, Burnz, Darwin, Tennyson, and all the great reformers on both sides of the Atlantic were "enuf to carry on an effectiv campaign."

Part III

Washington, D.C., 1906

President Theodore Roosevelt, dressed in his evening best, arrives at the New Willard Hotel for the annual Gridiron Dinner, a white-tie D.C. tradition for journalists and politicians. He has a general idea of how the night will go: there'll be comedy skits and musical performances, filet mignon and cherrystone oysters, and that always mysterious social lubricant known as "Gridiron Punch."

But as he enters the reception hall, Roosevelt encounters an unsettling sight: a slim hardcover book in the hands of smirking Cabinet members, foreign ambassadors, and *Herald* reporters. Someone hands him a copy. He looks at the title: *The Simple Speller and Gridiron Dikshunary*. Before he opens it, he knows what it is. It is the parting shot in his monthslong battle with the press. It is the culmination of every jest and jibe splashed across national headlines, immortalized in a token he now holds. And it is aimed at his recent foray into simplified spelling.

Roosevelt cracks it open and begins reading:

> [We] have endeavored in this Volume to gather the Wordz
> most kommonly misspelt and erroneously defined during the

long period of Intellektual Darkness preseding the Assumpshun
uv Universal Supervizhun by Theodore Rozavelt . . .

In order to give Permanentz to [our] Laborz [we] have dillijently
set down not only the korrect Spelling which iz hereafter to
prevail, but also the Definishunz which must be aksepted by
Rekognized Authoritiez.

Like many reform-minded intellectuals this year, Theodore Roosevelt
has been captivated by the simplified spelling movement. He has
begun writing his correspondence in simplified spelling. He has ordered his office to render all government documents in simplified
spelling. Congress is fighting back. Reporters and cartoonists are
having a field day.

Roosevelt scans through the entries in this parody dictionary:

klub. (n) A weppun. Obsoleet sintz the appearance uv the Big
    Stik.
yawn. (n) A speciez of applauze rezerved in Kongress az a
    spechul honor for the Prezident'z message only.
executive sesshun. (n) A mith.

Within a week of the Gridiron Dinner, Congress will officially vote
down "Ruzevelt Speling" and retain standard orthography as the law
of the land. Roosevelt will never speak publicly about simplified spelling again.

Ruzevelt Speling

B4 u take up this reformed spelin bizness u shud remember
that it iz going to be ruf saleing b4 u lern the nu kind.
—*Iola Daily Record*, 1906

Melvil Dewey spent the early years of the 1900s chasing Andrew
Carnegie's money. The wealthy Pittsburgh steel tycoon was among
America's most generous philanthropists, and Dewey believed that
with Carnegie's riches he might just breathe new life into the Spelling Reform Association. "The chief obstacle to getting the greatest
good from public libraries," he wrote to Carnegie in 1902, "[is] in
the absurd spelling of English . . . The greatest service that can be
rendered the race today at a moderate cost is . . . a wise, conservative campaign for the simplification of English spelling."

Dewey's cause intrigued Carnegie, but Carnegie wanted nothing to do with Dewey. By 1902, Dewey had developed a sordid
reputation in New York for his aggressive womanizing. Multiple
women came forward to tell their stories. Florence Woodworth and
May Seymour, two of Dewey's assistants, complained of Dewey's
unwelcome kissing and fondling. So did Adelaide Hasse, head of
document classification at the New York Public Library, who "ran
away so suddenly" after an unsettling car ride with Dewey that
the entire library industry began to whisper. As chief librarian at
Columbia University, and later as director of the New York State
Library, Dewey had been praised by progressives for his work in

recruiting female librarians into the male-dominated field. In time, as allegations surfaced, it became clear why Dewey had so eagerly populated his surroundings with women.

Dewey's behavior caught up with him in 1905. That summer, during a 10-day Alaska cruise organized by the American Library Association, Melvil Dewey sexually harassed four female librarians. They reported him to the ALA, and momentum against Dewey began to build. It was already his second scandal that year—in January, he made headlines for his open anti-Semitism—and as word of the cruise incident spread, Dewey knew his time in the library world was coming to an end. In 1905, the ALA expelled its co-founder, the New York State Library fired him as its director, and polite society chucked him like an expired library card.

As Dewey stepped back from the helm of the spelling crusade, Carnegie stepped in. That winter, Carnegie committed a $15,000 annual endowment to the creation of a new spelling reform organization. He leased offices on Madison Avenue in New York, appointed an executive committee to run operations, and assembled a team of scholars, teachers, judges, bankers, three dictionary editors, two university presidents, one rabbi, and Mark Twain. On March 11, 1906, a date that still lives in infamy among some language purists, Carnegie announced his latest philanthropic endeavor: the Simplified Spelling Board.

Ever since Carnegie sold his multimillion-dollar steel company in 1901 and began donating to educational and cultural causes, the press had adored him. But *this* cause, this fad of simplification, confounded American journalists. It certainly wasn't the typical Carnegie endowment (simplified spelling was no Carnegie Hall). Plus, the very idea of it seemed to undermine the skill set of the literary elite: their proud mastery of language. The press thus reacted with the predictable knee-jerk ridicule: "Carnegy Wil Teach the Nashun to Spel," laughed the headline of the March 12 *Lexington Herald*. "Kampane of Edukashun to Korect Speling Now On," wrote the *Lincoln Journal Star*. In cheekily misspelled articles, journalists parodied the Board and its lofty objectives. On March 25, the *Kansas City Star* reimagined the Simplified Spelling Board as the "Societe for the Distrukshun ov the English Langwij" and wrote a fictional account of one of its meetings:

> The meting ov the Societe for the Distrukshun ov the English Langwij, which waz held last nit in the privat apartments of [Board Chairman] Brander Mathuz, waz wel atended. The meting waz purly informal and brot out sum intresting diskushun.
>
> "Felo fanatiks," sed Mathuz, "we ar gatherd her to formulat and perfekt an organizashun that wil in tim wip the English langwij frum the fas uv the rth and frum the memory ov the inhabitants thereov. The nu langwij wil hav its on literachur begining frum now. Al that haz gon befor is ded. We wil mak bonfirz ov Chawser and Shaksper and Dikenz and Thakere and al ov them. I xpekt to sufr also on mi on akownt, but I mak this sakryfis withowt a ter in mi i. Mi on prevyus wurkz wil be burnd with the rest and I wil sa that what the wurld luzes bi this wil be mad up bi me in the brilyans ov mi fuchur writyngz in the nu langwij."

This was the age of Yellow Journalism, the heyday of half-truths and flashy headlines, and reporters hungered for any linguistic gimmick to hook their readers. Simplified spelling provided it on a silver platter. As the humor flowed and Carnegie took his hit pieces on the chin, it became clear that the next battle for spelling reform would be waged not in classrooms or academic symposia but in the colorful pages of the daily press—the black, white, and yellow of newspapers.

Mark Twain, a former newspaperman himself, made an early play at the press. That summer, as a delegate of the Simplified Spelling Board, Twain attended the annual dinner of the Associated Press to make a direct plea to journalists:

> I am here to make an appeal to the nations [on] behalf of the simplified spelling . . . There are only two forces that can carry light to all the corners of the globe—only two—the sun in the heavens and the Associated Press down here . . . If the Associated Press will adopt and use our simplified forms, and thus spread them to the ends of the earth, covering the whole spacious planet with them as with a garden of flowers, our difficulties are at an end.

Twain assured the room of reporters that a short experimental stint of simplified spelling in their papers—"Only three months, it is all I ask"—would surely lead to its acceptance among readers. After those three months,

> all eyes here and above and below will have become adjusted to the change and in love with it, and the present clumsy and ragged forms will be grotesque to the eye and revolting to the soul. And we shall be rid of phthisis and phthisic and pneumonia and pneumatics, and diphtheria and pterodactyl, and all those other insane words which no man addicted to the simple Christian life can try to spell and not lose some of the bloom of his piety in the demoralizing attempt.

Not every paper joined the revolt against simplification. The *New York Times* initially came out in support of Carnegie's mission (though it would later backtrack), and the *Chattanooga Daily Times* playfully encouraged its readers to "Tri ure own han on the nu stile. Altho it iz arkard at furst it wil ad to the gayty uv the nashun—'Kist' bi eny uther spelin tastes az sweet." In amassing media support, it helped that Carnegie already enlisted so many elite members. The freshman class of the Simplified Spelling Board read like a Who's Who of American intelligentsia: William James, philosopher and psychologist at Harvard University; David Jordan, president of Stanford University; Nicholas Butler, president of Columbia University; David Brewer, U.S. Supreme Court justice; Lyman J. Gage, former secretary of the Treasury; William T. Harris, U.S. Commissioner of Education; Charles E. Sprague, president of the Union Dime Savings Institution; Henry Holt, founder of the Henry Holt and Company publishing house; and Mark Twain, former Phunny Phellow, now committed reformer. (Melvil Dewey, too, was listed as a member, but with lower billing, and his desired chairmanship went instead to Brander Matthews, professor of Dramatic Literature at Columbia University.) As one paper put it: "That the matter of simplified spelling is one well worth serious consideration is, as we say, evidenced by [its] members . . ."

It also helped that Carnegie vowed a moderate approach to reform. He had seen plenty of well-meaning radicals charge into simplified spelling only to trip over their own eagerness. To avoid the usual pitfalls, Carnegie set two rules: First, the Board would focus solely on *subtracting* letters, not adding new ones. ("Simplification by omission," as chairman Brander Matthews wrote. "This is its platform; this is its motto.") And second, the Board would avoid the word *reform* entirely. People didn't like that word, Carnegie decided. It evoked ideas of revolution and upheaval, a disruption of the comfortable status quo.* No, Carnegie wasn't trying to *reform* spelling; he was just trying to simplify it.

On March 21, the Board released a list of 300 recommended respellings for the public to begin peppering into their writing. Along with this list came a pledge: "I will use in my correspondence, as far as may be practicable, the simpler spelling recommended by the Simplified Spelling Board in its circular of March 21, 1906." By mailing this pledge on a postcard to 1 Madison Avenue, the sender would be automatically subscribed to all future mailers of the Simplified Spelling Board. In all, some 40,000 pledges were sent in.

The words in Carnegie's list were a mix of the comfortably familiar and the gently innovative. Nearly half were already in common use in American newspapers—words like *theater* (with an *-er*), *honor* (without a *U*), and *medieval* (without its olden *æ* digraph). The other half, though less familiar, were no great leap for the phonetically uninitiated: *thru, tho, surprize, kist, lookt, fantom, subpena*. This tactful blend was deliberate: By accepting the already popular spellings, the public might be more amenable to the remaining recommendations. You already write *color* without a *U*, so went the logic—why not try *rhyme* without an *H*?

While reporters unleashed their barrage of snark upon Carnegie, teachers and students flocked to the cause. In June, the Board of Superintendents recommended Carnegie's 300 words to the New York City Board of Education. Schools across the city heeded the call, and within weeks, hundreds of schoolteachers had signed the

---

*   "A man might say: 'I'm against reform,'" explained the Board's Charles Sprague, "and he'd get some sympathy. But it doesn't sound so well to say, 'I'm against simplification.' . . . Some men have a congenital opposition to reform . . . and they just don't like the word."

Simplified Spelling Board's pledge, vowing to implement the new orthography in their classrooms. At Columbia University, students formed the "Fonetic Speling Assosiashun of Kolumbia University" and published their charter in the school paper:

> Resolvd, that we, students of Kolumbia University, today assembld, do hereby form ourselvs into an organizashun to be non as the 'Fonetic Speling Assosiashun of Kolumbia University'; and be it further
>
> Resolvd, that we herby bind ourselvs to abid by the desishuns of the 'Simplifid Speling Board,' resently organizd bi Androo Karnigy, wen mad public, and adopt the folloing prinsipls to be a gid in al privet korespondenz and in our kolij xaminashun papers: First, that al silent letterz be dropt; sekond, that al dipthongs be replased by singl vowlz wherever possibl; and, third, that the fonetic sistem of speling be adopted.

As the fervor for this stripped-down spelling swelled, a person of note was swept up in the tide: Theodore Roosevelt. The 26th president of the United States had always fancied himself a reformer; statues invariably portray him on horseback, galloping bravely into the unknown, and in 1906 he galloped straight into the strange land of spelling reform. Roosevelt, impressed by the early work of the Simplified Spelling Board, which was chaired by his friend Brander Matthews, directed his stenographer to recast the voice of the president in simplified spelling. "Mr. Loeb, himself an advanced spelling reformer," Roosevelt wrote to Matthews in August 1906, "will hereafter see that the President, in his correspondence, spells the way you say he ought to!"

He didn't stop there. Two days later, Roosevelt expanded his initiative to include the entire Government Printing Office. Henceforth, by order of the U.S. president, all communications of the federal government must be written in simplified spelling.

He informed his Public Printer, Charles Stillings, of his decision by letter:

My dear Mr. Stillings:

I enclose herewith copies of certain circulars of the
Simplified Spelling Board, which can be obtained
free from the Board at No. 1 Madison Avenue,
New York City. Please hereafter direct that in
all Government publications of the Executive
Departments the 300 words enumerated in Circular
No. 5 shall be spelled as therein set forth . . .
    There is not the slightest intention to do anything
revolutionary or initiate any far-reaching policy. The
purpose simply is for the Government, instead of
lagging behind popular sentiment, to advance abreast
of it and at the same time abreast of the views of
the ablest and most practical educators of our time
as well as the most profound scholars . . . [These
changes] represent nothing in the world but a very
slight extension of the unconscious movement which
has made agricultural implement makers and farmers
write "plow" instead of "plough;" which has made
most Americans write "honor" without the somewhat
absurd, superfluous "u;" . . . which makes us write
"public," "almanac," "era," "fantasy," and "wagon,"

instead of the "publick," "almanack," "aera," "phantasy,"
and "waggon" of our great-grandfathers . . .

Sincerely, yours,
THEODORE ROOSEVELT

Roosevelt had been riding his rugged-outdoorsman, big-game-
hunting image to five years of popular support. But in one fell executive swoop, he made himself a target for the hungry press. The *New
York Times,* once a supporter of simplified spelling, now called the
president a "laughing stock" for leaping hastily into language reform.
The Worcester Evening Gazette, once a pro-Roosevelt Massachusetts
paper, declared with an editorial smirk that it will "continue to be
printed in the English language, not in 'Karnegi,' [or] 'Ruzvelt' . . ."
The most colorful response came across the pond from London's *Sun:*

> Mr. Andru Karnegi (or should it be Karnege?) and Presi-
> dent Rusvelt (or is it Ruzvelt?) are doing their (or ther) best
> to ad to the gaiety of nations (or nashuns) by atempting to
> reform the speling of the English langwidge. No dowt their
> (or ther) intentions (or intenshuns) are orl rite, but their
> (or ther) objekt is orl rong, not to say silly (or sily).

"Had President Roosevelt declared war against Germany," the
Washington Times chided, "he could not have caused much more
agitation . . ."*

By all appearances, journalism and simplified spelling should make
a handsome pair. Shorter spelling allows for more efficient use of col-

---

* Teddy's wife, Edith, suggested that the president only backed reform because he didn't
know "how to spell anything, and wish[ed] a wide latitude in consequence."

umn space. It's gentler on the typist's hands. And, clearly, it's a boon for headlines. Yet, tradition holds a tenacious grip, and old habits, especially in the realm of language, die hard. The press and the president would thus battle each other over spelling reform for months, with journalists jabbing their yellow pens into the president's project on a semiregular basis and in semi-phonetic spelling.

Then came the blitz of political cartoons:

SANKSHUNS NU WA OV SPELING

Ruzevelt Wil Spel Wurds Akording tu Fonetik Sistem Advokated bi Speshul Komite.

Akshun ov the Nashun's Chief Exekutiv Wil Hav a Grate Influence in Efekting Reform in Prezent Stile ov Speling.

The *Biggs Weekly Argus*, August 31, 1906.

THIS DOES SETTLE IT.
President Roosevelt positively cannot accept the nomination for a third term; he has undertaken the introduction of spelling reform, and that is trouble enough for one man.

Figure 1

Figure 2

Figure 3

Figure 4

Figure 5

Figure 1: *Minneapolis Journal*, August 27, 1906. Roosevelt "bizy" at work on simplified spelling. Figure 2: *Philadelphia Item*, September 2, 1906. "Prezident Rozyvelt" teaches a professor, an editor, a teacher, and an author his "reform speling." Figure 3: *Collier's Weekly*, September 22, 1906. Roosevelt fires a revolver into a dictionary using "amunishon" sent by "A. Carnege." The ghosts of Chaucer, Shakespeare, and Samuel Johnson look on. (Look closely and you can see the bullets have pierced the words *through, though, thorough, thief, thigh,* and *thistle*.) Figure 4: *New York Globe*, December 13, 1906. Roosevelt and Congress both take aim at the Public Printer. Roosevelt's gun shoots words like "mixt" and "ript." Congress's shoots "mixed" and "ripped." Next to the president is a small figure labeled "Andy." Figure 5: *Plain Dealer*, December 15, 1906. Uncle Sam and a schoolteacher prevent Roosevelt from entering a schoolhouse.

Roosevelt's war with the media finally reached peak pettiness at the December 1906 Gridiron Dinner, the D.C. schmooze-fest that laid the groundwork for today's White House Correspondents Dinner. That night, all guests, including Roosevelt, went home with a souvenir: a simplified spelling "dikshunary" mocking Roosevelt's sojourn into the world of spelling reform. Roosevelt's real humiliation came five days later. On December 13, the chairman of the House Committee on Printing introduced a resolution demanding that all documents "emanating from any executive department or bureau of the Government . . . observe and adhere to the standard of orthography prescribed in generally accepted dictionaries of the English language." The House of Representatives approved the resolution, 142 to 24, and by Christmas Day the old spelling once again reigned in D.C. The *Philadelphia Press* ran a snarky obituary:

> DECEMBER 13, at the home of its adopted father, Theodore Rusevelt, Washington, D.C., after ate munths of sufering, Simpul Speler, belovd foster child of Androo Karnagy and Brandur Mathuse. Obseekwiz privut. Pleez omit flours.*

It was precisely what Carnegie had hoped to avoid: the rapid flare and fizzle, the fleeting boom and bust, the gallons of ink spilt in mockery of a worthy cause. Carnegie's slow, cautious reform was dead, demolished by Roosevelt and his bulldozing impatience to change the language with the stroke of an executive pen.

"Ruzevelt Speling," as the press now pejoratively called the

---

* Tr: "DECEMBER 13, at the home of its adopted father, Theodore Roosevelt, Washington, D.C., after eight months of suffering, Simple Speller, beloved foster child of Andrew Carnegie and Brander Matthews. Obsequies private. Please omit flowers."

Figure 1

Figure 2

Cartoonists mocked Roosevelt's spelling even after its demise. Figure 1: *Detroit News*, December 1906. Roosevelt sits stunned in a boxing ring after losing his match with the dictionary. Stars flutter around his head like thought bubbles: "Kissed not kist," "though not tho," "through not thru," "rhyme not rime." Figure 2: *New York Globe*, December 1906. Roosevelt and Carnegie visit the grave of simplified spelling. The tombstone reads: "Sakrud to the memry of Simpul Speler. Born Nu Yawk March 06. Died in Washington Desembur 1906. Wi morn owr loss." This copy originally belonged to Roosevelt. The message at the top, written to Roosevelt by a friend, reads: "Bare up thru it."

Board's proposal, had so contaminated the movement that by the next year even Mark Twain tried to distance himself from simplified spelling. "You might think that [Carnegie] had never committed a crime in his life," Twain joked at a club dedication ceremony, "but no—look at his pestiferous simple spelling . . . He's got us all so we can't spell anything."

By 1908, Ruzevelt Speling had become a symbol of overreach, a warning against the perils of unchecked zeal in reform. It wasn't merely a list of 300 words anymore; it was a cautionary tale told to every new generation of simplifiers, a reminder of the need for patience and practicality in the fight for reform. As the Simplified Spelling Board regathered and reset, Roosevelt moved on from the fiasco and never publicly addressed simplified spelling again.

On March 4, 1909, Roosevelt left office. The newspapers that week took a reverential tone toward the outgoing president, highlighting his accomplishments and minimizing his failures. They mentioned little about his foray into spelling; after all, it was a relatively minor blip in his presidency, four short months out of his eight-year term. The exception was Roosevelt's hometown New York paper *The Sun*. On page 6 of its March 4 issue, in a single line below the fold, the *Sun* memorialized Roosevelt's bumpy presidency in a perfectly succinct manner:

"Thru!"

Ye Olde or the Nu?

My spelling 'tis of thee,
Sweet land of spelling-bee,
Of thee I sing.
Land of the pilgrims' pride,
Land where my fathers dide.
For spelling simplifide
Let freedom ring.

—Owen Wister, "How Doth
the Simple Spelling Bee," 1907

At that precise historical moment when the spelling debate was at its most political, America held its first national spelling bee.

Outside the Hippodrome Theater, in downtown Cleveland, the streets were decorated as if for a holiday. Colorful banners hung from windows, streamers draped down from rooftops, and $25,000 worth of fireworks lay in wait in University Square, ready for the close of the contest. It was a festival of orthography—a celebration not only of the young spellers who had honed their craft but of the language itself, which had withstood the attacks of the Carnegies and Roosevelts, the Deweys and Twains, and remained proudly as complicated as ever.

Spelling bees have existed in America since at least the mid-1800s, when the post-Webster dictionary boom sparked a competitive urge for orthographic mastery among young spellers. The early contests were small affairs, often confined to a single town, and competitors usually came from local schools. But as Carnegie's spelling agitators stirred fresh interest around orthography in 1906, the National Education Association recognized a demand for a large-scale spelling competition. It booked the 6,000-capacity Hippodrome and invited teams of eighth graders from around the United States to compete in the first national contest on June 29, 1908.

With Ruzevelt Speling still fresh in the public's memory, however, suspicions began to stir. Was this spelling bee a ploy by the simplifiers? Were Carnegie and his Board pulling the strings? Paranoia of this sort had been bubbling since 1906, when the *Rochester Post Express* first proclaimed simplified spelling to be a vast conspiracy orchestrated by "large publishing interests, and designed to carry out an immense project for jobbery in reprinting dictionaries and school books." (Naturally, the NEA was also part of the conspiracy; it must have raked in billions with its "Twelv Words" campaign of 1898.) As the June contest approached, the question lingered, terrifying the anti-reformers and fueling speculations over the NEA's agenda: *Which spelling would the spelling bee be held in?*

Speculations became rumors, which became gossip, which turned into newspaper scoops, as baseless claims of a "simplified spelling bee" spread from paper to paper. The *Mans-*

YE OLDEN STYLE OF SPELL-ING OR THE NU.

The world eagerly awaits the later announcements af the national spelling bee, which it is proposed to hold in Cleveland, Ohio, in the very near future.

The scheme can hardly be endorsed enthusiastically until it is definitely learned whether the ideas of Webster and others who advocate ye olden style are to be re-established, or whether it is a boom for the Carnegie-Roosevelt method of "geting thru with as few leters as posibl."

The Elgin Review, May 8, 1908.

field News, tongue fully in cheek, endorsed the novel idea. "It would probably make [the contest] more exciting," they wrote, and, in a backward way, would give "the worst spellers . . . the best chances." The *Pittsburgh Post-Gazette,* tongue nowhere near the cheek, opposed the "freakish idea" and promised that if "any simplified spellers appear at the Cleveland contest, they would be laughed out of the hall." Somewhere between these views stood a reform-leaning school principal from New York; in his mind, nothing would better help the simplified spelling movement than holding the bee in traditional spelling:

> What better time could there be for demonstrating the absurdity of the present cumbersome system of orthography? For months the boys and girls of principal American cities will have been wrestling with the antiquated spelling which is contrary to all logic. Like parrots they will have committed to memory the written symbols of sounds, including thousands of useless letters. Think of the waste of time and the tax on the mental powers, all of which could be avoided by the adoption of simplified spelling.

The debate spilled into schools, where local spelling bees became battlegrounds for minor protests. That March, at a Pennsylvania competition, a girl caused a scene in support of simplified spelling when she refused to spell *honest* with an *H*. (This was "an old-time bee," the host reprimanded her, and "the spelling must be done in the old-time way.") Two months earlier, the winner of an Indiana bee had taken a defiant stand *against* simplified spelling by refusing her first-place prize—a photograph of the simplifier-in-chief himself, President Theodore Roosevelt. (When she offered it to her fellow contestants, none of them would touch the tainted prize either.)

And so, as traditionalists and modernists sharpened their arguments in the press, and grade-schoolers waged their protests from the spelling stage, the nation held its breath, waiting for the NEA to choose: Tradition or reform? Chaucer or Carnegie? Ye olde spelling or the nu?

Within this charged orthographic climate, the rumor had spread so freely, so naturally, that few bothered to question its plausibility. A simplified spelling bee? How would the NEA conduct such a thing? Without an authoritative simplified dictionary, whose version of *chiaroscurist* would be correct—the girl who spells it *kiaroskurist* or the boy who spells it *kiaroskyurest*? What about the judge who spells it *keearoskyerist*? How could a competition based on objective standards accommodate different phonetic interpretations?

With nothing concrete to sustain the rumor, newspapers eventually lost interest, the story petered out, and the spelling bee moved ahead as always planned, in traditional English, untouched by the fleeting whims of radical reform. Other controversies, of course, would take its place.

~~~~~

On the afternoon of June 29, sixty boys and girls took the stage at the Hippodrome as America's first national spelling bee began. In the opening written round, contestants silently wrote out tricky English words like *umbrella, cemetery, mischief, chimney, potato, lettuce, professor, February, pumpkin, balloon, conscience,* and *embarrass*. Next came the real spectacle, the showcase that 6,000 spectators had come to see: the oral round. Ten children at a time lined up center stage as the officiant delivered each their word. "Neuralgia," he would read from a preapproved list, and the contestant would carefully spell out *N-E-U-R-A-L-G-I-A*. "Fairies," he would say, and the child would spell out *F-A-I-R-I-E-S*.

To put the young contestants at ease, the officiant of the bee, S. H. Clarke, made feeble attempts at humor. He teased one contestant that his pants were too big. He told another that he would give him a quarter to get a haircut. His jokes were bad—but his pronunciations were worse. "On one occasion," reported a journalist, "we could not for the life of us determine whether he said *foreigner* or *cardinal*." In defiance of the contest organizers, Clarke also repeatedly provided word definitions off the top of his head, many of them imperfect and confusing. When asked to use *capitol* in a sentence, he confidently stated that "Washington is the *capitol* of the United States," which led to a minor crisis among the judging panel. The word on Clarke's list was indeed *capitol*—but that didn't fit his improvised example. Some judges therefore marked both *C-A-P-I-T-O-L* and *C-A-P-I-T-A-L* correct. Others deferred to the official list and only marked *C-A-P-I-T-O-L* correct. "These errors were not the fault of the Cleveland officials," the event organizer later assured the public, "but were due entirely to the man who pronounced the words."

From the start of the bee, one contestant stood out starkly from the rest: 13-year-old Marie Bolden. The daughter of a Cleveland postal worker, Bolden had learned to spell by reading local newspapers. By the age of 13, she was one of the best young spellers in Cleveland. And on this day, with her family watching from the crowd, Marie Bolden stood onstage at the Hippodrome as the only Black competitor in the national spelling bee.

"Several of the New Orleans children balked at the idea of spelling against a negro girl," reported the *Cincinnati Enquirer*, and in the days before the bee, many people demanded Bolden's removal. When the Cleveland organizers refused, the New Orleans team threatened to boycott. New Orleans was one of only four teams at the contest (along with Pittsburgh, Erie, and Cleveland); the organizers knew that losing a quarter of the field (and the only southern contingent) might dampen the entire event. But then, so would capitulating to segregationist demands. The Cleveland organizers wouldn't give in. New Orleans wouldn't back down, and the standoff persisted until the eve of the bee. Finally, with pressure mounting and time ticking, Warren Easton, the New Orleans superintendent, dropped the threat (a decision that his own school board would later censure him for). His 15 contestants would remain in the competition. So would Marie Bolden, who took her rightful place among the ranks of hopeful young spellers.

~~~~~

Over several grueling hours, America's best and brightest spelled and misspelled, S. H. Clarke defined and misdefined, and thousands followed along in rapt attention. *Restaurant* turned out to be a stumbling block for many spellers. So did *sovereign* and *ceiling*. On the other end of the spectrum, one Pittsburgh boy was so shocked to get the word *gas* that he assumed he had misheard. ("Gas?" he repeated. "*Gas?* Why, G-A-S, *gas.*") And, fittingly enough, one of the most frequently misspelled words of the day was, of course, *misspelled.*

When the final word had been delivered and the scores all tallied, the judges announced the results.* Erie finished fourth with 85 misspelled words. New Orleans finished third with 66, and Pittsburgh placed second with 47. Cleveland, with only 40 errors, took the team prize, and the individual prize came down to two spellers: Mae Thursby of Pittsburgh and Marie Bolden of Cleveland. They were the only two contestants to record perfect scores. In the event of a tie, the rules favored the contestant from the stronger team. And thus, Marie Bolden—the best speller on the best team—became America's first national spelling bee champion.

"The convention was swept with a storm of applause," reported the *Oskaloosa Herald*, as journalists, spectators, and even some spelling peers (with notable exceptions) swarmed Bolden to congratulate her. The next day, newspapers across the country lavished Bolden with praise, and Booker T. Washington (who had sparked racial controversy himself in 1901 when he became the first Black person invited to dine at the White House) applauded the young victor in a speech. "You will admit," he told his majority-white audience, "that

MARIE C. BOLDEN, CHAMPION SPELLER

---

* Modern spelling bees follow a different format than the 1908 competition. Today, a misspelled word generally results in immediate elimination. In 1908, a misspelled word counted toward the final tallies, but all contestants remained in the bee until the very end. Winners were determined by score, not by elimination, and spellers competed as teams, not as individuals.

we spell out of the same spelling book that you do. And I think you will also admit that we spell a little better."

~~~~~

In the aftermath of America's first national spelling bee, each losing team offered a different excuse for its defeat. New Orleans, according to its *Daily Picayune*, blamed the loss on its "clash with race prejudice in the Northern city," which had unfairly handicapped it. Erie faulted its own selection process, which relied on teacher nominations rather than competitive preliminaries. And Pittsburgh put the fault, naturally, on simplified spelling. According to its superintendent, Pittsburgh had been led astray by the language reforms of its most famous resident, Andrew Carnegie. Apparently, Carnegie's spelling had confused the young minds of his city, clouded their lexical judgments, and now embarrassed them on the national stage.

13

Our Drunken Alphabet

The da ma ov koars kum when the publik ma be
expektd to get rekonsyled to the bezair asspekt of the
Simplified Kombynashuns,* but—if I may be allowed the
expression—is it worth the wasted time?

—Mark Twain, 1899

During his speech at a Hartford spelling bee in 1875, Mark Twain,
the future face of the simplified spelling movement, questioned the
very concept of competitive spelling:

> I don't see any use in having a uniform and arbitrary way
> of spelling words. We might as well make all clothes alike
> and cook all dishes alike. Sameness is tiresome; variety is
> pleasing. I have a correspondent whose letters are always a
> refreshment to me, there is such a breezy unfettered origi-
> nality about his orthography. He always spells *Kow* with a
> large *K.* Now that is just as good as to spell it with a small
> one. It is better. It gives the imagination a broader field, a
> wider scope. It suggests to the mind a grand, vague, im-
> pressive new kind of a cow.

---

* Tr: "The day may of course come when the public may be expected to get reconciled
to the bizarre aspect of the Simplified Combinations . . ."

Perhaps no one in history has wavered as much on spelling reform as Mark Twain. In his days as a so-called Phunny Phellow, he declared that everyone should spell as they like, language authorities be damned. Eventually, he threw in his hat for standardized spelling reform; then he took it out, then in, then out again. "I disrespect our orthography most heartily," he wrote in his autobiography. And yet that critical question of what to *do* about our orthography continually stumped him.

"Free spelling"—sometimes known as "inventive" or "flexible" spelling—is the concept that we should all spell according to our own phonetic interpretation or convenience. Free spelling aligned with Twain's general disdain for rules and conformity. He was especially fond of the wild spelling idiosyncrasies of his wife, Olivia: "Maybe it is wrong for me to put a premium on bad spelling," he wrote to her, "but I can't help it if it is. Somehow I love it in you—I have grown used to it, accustomed to expect it, & I honestly believe that if, all of a sudden, you fell to spelling every word right, I should feel a pain, as if something very dear to me had been mysteriously spirited away & lost to me."

In the 1870s, Twain took his first step toward linguistic brevity. One day, while freelancing for a paltry seven cents per word, Twain was assigned to write 10 magazine pages on the following dizzying prompt: *"Considerations concerning the alleged subterranean holophotal extemporaneousness of the conchyliaceous superimbrication of the ornithorhyncus, as foreshadowed by the unintelligibility of its plesiosaurian anisodactylous aspects."* Twain marched straight to his editor. "You want ten pages of those rumbling, great long summer thunder-peals and you expect to get them at seven cents a peal?" "A word's a word," said his editor, "and seven cents is the contract; what are you going to do about it?" "Jackson," Twain replied, "this is cold-blooded oppression."

Twain vowed, then and there, to never use a long word where a short word would do:

> I never write "metropolis" for seven cents, because I can get the same money for "city." I never write "policeman," because I can get the same price for "cop" . . . I never write "valetudinarian" at all, for not even hunger and wretchedness can humble me to the point where I will do a word like that for seven cents; I wouldn't do it for fifteen.

On the hunt now for brevity and directness (particularly where money and labor were concerned), Twain began to see the wisdom in universal spelling reform. In 1899, he confessed he was developing "a kindly feeling, a friendly feeling, a cousinly feeling toward Simplified Spelling," but nothing more. To him, simplified spelling seemed to only "substitute one inadequacy for another; a sort of patching and plugging poor old dental relics with cement and gold and porcelain paste." What English really needed, he believed, "was a new set of teeth. That is to say, a new ALPHABET."

Twain's utopian ideal was the phonographic shorthand of Isaac Pitman. It was "the only competent alphabet in the world," he wrote—and he did the math to prove it:

> To write the word "through," the pen has to make twenty-one strokes.
> To write the word "thru," the pen has to make twelve strokes—a good saving.
> To write that same word with the phonographic alphabet, the pen has to make only THREE strokes.

To write the word "laugh," the pen has to make FOUR-TEEN strokes.

To write "laff," the pen has to make the SAME NUM-BER of strokes—no labor is saved to the penman.

To write the same word with the phonographic alphabet, the pen has to make only THREE strokes.

The cursive *M,* which requires five movements of the hand—down, up, down, up, down—"The phonographic alphabet accomplishes . . . with a single stroke," Twain explains, "—a curve, like a parenthesis that has come home drunk and has fallen face down right at the front door where everybody that goes along will see him and say, Alas!" Twain often used drunkenness as a metaphor to describe English's impaired orthography. Ours is a "drunken old alphabet," Twain said, "invented by a drunken thief," and Twain's job was to reform it "by reducing his whiskey." Simplified spelling is a start, but it will only make our alphabet *half drunk.* To fully rehabilitate it, we must "take away his whiskey entirely, and fill up his jug with Pitman's wholesome and undiseased alphabet."

Twain would eventually join the Simplified Spelling Board in the spring of 1906, but a month later he was already having doubts. The Board's ambitious goal of a simplified revolution "won't happen," he admitted to a newspaper in April, "and I am sorry as a dog. For I do love revolutions and violence." The following year, at a New York dinner ceremony for Andrew Carnegie, Twain twisted the knife further. "Simplified spelling is all right," he snickered, nodding toward the man of honor, "but, like chastity, you can carry it too far."

There's not a vowel in [our alphabet] with a definite value, and not a consonant that you can hitch anything to. Look at the "h"s distributed all around. There's "gherkin." What are you going to do with the "h" in that? What the devil's the use of "h" in gherkin, I'd like to know.

—Mark Twain, 1907

In November 1906, three months after President Roosevelt joined the cause and three weeks before he left it, Twain satirized his own Simplified Spelling Board in a short story set around 1000 B.C.E., during Egypt's transition from hieroglyphics to the "simpler" Phoenician alphabet:

The first time I was in Egypt a Simplified Spelling epidemic had broken out, and the atmosphere was electrical with feeling engendered by the subject . . . The Simplifiers had risen in revolt against the hieroglyphics. An uncle of Cadmus who was out of a job had come to Egypt and was trying to introduce the Phoenician alphabet and get it adopted in place of the hieroglyphics. He was challenged to show cause, and he did it to the best of his ability. The exhibition and discussion took place in the Temple of Astarte, and I was present.

Twain, the omniscient narrator, describes the proceedings of the "Simplified Committee" (a parody of the Simplified Spelling Board) led by King Croesus (Andrew Carnegie) and Viceroy Khedive (Theodore Roosevelt):

Croesus [was] foreman of the Revolt—not a large man physically, but a simplified speller of acknowledged ability . . . The Khedive was the main backer of the Revolt, and this magnified its strength and saved it from being insignificant. Among the Simplifiers were many men of learning and distinction, mainly literary men and members of college faculties; but all ranks and conditions of men and all grades of intellect, erudition, and ignorance, were represented in the Opposition.

In a demonstration before the Egyptian authorities, Uncle Cadmus—the mastermind of this revolt and a proxy, perhaps, for all spelling visionaries since Ormin—writes on a blackboard two versions of the Lord's Prayer (what else?). First, he draws an Egyptian man in profile. He surrounds him with birds, a house, two dinner pails, a lion, a javelin, a toothed line, an army of men shooting arrows, an army of men in a tower, a wheelbarrow, a large king, and assorted men in frocks. It takes him 45 minutes. Next, he writes the same Lord's Prayer in the simpler Phoenician alphabet. It takes four and a half minutes.

Uncle Cadmus sat down, and the Opposition rose and combated his reasonings in the usual way. Those people said that they had always been used to the hieroglyphics; that the hieroglyphics had dear and sacred associations for them; that they loved to sit on a barrel under an umbrella in the brilliant sun of Egypt and spell out the owls and eagles and alligators and saw-teeth, and take an hour and a half to [write] the Lord's Prayer, and weep with romantic emotion . . .

Twain's story trails off ambiguously, without resolution, a reflection perhaps of his own unresolved stance toward simplified spelling. He died in 1910, four years after the Board's founding. By then the jokes and jibes had slowed the movement to a near standstill. To his last days, Twain oscillated. Back and forth he went, from free spelling to simplified spelling to phonographic spelling, never settling on a single approach to sobriety.

Hi Soesiety

Thinc ov it! Iz it not a thing wurth thincing ov?
—*The Pioneer ov Simplified Speling*,
Vol. 1, No. 1, March 1912

As the national fervor for spelling bees grew, it eclipsed the once-trendy excitement for simplified spelling. Now, instead of recoiling from English's arcane quirks, children sought to conquer them with competitive zeal. Local spelling bees skyrocketed as students immersed themselves in obscure etymologies, Latin prefixes, homophones and homonyms, relishing the challenge of mastering our irregular system. The old guard of traditional orthography was back. Simplified spelling waned.

During those four reckless months of 1906, Theodore Roosevelt had done more to harm simplified spelling than even the Phunny Phellows had, spoiling Andrew Carnegie's careful planning and turning his vision for orthographic utopia into fodder for cartoons and punch lines. As the Simplified Spelling Board lost momentum, Carnegie raised his annual endowment to $25,000. It made little difference. Hoping to bolster Carnegie's confidence, Brander Matthews sent his benefactor a list of American newspapers that had adopted some of the Board's 300 spellings. Carnegie responded sternly: "Please note, not one Eastern paper. I see no change in New York and I am getting very tired indeed, of sinking twenty-five thousand dollars a year for nothing here in the East."

Across the Atlantic, England had watched this all unfold. It had watched as America's president crashed and burned, the press sneered and scoffed, and America's greatest author soured on the organization he'd helped found. The fumbling American movement only energized England more. In September 1908, three months after Marie Bolden's victory in Cleveland, ten Londoners gathered at the Holborn Restaurant to create a British counterpart to the Simplified Spelling Board. They called it the "Simplified Spelling Society"—soon to be respelled as the "Simplified Speling Soesiety"—and amassed a membership of luminaries to rival the Board's. George Bernard Shaw and H. G. Wells joined up. So did Charles Darwin's grandson, Charles Galton Darwin, a pioneer in quantum physics and X-ray technology. And with a donation of £1,000, Andrew Carnegie bought himself a seat as co–vice president, hedging his bets between England and America in the race for reform.

The Soesiety began printing a monthly journal, *The Pioneer ov Simplified Speling*, which set the bar high in its opening editorial:

TU THE REEDER.

WE recomend yu tu prezurv cairfuly this furst number ov "The Pioneer." Oenly a limited edishon ov it haz been printed; and it mai wun dai becum a priesles rarity az the furst peeriodical publisht in rashonaly-spelt English.

Among the journal's features were a "Noets and Nyuez" column, a "Praiz and Prejoodis" press section, and a monthly "Esai Competishon," all rendered in what it called the "wun sound wun simbol" principle:

ESAI COMPETISHON.

ESAIZ on the subject ov *The Edyucaishonal Advaantijez ov Simplified Speling* ar invieted bi the Comity ov the Simplified Speling Soesiety. A priez ov FIFTEEN GINIZ wil be aworded to the rieter ov the best esai in eech ov the foloing claasez :—

I. Teecherz in Scuulz (Men).
II.   „   „   „   (Wimen).
III. Non-Teecherz.

On the recomendaishon ov the jujez an adishonal priez ov fiev giniz mai be aworded in eech claas.

The Competishon iz oepen tu aul British subjects and tu forin memberz ov the Soesiety. Thair iz no entrans fe.

In many ways, Britain's new spelling society was the opposite of its American counterpart. While Carnegie's Board introduced its changes gradually (or tried to), the Soesiety committed to writing *everything* in simplified spelling. The London County and Westminster Bank was surprised and confused when, in 1913, the Soesiety started issuing certified checks in its new orthography. The bank requested an indemnity agreement to protect it against financial mishaps that might arise from these misspellings. True to form, the Soesiety wrote up the contract in its own style:

> In consideraishon ov yur paiing our checs maid out in wurdz in our oen moed ov speling we heerbie agree tu hoeld you harmles & indemnifie yu against eni claim which mai ariez thru the speling ov the amount being misunderstood.

The Soesiety took a democratic approach to new spellings. If a member wished to alter the orthography, they would submit their suggestion in writing. Fellow members would then vote on the change, and the majority would decide. On the question of whether *pure* should be rendered *puer* or *puur*, the Soesiety voted for the latter. Regarding whether *secretary* and *committee* should end in *I* or *Y,* it settled on the former. And in the matter of the word *private,* 55 voted to spell it *privet,* 46 for *privit,* 15 for *privut,* two for *privat,* and one each for *privaet* and *priveut.* The Soesiety's greatest advantage was its access to Britain's empire. Just as England once colonized the world with its language, the Simplified Speling Soesiety now dispatched missionaries around the globe to lecture on simplified spelling. "The Indianz wer enthyuziastic in regard tu the reform ov English speling," reported back Daniel Jones, the Soesiety's India ambassador, and following his trip it "woz agreed that the Secretari maic encuieriz az tu the posibility ov establishing Foecal Braanchez in Bombay and Lahore." In 1912, amid efforts to establish an outpost in South Africa, the Soesiety received a letter of gratitude from a Johannesburg resident:

> While the Soesiety acknowledged that some puritans might view its spellings as "groetesc," a "bad joec," or the "profesi ov a monomainiac" (their words), they assured critics that it was all for the benefit of the children:
>
> [Our spelling] cumz neer enuf tu acyurasy and consistensy tu saiv, on an averij, WUN HOEL YEER IN THE SCUUL LIEF OV EVERY ENGLISH-SPEECING CHIELD THRU AUL THE CUMING JENERAISHONZ.
> Thinc ov it! Iz it not a thing wurth thincing ov?

I am delieted at [the spelling's] amaizing simplicity. I beleev if such a sistem had been in voeg dyuering the laast 200 yeerz English-speecing peepl wood hav lurned tu reed az eezily az thair children lurn tu wauc and elementary scuulz wood hav had tu justifi thair egzistens bi teeching mor dificult subjects. I feel deeply thancful tu aul the men hu hav contribyuted tu this wurc ov simplificaishon and I hoep very suun tu se our peepl in ever-increesing numberz adopt it with enthyueziazm and alacrity.*

Meanwhile, Carnegie's impatience with the Simplified Spelling Board—and the Americans entrusted to lead it—continued to grow. In a 1915 letter to Henry Holt, Carnegie blamed the Board's failures and wasted dollars on its members: "A more useless body of men never came into association, judging from the effects they produce. Instead of taking twelve words and urging their adoption, they undertook radical changes from the start" (a strategy, it should be noted, that England's Soesiety undertook with greater success). By now, Carnegie had sunk more than $200,000 into the Board, with few tangible results. "I think I hav been patient long enuf," he added to Holt, in the spelling he so bittersweetly loved. "I hav much better use for twenty thousand dollars a year."

The Simplified Spelling Board made one last-ditch effort to revive itself. In the spring of 1916, for the first time since its founding, the Board added new recommended spellings to its list. "Words, like women's skirts, are to be shorter this spring," one Indiana paper quipped, and the line spread like an infectious jingle, reprinted by dozens of publications, before fading into the oblivion of yesterday's news. When this revamp didn't

---

* Tr: "I am delighted at [the spelling's] amazing simplicity. I believe if such a system had been in vogue during the last 200 years English-speaking people would have learned to read as easily as their children learn to walk and elementary schools would have had to justify their existence by teaching more difficult subjects. I feel deeply thankful to all the men who have contributed to this work of simplification and I hope very soon to see our people in ever-increasing numbers adopt it with enthusiasm and alacrity."

**A teacher whose spelling's unique
Thus wrote down the days of the
  wique:
The first he spelt "Sonday,"
The second day "Munday,"
And now a new teacher they sique.**

—Anonymous, *Lake
Placid News*, June 19, 1931

work, Brander Matthews tried a personal rebranding. "Melville Dewey has already trained down to Melvil Dewey," reported a Kansas newspaper, "and it is rumored that Brander Matthews, chairman of the board's trustees, will here after answer only to the name Brandr Mathus."

No gesture or gimmick was enough to shift the needle for Carnegie. His funding finally dried up in 1917, and when the philanthropist died two years later, he left nothing behind for the failing American project. The Simplified Spelling Board officially dissolved in 1920.

With the demise of the Simplified Spelling Board and the closing of its New York offices, America's spelling reformers sought new headquarters. They found it in a high-class resort in the Adirondack Mountains called the Lake Placid Club.

Long before his fall from grace, Melvil Dewey had founded the Lake Placid Club on Mirror Lake in Upstate New York, and when society turned on him in 1906, he turned to Lake Placid for ref-

Lake Placid Club
Supper

Tuesday 3 April 1928   Simpler spelling

Milk, vejetabls and flowers from Club farms, gardens and greenhouses
Orders not on menu and food taken from dyning room ar charjd

Cream of cres soup

Bran zos   Krumbls
_____
Club farm tomato pikl
_____
Broild steak
Lam crokets with nu peas
Freſ vejetabl patti
Finan hadie in cream
Eg Washington
Cold: Röst beef, Tuŋ, Ham
Baked potato   Brocolli Hollandaise
Scalopt potato   Slyst nu carots
_____
Egs to order
Drest letis   _____   Jerusalem artichök salad

Whyt, Graham, Bran, Corn and Yesterdays bred
Tost: Dry, Buterd, Milk, Dipt

French röls   Rys muſins
_____
Slyst banana and cream
Chocolat eclairs
Dundee cup cakes
Cotaj cheez with curant jeli and Melba töst
_____
Sweet and salted butr

Tea   Cefi   Coco   Postum   Sertifyd milk
Butrmilk

Afternoon tea 4.30-5.30 in Birdroom at Forest. All Club members
gests and children 12 and over invyted
over

Supper menu from the Lake Placid Club, April 3, 1928.

uge. Here, in the gated confines of his Adirondack estate, Dewey subjected all his paying guests to simplified spelling. A typical "brekfast" menu at Lake Placid included "bredcrum gridl cakes," "broil ham," "dyst potato," "buterd tost," and "egs to order." In the evening, after a hearty dinner of "rost goos" and "spyst figz," guests were encouraged to watch "the butiful after-glo" as the sun set over the mountains. "One of the hardships which visitors have to put up with," reported the *Brooklyn Daily Eagle,* "is to read the menu card and the music program and such other literature as the club puts out printed in Dr. Dewey's simplified method of spelling. Sometimes a guest is apt to go hungry, rather than try to decipher the bill of fare."

Amid the pristine views and quiet of nature, simplified spellers found a respite and a rallying point, a serene place to plot the future course of their linguistic crusade. The Lake Placid Club became the de facto center of America's simplified spelling movement. Dewey, now at the helm, tried to resurrect the defunct Simplified Spelling Board as the "Simplified Spelling Leag." In collaboration with the Simplified Speling Soesiety, he also began publishing a quarterly magazine, *Spelling,* to promote a new orthography called "Anglic":

Lincoln's Gettysburg speech
(*Anglic*)

Forskor and sevn yeerz agoe our faadherz braut forth on this kontinent a nue naeshon, konseevd in liberty, and dedikaeted to the propozishon that aul men ar kreaeted eequel.

Now we ar engaejd in a graet sivil wor, testing whedhr that naeshon, or eny naeshon soe konseevd and soe dedikaeted, kan long enduer. We ar met on a graet batl-feeld of that wor. We hav kum to dedikaet a por-shon of that feeld as a fienl resting-plaes for those who heer gaev their lievs that that naeshon miet liv. It is aultogedhr fiting and propr that we shood do this.

For most paying guests, the primary allure of the Lake Placid Club lay in its luxurious amenities and first-rate winter offerings. With a full supply of "sno-shoes," "hoki" sticks, skis, and sleds, Dewey turned the Lake Placid Club into a world-class winter resort, soon to become the skiing capital of the East. He expanded with the purchase of the nearby Adirondack Lodge—quickly Dewey-fied into the "Adirondak Loj"—and by 1920 newspapers were referring to Lake Placid as America's Switzerland.

Dewey spent the last years of his life campaigning for the Olympic Committee to hold the Winter Games at his Adirondack resort. He nearly lived to see it happen. In February 1932, just weeks after Dewey died of a stroke while vacationing in Florida, the Lake Placid Club hosted the Winter Olympic Games—the first international Olympic competition ever held on U.S. soil.

Dewey's spellings were curtailed for the Games—in official publications *sno* is back to *snow* and *hoki* is *hockey*—but the menus remained untouched, and for two weeks the greatest winter athletes in the world feasted on "gridl cakes" and "buterd tost." After a visit to the Lake Placid Club, one visitor remarked that he might never be able to spell *mayonnaise* properly again.

Part IV

Washington, D.C., 1962

John F. Kennedy sits in the Oval Office, staring at the letter in his hand. This isn't the first time he's been sent unsolicited political advice. Months earlier, a sixth-grade student mailed him three crayoned pages outlining her strategy to replace all military weapons with musical instruments. Another girl advised Kennedy to make summer vacation nine months long. And one particularly confident letter came from a boy in the wake of the Bay of Pigs: "I know how busy you are, but if you could get me to the White House I'll explain my plan for the Cubans."

But this one is different. This letter comes from a Pulitzer Prize–winning author, a man with a reputation for stirring up public outrage and shaming lawmakers into supporting progressive causes—a man who knows a thing or two about reform.

Upton Sinclair is a "muckraker"—a journalist who "rakes up" and exposes the unethical, inhumane dirt of society. Back in 1905, he reported on the filthy conditions of America's meatpacking industry in his bestseller *The Jungle*. In 1926, he took on Big Oil in *Oil!* (adapted into the film *There Will Be Blood* in 2007). Now, in 1962, at the age of 83, Sinclair has one last muck to rake: the spelling of the English language.

"[This is] a subject of vast importance," Sinclair begins, "[and] what I invite you to do . . . will immortalize your name as much as if you had written the Declaration of Independence." The plan:

> Select a group of scholars . . . and commission them to lay out a program for a minimum reform of orthography within a reasonable time . . . It will not be long before the public gets over the shock, and realizes the nightmare from which it has been wakened . . . It is clear that English may become the future international language; and nothing can stand in the way but the fantastic absurdities, the chaos and disorder, which have come down to us from the ignorance of the past centuries in which our language was formed.

Sinclair knows how to craft content that moves policymakers. When Theodore Roosevelt first read *The Jungle*, he was so repulsed by its graphic depictions of meat factories that he immediately pushed Congress to pass the Meat Inspection Act. If Sinclair wants to provoke a similar emotional response in Kennedy, he'll need an equally odious depiction of English spelling. So the 83-year-old author constructs the most phonetically horrifying, orthographically stomach-churning sentence he can think of:

> "A rough cough and a hiccough plough me through."

"There are five different ways you can read the sentence," says Sinclair, "and you can throw any company into 'stitches' by reciting: 'A ruff cuff and a hiccuff pluff me thruff,' or 'A roo coo and a hiccoo ploo me throo,' and so on. But to a foreigner these problems are not funny; he finds it hopeless to disentangle them, and may give up in disgust and go home to his native tongue. But your grandchildren and my great-grandchildren cannot do that; they have to learn thousands of exceptions to spelling rules, and all their lives have to know that if they slip up with a written or spoken word, they will be taken for illiterate."

Everything about Sinclair's letter is calculated—he knows, for instance, Kennedy is a poor speller himself (Jackie often called him out on it)—and his final gambit is brazen flattery: "There is nobody in the land who can do this job but you, Mr. President; and there is little chance that you could do anything else that will give such benefit to the human race."

Four weeks later, Sinclair receives a reply. It's from Kennedy's assistant. The president will forward the matter to the Office of Education, he assures Sinclair. And poof, there it goes—into a closet, a drawer, an administrative abyss. Two months later, Kennedy is deep in the muck of midterms and missile crises, and plenty more letters with advice for saving the world.

Mad Men

> About the only noticeable legacy of the simplified spelling
> movement which reached its peak in the presidency of
> Theodore Roosevelt . . . [is in] Holsum Bred, Rite-Way
> Products, Hol-Hi golf balls, Kleer-Site golf irons, Kreep-
> A-Wa slippers.
>
> —Louise Pound, 1923

As mass media exploded in the 1920s, it launched a new age of
commercial and consumer culture. Magazines, newspapers, and
the revolutionary phenomenon of radio now offered the public a
continuous stream of news and entertainment. In the fight for human attention, the advertising industry had to innovate and adapt.
Ads became punchier, sharper, more succinct. Language was dis-
tilled to its most engaging essence.

Always on the lookout for novel ways to attract consumers, advertisers locked onto simplified spelling as a playful method to
convey their messages quickly and quirkily. By the 1920s, brands
such as Phiteezi Boots, Uneeda Biscuit, Tastykake, Kleenex,
Cheez-It, and Nuklene Shoe Whitener had discovered the commercial power of comically phonetic spelling, and local shops
profited with punchy signs that read "Oysters R Now in Season"
and "R U Interested in a Rummage Sale?" If the goal of advertising is to catch the attention of prospective consumers—make
them linger a bit longer over your signage—then a simple switch

to "X-L-ent Salmon" or "Uneedme Chair Pad" could be just the gimmick needed.

Magazine ad for Tak-hom-a Biscuit ("take home a biscuit"), *Ladies Home Journal*, 1921.

Linguists took notice. Louise Pound, a professor at the University of Nebraska,* lamented in 1923 about the growing use of whimsical misspelling "as a device to catch the eye in advertising" and "in the coinage of trade names." She blamed the trend in part on the Roaring Twenties: the culture's "fading of awe for formalities and conventions" had also led, apparently, to a fading of established word formations. But she laid the fault largely upon the simplified spellers of her era—the Mark Twains and Andrew Carnegies who founded the Simplified Spelling Board, the Melvil Deweys who ushered its spellings into the hallowed halls of libraries, and the Theodore Roosevelts who brought them, briefly, into the high-

---

* Louise Pound was not only a linguist but a competitive golfer, cyclist, figure skater, tennis player, and basketball player. While working on her philology PhD, Pound was rated the top tennis player in the U.S. (among all genders), and later became the first—and as of this writing, the *only*—woman inducted into the Nebraska Sports Hall of Fame.

est offices of the land. These orthographic agitators, evidently, had contributed more to the decline of conservative American culture than any short-skirted flapper.

Time and again, the simplifiers had failed in their quest for nationwide legislative reform. But their dogged campaigning in the early twentieth century (and the mocking headlines it inspired) had accustomed the public to the sight of unusual spellings. It left America with a taste for novel and creative orthography, which paved the way for the advertisers of the 1920s. An earlier generation of self-respecting consumers might have balked at perversions like Trufit Shoes or Sav-U-Time Heat Regulator. Now, in the "anything goes" Jazz Age, these spellings brought big returns.

~~~~~

Simplified orthography for advertising is perhaps the most important legacy of the defunct spelling reform movement.

—Louise Pound

K doesn't start many words, and when it does, it's often silent. But take a stroll through the supermarket and you'll see hard *K*'s dominating brand names on every shelf, from Kool-Aid to Kleenex to Krispy Kreme to Kit Kats. This "Kraze for *K*," as Louise Pound called it, stretches back to the 1860s, but in the 1920s it exploded into every cor-

ner of American consumer culture. Pound lists her era's worst offenders:

> Kiddies' Koveralls. Kiddie Kars. Kiddie Klothes. Kleen
> Kwick Auto Emergency Klenzer. Krank's Kreem for Shav-
> ing... Korrect Koats. Kollege Kut Klothes. Keene's Kwality
> Kindles at the Kanditorium. Klay Kompact for Komplex-
> ions... Klip-Klap Snaps for Rings. Kut-Kwik Razor Strop.
> The Klose Kloset Hamper. Klever Klippers for Bobby Hair.
> Kosy Klosure Ideal Auto Tops for Winter. Kurz Kitchen-
> ettes Kant-Leak Kontainers.

The *K* phenomenon, says Pound, is the predictable by-product of
the "agitation for simplified spelling," which had been pumping words
like *karacter* and *korus* into the American mainstream since the days
of Noah Webster. The letter
K resonates with customers
on a subconscious level; due
to its rarity in the language,
it infuses a sense of novelty
into an otherwise mundane
product, elevating the brand
to something katchy and
kool. And yet, *K* occurs far
more frequently in English
than *Z*. Why doesn't *Z*, the
phonetic plural for so many
reformerz, receive the same
commercial prominence?
What's so special about *K*?

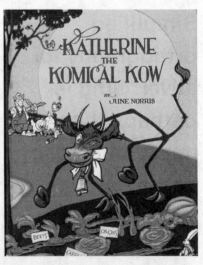

A shining example of the "Kraze for *K*."
Katherine the Komical Kow by June Norris,
1926.

Among comedians and comedy lovers, it's a truth universally acknowledged that *K* sounds are funny. *Kook, klutz, clank. KaBOOM, kaPOW, kerPLUNK.* Krusty the Clown. Cosmo Kramer. *K* has a *kick.* In Neil Simon's 1972 play *The Sunshine Boys,* a veteran comedian explains the art of the *K*:

> Fifty-seven years in this business, you learn a few things. You know what words are funny and which words are not funny. . . Words with 'k' in them are funny. Casey Stengel, that's a funny name. . . Cookie is funny. Cucumber is funny. . . Cleveland is funny. Maryland is not funny. Then, there's chicken. Chicken is funny. Pickle is funny. Cab is funny. Cockroach is funny—not if you get 'em, only if you say 'em.

"All in all," Pound writes, "there is no mistaking the kall of 'k' over our kountry, our kurious kontemporary kraving for it, and its konspicuous use in the klever koinages of kommerce."*

~~~~~~

While many commercial brands embraced these new fun fonetiks, others preferred to project an image of tradition and reliability. They believed in good old-fashioned orthographic values. They believed in *Webster's Dictionary.*

Beginning in 1889, when Charles and George Merriam (the

---

* Louise Pound suspected that some of the Ku Klux Klan's appeal (see Chapter 9), which peaked in the early 1920s, stemmed from its "curious, better perhaps kurious, nomenclature" of *K* sounds, which has "helped its rapid spread." The Klan's lexicography of *K* terms included *klectoken* ("an initiation fee"), *klaliff* ("vice president"), and *klonsul* ("attorney").

Massachusetts siblings who acquired Webster's dictionary rights upon his death) lost their copyright on the Webster name, a surge of brands suddenly leapt to attach themselves to Webster. Shoe sellers printed up promotional "Webster's Dictionary" giveaways for young customers, stamped with their own logos and taglines. *Buster Brown Webster Select Dictionary,* read one title—"Especially Prepared for the Wearers of Buster Brown Shoes." *Webster's Ever-Ready Dictionary,* read another—"Specially Prepared for Forest Grove Shoe Store." The *Coca-Cola Webster's* arrived in 1924, distributed for free to wholesale buyers, and in the 1930s the Standard Oil Company came out with the *Standard Oil Webster's,* an all-American blend of commerce and intellectual nourishment sold at gas stations.*

At the same time, so-called coauthored dictionaries, funded by men of means looking to raise their status, appeared under titles like *Hurst's Webster's Dictionary* (1889), *Hill's Webster's Dictionary* (1899), *Peabody's Webster's Dictionary* (1905), *Donohue's Webster's Dictionary* (1917), and *Abbott's Webster's Dictionary* (1933), to the point where Merriam-Webster—still the *official* Webster's—was eventually forced to use a tagline to distinguish itself from the fakes: *Not just Webster. Merriam-Webster*™. Today, "Webster's Dictionary" is considered a genericized trademark in the United States, which means it is not protected by copyright. Technically anyone can publish their own dictionary and call it "Webster's."

~~~~~

---

* Dictionaries often occupied a prominent place in the home (Google "antique dictionary stands"), and thus offered excellent opportunities for brand advertising. On the inside, these books were just like any other abridged *Webster's*. On the outside, they were *Buster Brown, Coca-Cola, Standard Oil,* and (insert brand name here) *Webster's*.

Other familiar ad gimmicks appeared in the 1920s—"EZ" for "easy," "xtra" for "extra," "rite" for "right"—but the most popular, outshining even the almighty *K*, was the solitary *U*. It greeted Americans on highway billboards ("Body and Fender Repairing While U Wait") and in candy shops ("U-Bet-U It's Good Candy"), street signs ("U R now in Emmet County") and roadside maps ("U R Here"). It even goaded them into purchasing new homes ("I. C. U. R. ready for our real estate"). In his 1929 article "Why Not 'U' For 'You'?" in *American Speech*, Donald M. Alexander notes the "considerable use . . . of the capital U by those who have either some commodity or service to offer the public" and lists a few galling examples:

> U Put It on Weather Strip, U-Do-It Graining Compound, Wear U Well Clothes, Wear U Well Shoes, U-Otto-Buy (used cars) . . . Sav-U-Time Heat Regulator, U-Serve Canned Goods . . . Hats Cleaned While U Wait, Suits Pressed While U Wait (sometimes varied to While U Rest), Motor Boats To Rent—U Drive, I'll Be Here When U Come Back . . .

Alexander, who makes a spirited case in support of *U*, notes that Benjamin Franklin himself tried to get *IU* to catch on as far back as 1768, and Andrew Carnegie had done the same with *YU* in 1906. Modern advertisers hadn't done anything except take the next logical step, simplifying the word to its basest form: *U*.

In fact, the first-person singular, *I*, had followed a similar evolution. In Old English, the word was written variously as *IC* or *ICH*, and the consonant was pronounced until it began fading around the twelfth century. By the fifteenth century, the stand-alone *I* emerged in the Northern and Midlands dialects, and a century later it spread to the rest of England. So, Alexander asks, if we did it with *I*, why not *U*?

The most analyzed, and least understood, *U* of the 1920s ad world appears in *Ulysses,* the story of an Irish advertising agent. A quarter way through James Joyce's 1922 novel, the hero Leopold Bloom encounters a friend, Josie. She informs Leopold that her husband has just received a postcard scrawled with an offensive message:

> —Read that, she said. He got it this morning.
> —What is it? Mr Bloom asked, taking the card. U.P.?
> —U.P.: up, she said. Someone taking a rise out of him. It's a great shame for them whoever he is.
> —Indeed it is, Mr Bloom said.

These four letters—"U.P.: up"—have mystified Joycean scholars for more than a century. What do they mean? What's so offensive about them? The Russian novelist Vladimir Nabokov suspected they referred to the English Midlands expression "U.P. spells goslings," a schoolboy taunt meant to demean the loser of a game. (U.P. stood for "up peg"; apparently the defeated party would be forced to remove a ground peg using only their teeth.) But in the context of Bloom's advertising world, many see "U.P.: up" as an orthographic abbreviation: "you pee up." Once again, no one quite knows what that means either. (This happens a lot with Joyce.) Some interpret it as a kind of sexual shaming, others as a pressing medical condition. I'll leave the specific visuals to your imagination. Your guess is as good as any.

~~~~~~

The catchy slogans, the shortened words, the cryptic insults—they all became part of the 1920s zeitgeist as simplified spelling found its place in the broader world of pop culture. It brought a sense of efficiency and novelty, of humor and wit, to a long-outdated language. It hijacked consumer attention, and the longer it held it—the longer a passerby paused over a signboard to contemplate the linguistic puzzle—the more it seeped into the American subconscious.

Louise Pound, for her part, feared where this insidious advertising might lead. "[There is] a possibility . . . that the language of advertising may, in its turn, have an influence upon the standard language. Many decades from now, it may be of interest to determine whether this reflex influence of the spelling reform movement (if there be such) did not prove to be greater than was its direct influence when the movement was at its height."

Cn U Rd Ths?

I never will need shorthand, as [Speedwriting] will cover all
my needs.

—Sylvia Plath

In 1924, a popular new spelling scheme began circulating in magazines and newspapers, purveying all the pesky ad lingo that Pound
warned about. That infuriating standalone *U* instead of *you*. That
equally infuriating *K* instead of *C*. And the reduction of a respectable
word like *college* to a state of abject indignity: *klj*. "Speedwriting" was
orthographic reform on steroids. It was simplified spelling turned up
to lvn.

Crafted by Emma Dearborn, a teacher at Columbia University
in New York, Speedwriting combined the best of shorthand (the
use of shortcut symbols to capture text at the rate of speech) with
the best of simplified spelling (the use of English letters rather than
shorthand squiggles). Taking the Simplified Spelling Board motto
"simplification by omission" to its minimalist extreme, Dearborn
cut nearly three-quarters of all English's vowels, chopping *rough*,
phone, and *school* down to *rf*, *fn*, and *skl*, and introduced a technique called "phrasing" that allowed multiple words to be written
without spaces between them. She also used a system of one-letter
signifiers for common words like *and* (*a*), *with* (*w*), *you* and *your*
(*u*), *in* (*n*), and *the* (*t*). Put all that together, and you can boil down
a sentence to its dozen most important letters.

Dearborn demonstrates in this November 1924 ad in *Popular Science Monthly* comparing Speedwriting with two other shorthands on the market:

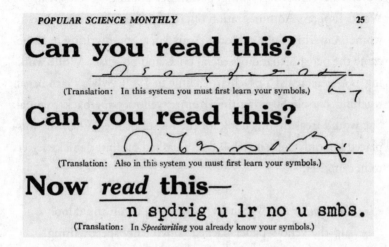

Can you read this?

(Translation: In this system you must first learn your symbols.)

Can you read this?

(Translation: Also in this system you must first learn your symbols.)

Now *read* this—

n spdrig u lr no u smbs.

(Translation: In *Speedwriting* you already know your symbols.)

Spelling reformers are notoriously pitiful at marketing, but Dearborn was a master. She embraced the advertising world in all its material offerings, placing glamorous full-page color ads in *Woman's Home Companion* and *Good Housekeeping* and corner-page classifieds in newspapers around the country. Amid glossy ads for hosiery and Frigidaires, Dearborn promised to teach anyone to "rt 120 wpm & gt a hi pa jb" in just 6 to 12 weeks. Between 1924 and 1931, more than 100,000 students (mostly women) signed up for Speedwriting. Nobody merged advertising and simplified spelling as well as Emma Dearborn did.

Speedwriting was designed for the business world—a tool for secretaries and stenographers to take notes quickly and efficiently— but it found admirers outside the office as well. In preparation for an antarctic expedition, Commander Richard E. Byrd and his crew took classes with Dearborn to learn how to record their scientific observations with speedy but legible efficiency. Theodore Roosevelt's son Theodore Jr. and their cousin Franklin Delano Roosevelt both endorsed Dearborn's spelling, and under Franklin's New Deal, the Works Progress Administration offered free Speedwriting classes to women entering the workforce. Years later, Speedwriting even became the pet shorthand of several poets and novelists. While working as a secretary at a psychiatric clinic in 1958, Sylvia Plath began teaching herself Speedwriting from a yellow paperback manual. She would treasure this book for the rest of its life. When she misplaced her only copy in 1960, Plath dashed off four panicky letters to her mother:

> *September 23:* "I wonder, by the way, if you could look up the yellow-paper-backed copy of my speedwriting book (it should be in my bookcase or drawers or closet, near the surface of piles of magazines or something) & send it on to me."
>
> *November 19:* "I hate to bother you about this again, but could you look around once more for that yellow paperbound Speedwriting book or beg, borrow or steal another copy & airmail it to me? . . . I'm dying to get hold of it."
>
> *December 14:* "Keep after that speedwriting book."
>
> *December 24:* "<u>Do</u> make a final search for that bright yellow paper-back speedwriting book! It <u>must</u> be at home . . . I am so frustrated without it . . . Couldn't you invent some pretext to get the book from the school as a teacher? . . . I just feel if I walked into the house I could put my hand on the speedwriting book!"

Plath's book never turned up, but her mother did manage to dig up a few tattered copies from other sources. She mailed her daughter every single Speedwriting book she found.

CAN YOU READ THIS?

thl nbu tmka kPsn v thssm w Os. spdrig dsn sf bt kPsn. ulr nolt Kaks mply trps-spdrig aks vta uk lrnt Q n n, Ossm. ukrit wpn sls pcl a lso oa tpRi wh gist agr avg amkst pob fu tnkrs uspd to a hi py.

VICTORIA SPEEDWRITING SCHOOL

755 Broughton Street   Phone 552

WATCH THIS SPACE TO-MORROW

Some Speedwriting ads, like this one, really challenge our decryption skills. "Can you read this?" it asks. Our resounding answer: No. (*Times Colonist*, September 9, 1927)

Emma Dearborn marketed Speedwriting as the more convenient alternative to the nineteenth-century shorthands of Pitman and Gregg. Speedwriting could be learned at home, by oneself, instead of at vocational school under an instructor. This is what Plath loved about it. Throughout her letters and fiction, Plath wrote resentfully of traditional shorthand. Because it was required for most office jobs available to women, Plath saw it as a symbol of chauvinism, a tool for molding girls into subservient secretaries to take the dictations of their male bosses. "I wanted to dictate my own thrilling letters," says one of Plath's fictional characters as she, like Plath, resists the call of the secretarial life. When Plath received her first yellow-backed Speedwriting book in 1958, a little yellow light went on. Speedwriting was *not* shorthand; it was a simplified *longhand*, an abbreviated version of the language she already knew. And since it was self-taught, it embodied a spirit of independence that shorthand never could. "I never will need shorthand," Plath wrote in a letter to her mother, "as [Speedwriting] will cover all my needs."

The Great Depression hit Emma Dearborn hard. As unemployment soared in the 1930s, the demand for stenographical tools like Speedwriting plummeted. At the same time, Dearborn's livelihood became threatened by copycats and counterfeits. When one of Dearborn's former students published a spelling system that looked suspiciously like Speedwriting, Dearborn took him to court. Despite overwhelming evidence of plagiarism, the circuit court judge ruled against Dearborn. "There is no literary merit," declared the judge, "in a mere system of condensing written words into less than the number of letters usually used to spell them out." This opened the floodgates, and after the court's decision a slew of shorthand systems emerged calling themselves "Speedwriting" and differing little, if at all, from Dearborn's system.

Emma Dearborn, like Sylvia Plath, spent her life inside what Plath called a "bell jar," the suffocating isolation of depression. When the economy entered a particularly cruel dip in 1937, Dearborn, along with many other Americans, slipped into a hopeless state. She never came out. On a single day in New York that summer, eight people plunged to their deaths from buildings. Emma Dearborn was one of them.

~~~~~

The Great Depression cast a long, dark shadow over the entire globe in the 1930s. The economy contracted. Employment plummeted. Breadlines grew. People starved.

With the crash of Wall Street in 1929 and the death of Andrew Carnegie, simplified spelling's greatest benefactor, a decade earlier, funding for spelling reform disappeared. Educational institutions, grappling with budget cuts, could no longer entertain the luxury of altering their curricula. Reformers who had once been on the cusp of revolutionizing the written word began to abandon the movement. The push for simplified spelling receded into the background, eclipsed by the pressing needs of a world in economic disarray.

~~~~~

In 1934, while struggling to keep his newspaper afloat, a lone media mogul with a reputation for innovation came up with a plan to save money. Shorter spellings, it seemed to him, would eat up less column space in his paper. It would extend the life of his lino-type machines, and might even increase sales by bringing a sensationalist, eye-catching *pop* to his above-the-fold headlines. He saw the great utility that brief but snappy language could serve for money-minded media men like himself. So, he undertook an experiment—and by the time it concluded 41 years later, Colonel Robert McCormick had carried out the most effective newspaper campaign in the history of simplified spelling.

In a prominent front-page article on Sunday, January 28, 1934, the *Chicago Tribune* introduced the first 24 words of a new paper-wide system it called "Saner Spelling." *Hocky, drouth, demagog, definitly, fantom,* and other "sane" renderings were now, suddenly, house style, and all writers at the *Tribune,* as well as readers at home, had to accept this abrupt overnight twist in orthography.

The man behind it, Robert McCormick, was a former U.S. Army officer in World War I and the owner of the *Tribune.* A die-hard

"America First" isolationist, McCormick was better known for his political conservativism than for his orthographic progressivism. But as he fought to keep his newspaper running during the Depression, it became a matter of economy. Simplified spelling saved money. Simplified spelling saved labor. Simplified spelling did more with less. Every man, woman, and child was tightening their belt in 1934. English might as well do the same.

McCormick's list began modestly—a lost *L* here, a dropped *UE* ending there. But with the zealousness that inevitably attaches to the simplified speller, the *Tribune* added another 18 simplifications in early February (*agast, pully, crum*), followed by 18 more in late February (*herse, staf, etiquet*), then another 20 in March (*doctrin, yern, jaz*), totaling 80 new spellings by winter's end. For the next four decades, McCormick's "saner spellings" populated the most widely circulated newspaper in the Midwest.

"The response was vehement," the *Tribune* recalled. "There was intelligent praise. There was intelligent blame. There was abuse more remarkable for virulence than for intelligence. A neutral observer . . . would have found difficulty in believing that etymology and orthography could enkindle such passion in the human breast."

McCormick had certain strange biases when it came to spelling. He specifically barred three of the more common simplifications, *tho, thru,* and *thoro,* from the *Tribune's* pages. Why these three in particular? The reason may be as simple as Bill Bryson hypothesized in his 1990 book *The Mother Tongue*: McCormick "just didn't like them, which of course is all the reason that is necessary when it's your newspaper." Five years later, by the same arbitrary rationale, McCormick suddenly decided he *did* like them—and just like that, the prohibition was repealed and *tho, thru,* and *thoro* joined the *Tribune* lexicon.

McCormick's phonetic logic could also seem random and capricious. Headlines like "Rookie Goalie Scores 6th Hocky Shutout" (1938) had readers wondering: Why shorten *hockey* but not *rookie*? Why not change *goalie* to *goaly*? The rules didn't seem to apply evenly. And if McCormick was truly committed to eradicating orthographic nonsense, why hadn't he refashioned his military title to the obvious *Kernel*? Or rebranded the *Tribyoon*? Again, to paraphrase Bryson: McCormick simply liked certain spellings and didn't like others. In the autocratic realm of his newspaper kingdom, that was all the reason he needed.

Where the *Tribune* succeeded over previous reforms was in its ability to inject simplified spelling into immediate daily circulation to all classes of the Windy City, high and low. Instead of a top-down approach, the *Tribune* made its changes from the bottom up. While the Simplified Spelling Board had focused its lobbying on the political upper crust (where the money and influence seemed to be), McCormick's spellings went directly to the people—to the breakfast table, the railroad car, the morning newsstands—and over the next 41 years the *Chicago Tribune* raised two generations of everyday Chicagoans in the orthographic creed of *jaz, lether, frate,* and *rifraf.*

To these daily readers of the *Tribune*, McCormick's changes

In 1939, the *Chicago Tribune* recounted the initial hostility toward Saner Spelling, which came from both beyond—and within—its walls:

Five years ago this February we turned [perhaps we should say we definitly and genuinly turned] humanitarian only to discover, as so many reformers have in the past, that the rifraf does not appreciate efforts put forward in its behalf. Even the staf was agast.

were startling, yet somehow expected. McCormick was always on the cutting edge. Ten years earlier, the *Tribune* had become one of the first newspapers to enter the "era in ether" when McCormick purchased an Illinois radio station* and turned it into the broadcasting arm of his publication. Since then, the paper had backed other innovations in technology and culture, sponsoring a pioneering aviation attempt along the Arctic Circle in 1929 and organizing the very first Major League Baseball All-Star Game in 1933. In fact, the *Chicago Tribune* had even taken up simplified spelling once before—or, as it was called then, "Briefer Spelling"—under the ownership of McCormick's maternal grandfather, Joseph Medill.

Like other reform-minded men of his time, Joseph Medill dabbled in various causes. He was an abolitionist and a teetotaler, an education reformer and a simplified speller, and over his 44 years at the *Chicago Tribune*, his causes tended to overlap on his pages. His pro-Lincoln newspaper often editorialized for "ablishun" (see Chapter 9), and Medill likened slavery to the "tyranny" of English orthography, which keeps "millions of English-speaking people in lifelong bondage." Spelling reform *is* social reform, Medill believed—and "lerning tu spel and red the Inglish langwaj iz the grat elementary task ov the pupol."

After a two-year stint as mayor of Chicago representing the short-lived Fireproof Party (formed in the wake of the Great Chicago Fire of 1871), Medill returned to the *Tribune* and began sprinkling more and more simplifications into the paper's house style. *Favorit, filosofy, liv, hav,* and *gon* took root in 1879. *Thru* and *rite* entered in 1880. "These reforms might be enough to begin with," read a

---

* He named his radio station WGN for "World's Greatest Newspaper."

Tribune editorial, "and, as newspapers rule the reading world, we think there should be a congress of newspapermen to decide the whole question."

It was under Joseph Medill's *Tribune* leadership that Chicago's first baseball team, the White Stockings, became known as the White Sox.* Named in 1870 for their iconic white hosiery, "White Stockings" proved cumbersome for headlines. Irving Sanborn, a sportswriter for the *Tribune,* started using the shorthand "White Sox," and it stuck. The phonetic abbreviation not only economized on precious print space, but added a contemporary and catchy flair to the team, helping to boost its appeal over crosstown rivals the Chicago Browns and Chicago Maroons (likewise named for their uniform hues). Fans loved the nickname. So did the upper echelons of the baseball world. In 1908, the Boston Americans adopted fresh red footwear and officially became the "Red Sox."

Newspapers certainly wield significant power in shaping the public vernacular. But Medill's grand vision of an enlightened "congress of newspapermen," rising up to rule and reform the English-speaking world, never came to pass. After Medill's death in 1899, the new editor-in-chief—Medill's son-in-law Robert Wilson Patterson—dropped his "Briefer Spellings" (except in the case of his beloved White Sox). And although all four of Medill's grandchildren ended up in the newspaper business (Joseph Medill Patterson founded New York's *Daily News*; Eleanor Medill Patterson published and edited the *Washington Times-Herald*; Joseph Medill McCormick became part-owner of the *Chicago Tribune*), only Medill's youngest grandchild, Robert McCormick, inherited his grandfather's affinity for briefer, saner, simpler spelling.

---

* At the turn of the century, Chicago actually had two professional baseball teams named the White Sox. Medill's White Sox, formed in 1870, changed their name to the Chicago Cubs around 1903. The St. Paul Saints, who also sported white hosiery, became the current Chicago White Sox around 1901.

How much better could life be if that lump of exhausted brain cells devoted to "cough," "island," "debut," "solder" and scores of other such curiosities were applied to improving the human condition?

—Eric Zorn, *Chicago Tribune*, 1997

Words came and went from the Colonel's paper. The *Tribune's* spelling of *iland* was back to *island* by the time Japan bombed Pearl Harbor in 1941, and *herse* was back to *hearse* by the assassination of John F. Kennedy in 1963. But *cigaret* was still the in-house style when the *Trib* reported its link to cancer in 1964, and *subpena* remained around long enough to track the Watergate investigations of Richard Nixon in 1973.

By midcentury, millions of Midwesterners were reading a modest form of simplified spelling every day. According to a poll, two-thirds of *Tribune* readers even *preferred* the new spellings over the old. The simplified revolution might have finally materialized were it not for McCormick's own editorial staff. They indulged the Colonel's experiment only as long as they had to, nodding and smiling through his reign of whimsy, but after his death they gradually reversed every one of his reforms. The last simplified words to join the paper—*tho, thru,* and *thoro*—were also the last to go. On September 29, 1975, a *Tribune* headline made it official:

Thru is through and so is tho

"Sanity some day may come to spelling," lamented the writer, "but we do not want to make any more trouble . . ."

Shaw(t)hand

My specialty is being right when other people are wrong.

—George Bernard Shaw

George Bernard Shaw wrote some 60 plays in his lifetime, and he would be the first to remind you that Shakespeare only wrote 38. When we think of Shaw, we typically think of the gruff, headstrong author of *Pygmalion,* the 1913 production that spawned the Tony-winning musical (1956) and Oscar-winning film (1964) *My Fair Lady.* But in the underground world of simplified spelling in the 1940s, Shaw was revered as a central leader of the cause, a phonetic warrior, a knight in the battle against superfluous letters.

In 1945, at the cusp of the atomic age, when esteemed political minds around the world were debating the ethics of The Bomb, Shaw was protesting the *spelling* of "bomb." "[It] is entirely sense-less," he wrote in a letter to the London *Times,* "it not only wastes the writer's time, but suggests an absurd mispronunciation, as if the word *gun* were to be spelt *gung.*" Shaw spent the final year of the Second World War fretting over this silent *B.* In December, he timed himself and found that he could write *bomb* eighteen times in a minute; when he spelled it *bom,* he could write it twenty-four times. "The waste of war is negligible," he declared, "in comparison to the daily waste of trying to communicate with one another in English."

Shaw was part of a British contingent of simplified spellers who made a play for reform in the mid-twentieth century, and he used his platform, the stage, to draw attention to the cause. *Pygmalion* was, in his own words, "an advertisement of the science of phonetics," a point he elaborates in his preface:

> The English have no respect for their language, and will not teach their children to speak it. They spell it so abominably that no man can teach himself what it sounds like . . . German and Spanish are accessible to foreigners: English is not accessible even to Englishmen. The reformer England needs today is an energetic phonetic enthusiast: that is why I have made such a one the hero of a popular play.

Pygmalion's hero, Henry Higgins, is modeled loosely on a man named Henry Sweet, a nineteenth-century British linguist and creator of "Current Shorthand," a competitor to the Pitman style.[*] In Shaw's play, Higgins is a language reformer on the smallest scale: over the course of five acts, he reforms the cockney-accented Eliza Doolittle into (*spoiler alert*) a polished example of linguistic refinement.

Shaw himself was a devout Pitmanite. He drafted his plays in Pitman shorthand and credited it for his prolific output. But while he appreciated Pitman's utility in playwriting, Shaw knew that it would never (and should never) replace traditional English entirely. The same went for simplified spelling; because its phonetic pruning relies on our current alphabet, Shaw knew the public would always view it as a kind of *mis*spelling, and thus would never take

---

[*] Henry Sweet referred to his rival's system as "Pitfall" shorthand.

it seriously. The only path to a phonetically pure spelling, Shaw believed, was to tear down all the old systems and start fresh with a new alphabet.

~~~~~

Shaw called upon the British government to take action on spelling reform, and surprisingly they did—or tried to—twice.

On a drizzly Friday morning in 1949, Montefiore Follick, a British Labour Party politician and friend of Shaw's, presented his "Spelling Reform Bill" to the House of Commons:

> I do not think that a Bill of this kind comes into this House very often, because this is a case where a man has devoted the whole of his life to one seemingly impossible object. From being a lone voice crying in the desert without any followers but for more than 40 years ploughing a way through upsets, despair and disappointments, I have at last brought my idea into this House of Commons. That is no small achievement.

Follick's legislation proposed, as a start, to cut out *C, Y, Q,* and *PH* from schoolrooms and government offices, along with double *L*'s (as in *traveller*) and double *F*'s (as in *staff*). The bill's staunchest opponent was none other than Winston Churchill; he had led England to victory in Europe and now, by God, he would defend it against the scourge of spelling reform.

Follick recalled Churchill cornering him one day in the Parliament smoking room:

Churchill, who was reading the *Daily Worker,* edged nearer to me and said: "You are not going to mess up the language of Shakespeare, are you?" I explained to him that I was not interfering with language at all, but that I only wanted the English language to have a consistent spelling . . . I am sure he was not very convinced. As the greatest English orator of the century, he seemed to think that there was something that bound beauty of language with the symbols that formed the written form of it. Whereas, in truth, beauty of language comes from the brain, the soul and, perhaps, as in his own case, long experience in the use of words and thoughts, whilst spelling is just the mechanical device that printers, writers and correspondents use in expressing and perpetuating that beauty . . .

Follick's bill lost by a vote of 84 to 87—just three *ayes* standing between simplified spelling and the King's English. Still, Follick counted it as a small victory. "That evening it was the first item on the six o'clock news of the B.B.C.," he said, "and again at 9 p.m. If we had not been lucky enough to wean those three votes from the

---

While making his case for reform before the House of Commons, Follick rested part of his argument on the poor spelling of his fellow Members of Parliament:

The other day a Committee of this House wasted a quarter of an hour arguing whether the word "nationalized" should be spelt with an "s" or a "z." That is true. That is what our spelling does for us. Amongst Europeans generally one of the greatest laughing stocks is our game of Spelling Bee. They ask, "Do not you people know how to spell your own language?" And the fact is we do not.

other side, we had at least given them a shaking that they had not expected."

The publicity helped build some interest in England's reform movement, and three years later, Follick presented his spelling bill again for another parliamentary shellacking. His fellow MPs treated this second attempt as a joke and sneered and jeered throughout Follick's speech. The parliamentary exchanges that unfolded seemed to be plucked straight from Monty Python:

> **Montefiore Follick:** This House is of the opinion that a great advantage would accrue, in the sending of despatches, signals, orders and messages, if some simplification of the English spelling were introduced . . .
>
> **Commander Harry Pursey:** The honourable Gentleman is the only one who says so.
>
> **Follick:** Which side is the honourable and gallant Gentleman on?
>
> **Pursey:** Not the honourable Gentleman's.
>
> **Follick:** Thank goodness the honourable and gallant Gentleman is not on our side. I am afraid that if he were, we should not get any votes at all.
>
> **Mr. Emrys Hughes:** The honourable Gentleman will not, in any case.

To the surprise of all these honorable gentlemen—most of all to Follick—the bill passed the Commons by 12 votes. The Ministry of Education, now in a panic and ready to deploy whatever legislative roadblocks it could, offered Follick a compromise instead. In exchange for his withdrawal of the bill, the Ministry would fund research into the effects of simplified spelling upon literacy

Mr. Shaw has found himself, led by the same mad imp of modernity, on the side of the people who want to have phonetic spelling. The people who want phonetic spelling generally depress the world with tireless and tasteless explanations of how much easier it would be for children or foreign bagmen if "height" were spelt "hite." Now children would curse spelling whatever it was, and we are not going to permit foreign bagmen to improve Shakespeare.

—G. K. Chesterton, 1909

and childhood development. Follick accepted the terms. Years later, this small concession would bloom into the controversial and far-reaching Initial Teaching Alphabet (ITA), which would spark fiery debates and polarize parents and educators around the world well into the 1980s. But we'll get to the ITA in due course.

~~~~~

George Bernard Shaw didn't live to see Follick's second bill, or any other fruit of his spelling labor, but he ensured that his influence in the movement would carry beyond his lifetime.

Upon his death in 1950, Shaw endowed a significant portion of his estate to the construction of a new "British Alphabet." He appointed his friend James Pitman, grandson of the shorthander Isaac (and an accomplished linguist in his own right), to head the project. In 1958, following a lengthy court battle over Shaw's estate (which culminated in the British Museum, the Royal Academy of Dramatic Art, and the National Gallery of Ireland chipping in to fund the alphabet), Pitman announced a global competition in the pages of *Star Weekly*:

WANTED: A NEW ALPHABET OF 40 LETTERS OR MORE. FOR DEVISING THIS THE WINNER OF A WORLD-WIDE CONTEST WILL BE PAID £500 OR ROUGHLY $1,300. MORE IMPORTANT, HE WILL HAVE THE CHANCE OF GAINING FAME IN THE HISTORY BOOKS, SINCE SUCH AN ALPHA-BET, IF GENERALLY ACCEPTED, COULD SAVE MORE THAN $3,000,000,000 EACH YEAR. THAT FIGURE, PLEASE NOTE, IS NOT MILLIONS BUT BILLIONS . . . THOSE DESIGNING SUCH A SYSTEM OF COMBINED WRITING AND PRINTING SHOULD SUBMIT THEIR BRAIN CHILD BEFORE NEXT NEW

Year's day to Britain's Public Trustee, Kingsway, London W.C.2, England.

Pitman's call echoed around the globe. Submissions flooded in from all over—every continent except Antarctica—and by New Year's Day, Pitman faced a daunting stack of 467 alphabets to consider. After two years of painstaking review, he picked his winner: a 48-letter alphabet based on the design of a Birmingham phoneticist named Ronald Kingsley Read. Read's system would come to be known as the "Shaw Alphabet."

When audiences at London's Drury Lane theater opened their programs for *My Fair Lady* in 1958, after first flipping past the face of a 23-year-old budding starlet named Julie Andrews, they found a two-page promotion for Shaw's British Alphabet, written by James Pitman. "My Fair Ladies—and Gentlemen," Pitman begins:

Shaw's interest in speech—shall we say pronunciation—and in its importance, was the origin of "My Fair Lady." Thanks to the musical version of "Pygmalion" this human problem has come to be widely recognized . . .

Shaw's intention was to do for *Roman letters* what the *new Arabic system* had *already* done for *Roman numerals*—give a better alternative which could be added to their repertoire by those intelligent enough to appreciate its advantages. "VI" is less good than "6" as a means of representing the number which follows "five." . . . Similarly, the four signs "SHAW" afford a poor way of representing the two units of the author's name . . . It is likely, then, that Shaw's Alphabet will yield at least a reduction in space occupied as did the introduction of the new Arabic numerals "1958" alternative to the Roman "MCMLVIII" . . .

In effect, he wants the Eliza Doolittles (and the Higginses) to have a good modern alphabet placed at their disposal.

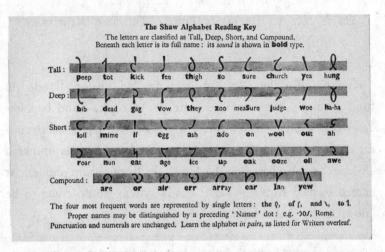

The Shaw Alphabet is divided into four categories—Tall, Deep, Short, and Compound letters. Vowels are Short. Voiceless consonants (Ch, F, K, P, S, Sh, T, and Th) are Tall. The remaining consonants are Deep (represented by a tall letter flipped upside-down), and compound sounds—the phonemes that get pronounced nearly twice as long as others, such as air, err, or ear—are Compound. ("The Shaw Alphabet Reading Key," published in *Androcles and the Lion*, 1962)

Working with Penguin Books, Shaw's estate put out a bi-alphabetic edition of his 1912 play *Androcles and the Lion*, featuring traditional spellings on the right side of each spread and Shavian spellings on the left. (*Shavian* is the Latinized adjective of "Shaw." The Shaw Alphabet was alternatively referred to as the "Shavian Alphabet.") "To communicate—more easily, more sensibly, more economically—is the whole purpose of Shavian writing," Penguin explained in an editorial note. Encouraged by early sales, Read, the architect of the alphabet, decided to take his idea one step further. "I have in mind the possibility of modifying a new machine," he wrote to James Pitman in 1962, and within a month Read had already sketched out the keyboard layout of the "Shaw Typewriter."

A year later, the Imperial Typewriter Company Limited began factory production of Read's Shaw Typewriter. "EVERYONE MAY

Keyboard layout of the Shaw Typewriter, with options for either English or Shaw letters (toggled via the shift key).

SOON BE DOING SHAW(T)HAND," announced the *Leicester Evening Mail* in giant, all-caps enthusiasm. "Leicester's typewriter designers have now evolved a machine that types in Shaw(t)hand!" The excitement didn't last long. By 1964, sales for *Androcles* had plateaued and the Shaw Typewriter, which sold for £29 (more than $600 today), was still searching for buyers. As Audrey Hepburn's *My Fair Lady* hit theaters that December and catapulted Shaw to a renown he'd never experienced in his lifetime, Shaw(t)hand ended its run without ceremony or applause. "With the publication of 'Androcles' in Shaw alphabet still unheralded," wrote the *Richmond Times-Dispatch*, "and the reforms of Sweet, Pitman, and Theodore Roosevelt all but forgotten, one wonders if . . . [phonetic spelling] is a dead issue."

In today's post-typewriter world, a singular artifact remains of the Shaw Alphabet—the lone typographical legacy of a playwright who believed that, with enough phonetic training, even the humblest street urchin could achieve linguistic excellence: a downloadable special-character font aptly named "Doolittle Garamond."

Kool Kidz

"I" before "C,"
Or when followed by "T,"
O'er the ramparts we watched,
Not excluding joint taxpayers filing singly.
EXCEPTION: "Suzi's All-Nite E-Z Drive-Thru Donut
Shoppe."

—Dave Barry

Let's take a drive.

The year is 1960. You start out in sunny Florida heading north. As you cross into Georgia, a large wooden placard announces that "U R now in Echols County." It's a sign—literally—that simplified spelling has penetrated even the most banal of cultural wordage. When you reach the Carolinas, roadside billboards tantalize you with hometown Bar-B-Q (an abbreviation that first appeared in print in 1932), and in Maryland you spot the sparkling flagship of a new retail chain called ToysЯUs, with a backward letter you've only seen in the crayon script of little children.

You get hungry. You stop at Dunkin' Donuts, a restaurant chain that smartly capitalizes on the phonetic simplification of *doughnut*. In your haste, you leave without paying. Now the sheriff's on your trail. He calls in the K-9 unit—a bit of military jargon from America's corps of trained canines in World War II. As you exit the thruway (a spelling that dates to 1930), you crash into one of those new three-wheeler Styl Kars. (Luckily, you were wearing your Saf-Tee-Belt, a $10 vehicle add-on that won't become mandatory in cars for eight more years.) At last, you reach New York, where the Times Square barkers welcome you with "Live Burlesk" and "All-Nite Peep Shows." You—and Noah Webster—are finally home.

~~~~~

The 1960s were a period of social upheaval and free expression that reached far beyond the realms of politics, art, and fashion. As the counterculture eroded societal boundaries and challenged Western norms, it developed a relaxed approach to language that favored creativity, playfulness, and independence over order and regularity. C. S. Lewis, the Irish-born author of *The Chronicles of Narnia,* described his own liberal attitude toward spelling on New Year's Day 1960:

> Nearly everything I have ever read about spelling reform assumes from the outset that it is necessary for us all to spell alike. Why? . . . Who would be a penny the worse if *though* and *tho, existence* and *existance, sieze, seize* and *seeze* were all equally tolerated? . . . As things are, surely Liberty is the simple and inexpensive "Reform" we need?

Liberty to spell correctly. Liberty to spell inkorectli. Liberty to write *Tuesday* as *Teusday* with no rhyme, reason, or phonetic basis. This was an age of peace, love, and artistic rebellion. No one should tell you how to live your life, and no one—not Noah Webster or the president of the United States—should tel u how to spel it.

Whether he knew it or not, C. S. Lewis, writing on the first morning of the '60s, was conveying a theory of childhood learning known as "inventive spelling" (sometimes "free" or "flexible" spelling; see Chapter 13). At the heart of this theory is the belief that children should spell how they want, free from correction or criticism. By encouraging orthographic independence, parents could better nurture their kids' creativity, boost their self-esteem, and create a more inclusive environment. Successful parenting, the theory posited, began with abandoning rigid orthography in the nursery.

Ron Tandberg, *The Age*, June 26, 1973.

For better or worse, inventive spelling would come to infiltrate classrooms on both sides of the Atlantic through the 1960s and '70s. For better or worse, the legacy of "spell-as-you-wish" learning still trickles through curricula today.

One of the leading voices for inventive spelling was Dr. Carol Chomsky, a renowned Harvard linguist and educator. In her 1971 essay for the journal *Childhood Education,* she explains: "Children ought to learn how to read by creating their own spellings for familiar words as a beginning . . . Allowed to trust their own ears and their own judgments, many children show amazing facility as they begin to spell." This experimentation phase is necessary, writes

Chomsky; it is the substructure of language acquisition and "forms an excellent basis for reading later on" when children ultimately train up to traditional English spelling. Until the mid-twentieth century, conventional wisdom held that a child must learn to read before they can learn to write. Chomsky flipped the theory on its head: "Write now," she said. "Read later."

She tells a story about her three-year-old son, Harry. In his toddler speak, Harry confuses the sounds for R and W. He pronounces his name "Hawwy" and spells *wet* with an *R*:

> Now *r* is correct for him, as a matter of fact. In this child's pronunciation, *r* and *w* are alike when initial in the syllable. For him *wet* begins the same as the second syllable of his name . . . Had I said "No!" when Harry chose the *r* and insisted on *w* (which corresponds to no reality for him), he would have gotten that sad message children so often get in school: "Your judgments are not to be trusted. Do it my way whether it makes sense or not; forget about reality."

By giving children the latitude to explore language with confidence, Chomsky believes we empower them to question and discover. They learn that language is not a rigid, unyielding structure, but a dynamic, living entity that invites creativity and adaptation. When we allow little Hawwy to spell *wet* with an *R* and *rug* with a *W*, we send him a powerful message: his voice is valued, ewwows and all.

Some parents found this idea not only ridiculous but dangerous. To the tough-love generation raised with strict rules and corporal discipline, inventive spelling seemed like a crumbling of educational standards and a surefire recipe for raising self-absorbed children. Spelling *does* have rules. There *are* right and wrong ways to write words, and the sooner you learn them the sooner you'll master them. Some feared that this loosening of rules might lead to a disregard for *all* of society's rules, a collapse of order, and a rejection of traditional attitudes and beliefs—in short, a distillation of all the fears associated with the '60s counterculture itself.

Carol Chomsky's theories grew, in part, out of the research of her husband (and Hawwy's father), Noam Chomsky, the social activist and educator recognized today as the "father of modern linguistics." Among Noam's contributions to linguistics is the idea that children learn language by *internalizing* its underlying rules rather than by memorization and recitation. Spelling mistakes, therefore, reveal a deeper (if preliminary) grasp of the phonological structure of words. When a child spells *laugh* as *laf,* they are applying a consistent rule: using the letter *F* to represent the fricative *F* sound. And although the parent may be tempted to swoop in and correct a child's spelling or speech in such moments, they should pause and appreciate the underlying intelligence in these so-called "errors." The child is generating their *own* understanding of words. They are learning to navigate by their own phonemic compass.

As a practical mode of reform, inventive spelling doesn't work. If we all spelled as we liked, the linguistic landscape would quickly devolve into chaos (to say nothing of kaos and kayos). And yet, there is a charm in orthographic flexibility that enchanted many spelling reformers. Mark Twain, who fluctuated frequently on the subject, adored the unorthodox spelling of his children. "[Her] spelling is frequently desperate," he wrote of his daughter, "but it was Susy's, and it shall stand. I love it, and cannot profane it. To

You can't help respecting anybody who can spell TUESDAY, even if he doesn't spell it right; but spelling isn't everything. There are days when spelling Tuesday simply doesn't count.

—A. A. Milne, *The House at Pooh Corner*, 1928

me, it is gold. To correct it would alloy it, not refine it. It would spoil it. It would take from it its freedom and flexibility and make it stiff and formal."

Language, after all, is more than just a means for communication. It's a vehicle for art and expression. The uneven brushstrokes of a painting, the creative misspelling of little Susy Clemens—these are the fingerprints of the author. And in a world driven by standardization, the little imperfections have a beauty all their own.

~~~~~

The shift to inventive spelling in children's education coincided with a wave of creative orthography in the marketing of toys and sugary foodstuffs to kids. Some of these gems are still with us today:

Play-Doh (1956)
ToysЯUs (1957)
Cocoa Krispies (1958)
Pixy Stix (1959)
Froot Loops (1963)
Kream Krunch (1965)
Liddle Kiddles (1965)
Lite-Brite (1967)
Krazy Kar (1968)

As the counterculture rebelled against tradition, so did the marketing teams at Playskool and Mattel, who embraced the playful, free-spirited spelling of the time over the rigid orthography of yore. Television writers followed suit. On Saturday mornings, Froot Loops in hand, a child of the sugar-charged '60s could enter the world of Deputy Dawg, Ruff and Reddy, The Monkees, H.R. Pufnstuf, and Wile E. Coyote in between ads proclaiming "Beanz Meanz Heinz" (baked beans) and "Kool is the Coolest!" (cigarettes). These kidz never stood a chance.

In the years following World War II, as the Space Age turned our eyes skyward, we became fascinated with a particular genre of escapist entertainment: science fiction. We imagined worlds light-years and millennia away, far more advanced than our own, filled with robot maids, alien spacecraft, and, it turns out, fonetik speling. In their fantastical tales of space and time travel, sci-fi authors began utilizing simplified orthography as a visual cue to indicate a distant world, a distorted reality, or a high-tech future. In Ray Bradbury's "A Sound of Thunder" (1952), a time traveler inadvertently steps on a butterfly while hunting dinosaurs in the Late Cretaceous, which disrupts the timeline and alters the course of history. When he returns to the present, he finds that everything is just a little bit . . . *off*:

> But the immediate thing was the sign painted on the office wall, the same sign he had read earlier today on first entering. Somehow, the sign had changed:
>
> TYME SEFARI INC.
> SEFARIS TU ANY YEER EN THE PAST.
> YU NAIM THE ANIMALL.
> WEE TAEK YU THAIR.
> YU SHOOT ITT.
>
> Eckels felt himself fall into a chair. He fumbled crazily at the thick slime on his boots. He held up a clod of dirt, trembling, "No, it can't be. Not a little thing like that. No!"

To fans of the genre, the sign on the wall has a clear meaning: it means Eckels is now in an uncharted realm, a parallel timeline in which language has evolved on a different track. In 1953's *The Demolished Man*, Alfred Bester visualizes a twenty-fourth century of typographically simplified surnames—Atkins, Wygand, and Quartermaine are written as @kins, Wyg&, and ¼maine—and on a trip to the fifty-first century in a 1977 episode of *Doctor Who*, signage on the Titan Base reads "Imurjinsee Egsit," "Isolayshun Ward," and "Shutle Airlok."* Even *The Simpsons* played on the trope. In a 2014 Couch Gag, Homer sends himself to the year 10,535, where *A* has begun to upstage *E* in *Oktobar* and *numbar*, and viewers are invited

---

* Incidentally, this episode also marks the first appearance of the Doctor's robot dog K9.

to connect their neural netwarks to purchase "Sampsans"-brand helmats and lasar hats (now availabl in the Sampsans outernet markat).

A distant future. An outer dimension. A journey into a barely intelligible land whose boundaries are that of phonetics. That's the signpost up ahead! Your next stop: the Twilite Zön.

~~~~~

For certain sci-fi masters, simplified spelling is more than just a dialect for space aliens and beings of tomorrow. It's a noble pursuit for us Earthlings of today. As early as 1884, H. G. Wells, author of the classics *The War of the Worlds* and *The Time Machine,* and at one time the vice president of London's Simplified Speling Soesiety, was signing off letters "Yurs veri sinsjrli" and spelling his name with one *L,* Melvil Dewey style. With Wells's blessing, his fellow Soesiety members published one of his short stories, "The Star," in 1912 in the "advanst" style of their "simplifyd" movement. It begins most ominously:

> It woz on the furst dai ov the nyu yeer that the anounsment woz maid, aulmoest simultainiusli from thre obzurvatoriz, that the moeshon ov the planet Neptune, the outermoest ov aul the planets that wheel about the sun, had becum veri eratic . . . Such a pees ov nyuz woz scairsli calcyulaited tu interest a wurld the graiter porshon ov huuz inhabitants wer unawair ov the egzistens ov the planet Neptune, nor outsied the astronomical profeshon did the subsecwent discuveri ov a faint remoet spec ov liet in the reejon ov the perturbd planet cauz eni veri grait ecsietment.

Isaac Asimov, the genre's most prolific storyteller, with more than 500 published books, also harbored a resentment for the peculiarities of spelling:

> If you don't know in advance and just judge by the letters, can you know that "through," "coo," "do," "true," "knew," and "queue" all rhyme? If you don't know in advance and just judge by the letters, can you know that "gnaw," "kneel," "mnemonic" and "note" all start with the same consonantal sound? Why can't we say "throo," "koo," "doo," "troo," "nyoo," and "kyoo"? Why can't we say "naw," "neel," "nemonik" and "note"? It looks funny? Sure it does, because you've memorized the "correct" way—but millions are helped on the road to illiteracy because the "correct" way makes no sense.

Asimov's frustration with spelling began around the age of 3, when his family immigrated from Russia to the United States. Upon their arrival in 1923, his father mistranslated their Cyrillic surname to "Asimov" instead of the more phonetic "Azimov." Young Isaac became so embittered with strangers misspelling his name that he fantasized a tale of retribution. In the 1958 short story "Spell My Name with an S," a down-on-his-luck nuclear physicist, Marshall Zebatinsky, consults a numerologist for advice. The numerologist tells him to change his name to "Sebatinsky" with an S. So he does. And this seemingly arbitrary alteration triggers a series of wild events that, by tale's end, prevents a global nuclear disaster and secures Sebatinsky a pretty cushy career promotion. The moral of the story: Spell my name with an *S*, damnit!

Simplified spelling, to quote George Philip Krapp, is "the spelling of the future," and who better to paint a picture of our future than science-fiction authors? They are our cultural soothsayers, our prophets of progress. They extrapolate current realities into future possibilities. And to those with the forward-looking ethos, it makes sense that our spacefaring heirs would write in a language as slick and streamlined as their silver spacesuits. (No wonder the Sci-Fi Channel now goes by the *Syfy* Channel?) In our futuristic imaginings, simplified spelling is on a level with warp drive and dilithium crystals: slightly out of this world and eternally kool.

Εεzy Rεεding

Gwen Stefani has done more for the spelling of "bananas"
than all third-grade teachers combined.

—Mike Birbiglia

As inventive spelling took off in the 1960s, it triggered a wave of
"training wheel" alphabets designed to boost childhood literacy.
The idea was simple: Beginning around age 5, the child would be
taught a simplified orthography based on easy phonetics. This will
be their lifelong foundation for written language. After two years,
the training wheels come off and the child transitions to traditional
spelling. In theory, this intermediate step helps smooth the path
to literacy. It teaches preliminary sound-to-symbol relationships,
but without the ancient orthographic rules (and exceptions to the
rules) that so often frustrate young learners. The child cuts their
teeth, so to speak, on simplified spelling. After that, English orthography is a piece of cake.

Unifon

"Unifon" is the cult classic of training-wheel alphabets. It's still
cherished today by some die-hard boomers, who learned it in the
'60s and keep the dream alive in online nostalgia communities. It
began life around 1957 when the Bendix Corporation commis-
sioned a Chicago economist, John Malone, to design a 40-letter

phonetic alphabet for the aviation industry. (Pilots and air traffic controllers needed a shared international language to communicate clearly.) Malone spent months on the project before Bendix pulled the plug. Malone moved on from Unifon, until one fateful evening in 1958 while attending a theater production of *My Fair Lady*. He was struck by Eliza Doolittle's faltering attempts to learn English, and in a burst of inspiration Malone reenvisioned Unifon as a teaching tool for young learners. He brought Unifon around to local schools and found that many educators were receptive to this alternative teaching method. Unifon started to spread through Illinois.

In 1960, ABC took viewers inside a Unifon classroom. For three weeks, television cameras followed an Illinois schoolteacher as she taught four children to read using Unifon spelling. Though controversial to some viewers (particularly parents), the method stirred interest in educational circles, and by the end of the year the Chicago Public School system had begun weaving Unifon into its first-grade curriculum.

When it comes to new and improved alphabets, success largely depends on aesthetics (see: the disaster of Deseret), and Unifon had a kool, futuristic look that mirrored what kidz were seeing all around them in the 1950s and '60s. In Unifon, there are three versions of the letter *A*:

ΑΔΛ

And five versions of the letter *O*:

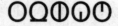

There is no *X*, but there *is* a backward *Z*, a typographical curiosity that would come to invade the logos of rock bands (Adam and the Ants, Kiss) and graffiti art in the 1970s. "Your child will discover," explains the schoolteacher in the ABC special, "there is a great similarity between Unifon and what he sees on TV screens, in comics or road signs, and on cereal boxes. Soon he finds with amusement that he can read the 'old people's alphabet' as easily as he can read and write in Unifon."

Words in Colour

As much as Unifon appealed to pop-cultured '60s youth, "Words in Colour" seemed even more primed to excite kids' sensibilities. Developed in 1962 by Dr. Caleb Gattegno, a professor at the University of London, Words in Colour assigned each sound a particular hue. The letter *A,* when colored white, represented the vowel in *bat.* When blue, it became the long *A* in *tame.* In English, that same long *A* sound can be spelled nearly a dozen ways. (*Cane, pain, rein,* etc.) In Words in Colour, it's always the same shade of blue.*

Words in Colour added a vibrant, kaleidoscopic layer to the age-old task of learning to read. The once monochrome blackboard was now a tapestry of hues. These days, Gattegno's color-coding method is still used in certain specialized settings—notably in dyslexia classrooms—but it never caught on in the mainstream curriculum. For one thing, regional accents make it impossible to standardize a color palette.† The speech patterns of a Londoner vs.

---

* "Close your eyes," a teacher might say to her class, "and tell me: What does brown, red, and purple spell?" A brownnoser in the front row responds: *Pet!*

† Navigating regional accents is tricky in any spelling reform, but the thought of Texans fighting Kansans over spelling pigments makes it all the more absurd.

a New Yorker, an Australian vs. a Canadian, a toh-MAY-to vs. a toh-MAH-to, quickly turn that rich tapestry into a confusing psychedelia. And what about the 8% of colorblind boys? Will they go through life mispronouncing shades of pink?

Initial Teaching Alphabet

The most successful of these '60s training-wheel alphabets was the "Initial Teaching Alphabet"—that is, if you measure "success" by the ability to thoroughly mangle an entire generation's ability to spell. How do you spot a former ITA user today? Count the number of red squiggles in their Word document, the beads of sweat on their brow before sending an important email. From 1961 through the mid-'80s, hundreds of thousands of English-speaking children learned to read using this short-lived, all-lowercase, 44-letter fad alphabet. Like Unifon and Words in Colour, the ITA was designed to be transitory, meant to be learned around age 5 and then unlearned at 7 once the child mastered letter-phoneme relationships. Unlike other phonetic alphabets, the ITA caught on in a major way among educational boards, spreading from Britain to America to Australia within five years. By the mid-'60s, the ITA had wrapped its orthographic tendrils around a generation of unsuspecting guinea pigs, simplifying—or, more often than not, complicating—wherever it went.

The alphabet was created by Sir James Pitman, grandson of Sir Isaac, and grew directly out of the parliamentary efforts of Montefiore Follick, who had tried and failed (twice) to pass his Spelling Reform Bill a decade earlier. Following in his grandfather's footsteps, James had joined England's Simplified Speling Soesiety in 1936 and spent the next three decades bringing Isaac's wisdom into the modern simplified spelling movement. He built the ITA upon Isaac's phonetic framework, with a one-to-one character-phoneme relationship—44 letters for the 44 sounds of English speech—adding nine new vowels, ditching two old consonants (*Q* and *X*), and otherwise purging all the spelling inanities that confound most children (and far too many adults). Like the kid-friendly Unifon, the ITA also added a nifty backward *Z,* called a "zess," to indicate plural *S* endings.

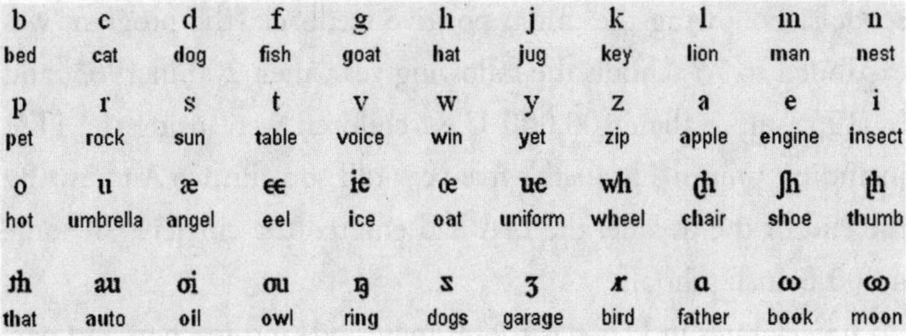
b bed c cat d dog f fish g goat h hat j jug k key l lion m man n nest
p pet r rock s sun t table v voice w win y yet z zip a apple e engine i insect
o hot u umbrella æ angel ɛɛ eel ie ice œ oat ue uniform wh wheel ch chair sh shoe th thumb
th that au auto oi oil ou owl ng ring z dogs ʒ garage r bird a father ω book ω moon

The 44-letter Initial Teaching Alphabet (ITA) devised by Sir James Pitman.

To reach his target kindergartener demographic, Pitman teamed up with Ladybird, a London children's book publisher, to reissue its iconic titles in the ITA in what came to be known as lædybird 'ɛɛzy-rɛɛdin' bωks. Its bestsellers were its "pɛɛpl at wurk" series, which gave kids a glimpse into the life of "the polɛɛsman," "the nurs," and "the fisherman":

> the life ov a fisherman iz a hard wun. hɛɛ spends mœst ov his tiem at sɛɛ in aull kiendz ov wether. hɛɛ wærs speshial clœthz tω kɛɛp him waurm and drie. when it is wet and stormy the fisherman wærs an oilskin mackintosh. hiz hat is mæd ov oilskin, tω, and iz caulld a sou' wester.

The long sɛɛ-bʊts a fiſherman wærs rɛɛch riet tʊ the top
ov his legz.*

James Pitman's résumé stretched nearly as long as his grandfather's.
After retiring from professional rugby at age 27, he served with
the Royal Air Force in World War II. Then he became director of
the Bank of England. Then a Member of Parliament. His broad
influence across England's most elite fields allowed him, in 1961,
to speed through a small pilot ITA program in 20 select English
schools. Following the initial positive feedback, the program was
expanded to 75 schools the following year, then 200 in 1963, and
by 1965 more than 100,000 U.K. children were using the ITA,
including Queen Elizabeth's five-year-old son, Prince Andrew. By
the end of the decade, the ITA had entered the curricula of some
4,000 British schools.

Literacy rates in ITA classrooms increased, and teachers and parents buzzed with tales of children who, once jaded readers, now devoured Ladybird books with gusto. Pitman took the early praise as
proof of the ITA's efficacy and in 1965, armed with data and anec-
dotes, began touring schools and conferences in Canada, Australia,
New Zealand, South Africa, and the United States, introducing the
globe to a novel spelling that, maybe for the first time since Pitman
shorthand, found a real-world application for simplified phonetics.
Grandpa would have been proud.

The first cracks began to show in 1963. After two years of immersion in Pitman's simplified alphabet, the first wave of ITA children
now had to *unlearn* it and switch to standard English orthography.
The off-ramp from ITA proved bumpier than the on-ramp. Just

---

* Transcribed as faithfully as possible using our limited modern fonts.

when these budding literati started to feel confident in their reading skills, they had to abandon the only orthography that made sense to them. Many struggled with the transition. Some would struggle for the rest of their lives.

To this day, ITA veterans carry the scars of their early education in a constant battle with spell-check. On College Confidential, an online community related to higher education, the forum on the ITA is filled with traumatic orthographic memories:

> "I was a lab rat for [ITA]. I was in first grade in Bethlehem PA in 1966 . . . I remember having reading difficulties in 2nd grade when we switched to regular reading. I was a horrible speller all my life. In 3rd grade I was in the lowest reading level and never really caught up . . ."

> "I was taught the ITA method in 1st grade in the 60's, but my family moved away the year after to a place where ITA was neither taught nor even heard of. Looking back, I remember the humiliation of failing nearly every spelling test in 2nd grade and of being laughed at when writing something on the blackboard. I haven't thought about those days for many, many years."

In retrospect, it's obvious: Unlearning a skill requires more effort than learning it. Removing a habit is harder than forming one. And as the first generation of inventive and ITA students came of age in the 1970s, they unwittingly carried the vestiges of their experimental education into lyric sheets and band tees, into backward *Z*'s and gratüitoüs ümlaüts, and into the misspelling pop mania that still rules the charts today.

Nothing Compares 2 U

You should never
Write words using numbers
Unless you're seven
Or your name is Prince.

—"Weird Al" Yankovic, "Word Crimes" (2014)

To be fair, pop stars have always played fast and loose with spelling. The Beatles dropped an *e* from *beetles* and replaced it with an *a*. The Byrds slipped in a *y*. The Turtles objected when their label tried calling them The Tyrtles, and The Monkees, well, did exactly what their label told them.

In an industry that depends on standing out, funky spellings can mean the difference between a hit and a flop. (Ever wonder what those two little dots mean in Blue Öyster Cult? They mean someone knows how to sell records.) For those of us grammar pedants struggling to remember where, exactly, the apostrophe goes in "Lil" rapper names,* or how to spell "Waka Flocka Flame," fortunately there are artists like Snoop Dogg to keep us orthographically informed. At every lyrical opportunity, he reminds us that his name—properly rendered in the traditional English style—is spelled *S-N-double-O-P* to the *D-O-double-G*.

The training-wheel alphabets, inventive-spelling experiments,

---

* No apostrophe for Lil Wayne; after the second *L* for Lil' Kim.

and kid-geared consumables of the '60s had subtly, but signifi-
cantly, reshaped an entire generation's attitude toward language.
Children grew up viewing spelling not as a fixed set of rules, but as
a flexible tool, open to personal interpretation. And as the children
of the '60s became the adults of the '70s, they began putting their
stamp on the culture.

From Kix to U2, Def Leppard to Split Enz, the music industry
plunged headlong into phonetic spelling. Sly and the Family Stone
contributed their classic phonetic puzzle in 1970—"Thank You
(Falettinme Be Mice Elf Agin)"—and beginning in 1971, Slade
went on an impressive run of *17 consecutive misspelled Top 20 hits*.
"Cum on feel the noize!" they implored their fans, and their fans
closed their dictionaries and obliged. To this day, Slade—or Slayed,
as they hinted on their third album—holds the record for the longest stretch of misspelled *Billboard* hits in music history.

In recent pop memory, no spelling gimmick has been trendier
than alphanumeric abbreviation, the practice of substi2ting words
with numbers and standalone letters, which came 2 define the
songs of the '90s and early '00s. Sinéad O'Connor kicked things
off in January 1990 with her rendition of "Nothing Compares 2
U." Five days later, MC Hammer released his own career-defining
track, "U Can't Touch This," and together these megahits set the
orthographic tone of the decade. The trend took off with:

- MC Hammer's "2 Legit 2 Quit" (1991)
- TLC's "Ain't 2 Proud 2 Beg" (1992)
- Toni Braxton's "Give U My Heart" (1992)
- Tupac Shakur's "Thug 4 Life" (1993)*

---

* Tupac dubbed himself "2Pac" in 1991 and later took the stage name "Makaveli," a
tribute in simplified spelling to Niccolò Machiavelli and his 1532 masterwork *The Prince*.

- Spice Girls' "U Can't Dance" (1996)
- A Tribe Called Quest's "1nce Again" (1996)
- Missy Elliott's "Sock It 2 Me" (1997)

then carried over into the new millennium with:

- Jay-Z's "I Just Wanna Love U (Give It 2 Me)" (2000)
- Usher's "U Remind Me" (2001)
- Aaliyah's "I Care 4 U" (2001)

before reaching a high-water mark around 2002 with that most notorious case of alphanumeric overzealousness, "Sk8er Boi" by Avril Lavigne.

Where did this simplifying fad come from? Which trailblazing orthographer is responsible for bringing it in2 the pop mainstream? Look no further than his highness himself, the sultan of symbols—the man who traded his name for an unpronounceable character and left us all scratching our heads and scouring our typewriters—the artist formerly, and now again currently, known as Prince.

Beginning in 1981 and for the rest of his career, Prince Rogers Nelson compressed, contracted, and simplified his songs at every titular opportunity. A decade before the trend reached Missy and the Spice Girls, Prince gave us:

- "All the Critics Love U in New York" (1982)
- "How Come U Don't Call Me Anymore?" (1982)
- "Take Me With U" (1984)
- "I Would Die 4 U" (1984)
- "Do U Lie?" (1985)
- "Boy U Bad" (1986)

- "U Got the Look" (1987)
- "I Wish U Heaven" (1988)
- "R U There?" (1989)

as well as Sinéad O'Connor's aforementioned hit "Nothing Compares 2 U," which Prince wrote in 1984 but didn't release his own version until 1993.

In a time of musical maximalism, when heavy metal bands crammed in superfluous markings (Queensrÿche, Mötley Crüe, Infernäl Mäjesty, Motörhead, ët äl), Prince mastered the art of minimalism. When everyone else was shouting, Prince was whispering. His simple spelling set him apart from the headbangers, and it became so entwined with his identity that it spread into his journals, handwritten letters, and album liner notes. ("Can u pass me the pepper?" he writes in a rambling poem on the back cover of 1984's *Purple Rain*. "Why, because u told me salt was bad 4 me.")

Prince's style is reminiscent of a writing system known as "logography." A *logograph* (or *logogram*) is a written symbol that represents a word or part of a word rather than the individual sounds within it. Modern Chinese and Ancient Egyptian are primarily logographic writing systems. English, by contrast, is an alphabetic system. But as communication in the digital age speeds up, and boundaries around orthography break down, we find ever more logographs infiltrating English. (Numbers serve as logographs in *b4* and *l8*, for example.) In fact, hardly a digital conversation goes by today (at least among certain demographics) without some permutation of *2, 4, 8, U, B, R, Y, &,* or @ working its way in.

One of rap's biggest rivalries started over spelling. Donwill, the Brooklyn rapper and host of *The Almanac of Rap* podcast, explains:

> At one point, spelling out words was the thing to do in hip hop. You'd have Master Gee going, "I said a M-A-S, a T-E-R, a G with a double E." But nobody really claimed it as their rapping style until K-Solo came along. The story goes that DMX and K-Solo were in prison together and they would have rap battles. K-Solo's whole style was "It's the K-S-O-L-O, you know, I F-L-O-W so well," stuff like that. And DMX got out of lock-up first and came up with a song called "Spellbound" that copied what K-Solo was doing. K-Solo hears this, gets out of prison, and releases his own song called "Spellbound." And there's this whole controversy about who patented the concept first.

The beef spanned thirty years, multiple diss tracks, and at least one inconclusive lie-detector test. K-Solo even challenged DMX to a boxing contest to determine, once and for all, who was the true innovator of *S-P-E-L-L-I-N-G O-U-T W-O-R-D-S* in rap lyrics. "To K-Solo's credit," Donwill continues, "DMX passed away and K-Solo still holds that grudge. He's still mad about it."

As a teenager, Prince idolized Joni Mitchell and often subjected her to his special logography. "Prince used to write me fan mail with all of the U's and hearts that way that he writes," Joni recalled. "And the office took it as mail from the lunatic fringe and just tossed it!" Prince wasn't part of the lunatic fringe (orthographically speaking, at least), but merely a child of the linguistically loose '60s, raised on Cap'n Crunch (his favorite cereal),* Sly and the Family Stone (one of his favorite groups), and the flexible, freewheeling spelling that saturated the culture around him.

According to his own handler, Prince had "the attention of a

---

* Prince served Cap'n Crunch instead of alcohol at his 1996 album release party for *Emancipation*.

10-year-old," and many might assume he had the spelling of one too. Alphanumeric writing generally comes across as childish, the province of texting teens and certain semiliterate politicians. But this is a fairly modern perception. In fact, Prince's 2U's, 4U's, and what-have-U's go back as far as Victorian England, a place where Prince might have felt poetically at home. This was a period of linguistic creativity—a time when poets played with the *look* of text on the page, and words and shapes freely merged and mingled. Some poets, like Lewis Carroll, sculpted verse into pictures, as when he typed his 1865 poem "The Mouse's Tale" into the shape of a long, winding mouse's tail.* Other poets inverted the concept: instead of using words to form shapes, they used existing shapes—pictures, numbers, and standalone letters—to form words. Here's a unique (but palpably Prince-esque) verse from 1867:

> From virt U nev R D V 8;
> Her influence B 9
> A like induces 10 dern S,
> Or 40 tude D vine.

This kind of linguistic riddle was known to nineteenth-century readers as a "rebus" or "enigmatic poem." Rebuses would circulate in newspapers the way crosswords do now, offering a playful reprieve from the news of the day. *The New Monthly Magazine* published one such ode, "TO THE MEMORY OF MISS ELLEN GEE, OF KEW, who died in consequence of being stung in the eye." It begins:

---

* Carroll was one of many playful bards who wrote pyramid-shaped poems about pyramids, circle-shaped poems about circles, wineglass-shaped poems about wineglasses—all falling under the umbrella (did I mention umbrella-shaped poems about umbrellas?) of "Emblematic Poetry."

PEERLESS, yet hapless maid of Q !
Accomplish'd LN G !
Never again shall I and U
Together sip our T.

For ah ! the Fates ! I know not Y,
Sent midst the flowers a B,
Which ven'mous stung her in the I,
So that she could not C.

And ends several verses later in a morbid state of affairs:

They bear with tears fair LN G
In funeral RA,
A clay-cold corpse now doom'd to B,
Whilst I mourn her DK.

Characters in these nineteenth-century poems routinely met a grim fate. Abey Isaacs (AB I6) dies of excessive O D V (*eau de vie* is a type of brandy) and Emily Kay (MLE K) catches fire while trying to place a : (a colon, or a *coal on*) the hearth during T with LN G.

Contemporary though they seem now, rebuses were poetically extraordinary for the nineteenth century and likely made a good challenge for the morning commute. Think you got the hang of it? Try this doozy, courtesy of the Victorian writer Charles Bombaugh:

He says he loves U 2 X S,
U R virtuous and Y's,
In X L N C U X L
All others in his i's.

This S A, until U I C,
I pray U 2 X Q's,
And do not burn in F E G
My young and wayward muse.

Now fare U well, dear K T J,
I trust that U R true—
When this U C, then you can say,
An S A I O U.*

As MC Hammer and Sinéad O'Connor carried his highness's spelling style into the new decade, Prince continued distilling his shorthand into ever smaller and more elemental language blocks. In 1988, he released a song that appeared on its vinyl sleeve as a single almond-shaped eye and the word "No"—a title meant to be pronounced as "I Know." This eye would appear in at least fifteen Prince song titles, and Prince peppered dozens more throughout his liner notes and autobiographical musings as he became ever more obsessed with symbol writing.

There is a word for these symbols too—*pictographs*—and together with logographs, they comprise a healthy portion of Prince's writing system.† Here again, Prince's linguistic playfulness seems to channel the creatives of Victorian England. Compare his pictographic writing to Lewis Carroll's letter to a young fan in 1869:

---

* Tr: "He says he loves you to excess, / You are virtuous and wise, / In excellency you excel / All others in his eyes. / This essay, until you I see, / I pray you to excuse, / And do not burn in effigy / My young and wayward muse. / Now fare you well, dear Katie Jay, / I trust that you are true—/ When this you see, then you can say, / An essay I owe you."
† To understand the difference between logographs and pictographs, take *Hamlet* as an example. If Shakespeare, in a moment of whimsy, wrote "2 B or not 2 B," he would be writing logographically. If instead of *B*'s the Bard drew cute little sketches of buzzing bumblebees, he would be writing pictographically.

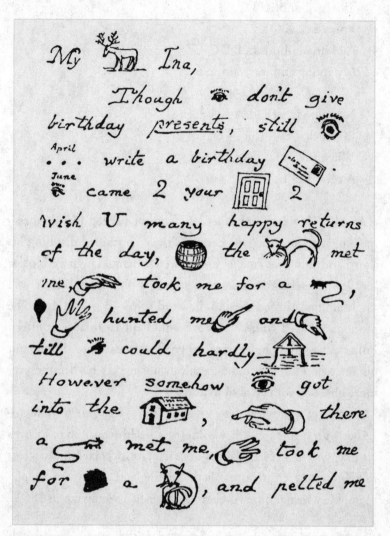

Letter from Lewis Carroll to Georgina Watson, October 1869. Tr: "My dear Ina, Though I don't give birthday <u>presents</u>, still I may write a birthday letter. I came to your door to wish you many happy returns of the day, but the cat met me, and took me for a mouse, and hunted me up and down till I could hardly stand. However <u>somehow</u> I got into the house, and there a mouse met me, and took me for a cat, and pelted me . . ."

Prince's spelling was an extension of his fashion,[*] an orthographic counterpart to his purple platforms and feather boas. But there may be more to his symbols than meets the ◉. For some contemporary artists, especially in America, creative spelling can be a subtle form of resistance—a reclamation of power from the land and language that stole it. Six of Prince's eight great-grandparents were born into slavery. And just as Malcolm X swapped the name "Little" for an "X," Prince shed both the surname (Nelson) and the orthography of his family's master. "In order for a man to really understand himself," Malcolm X said in 1963, "he must . . . [have] a language of his own." Malcolm might've admired a linguistic innovator like Prince—as well as others like 2Pac, ?uestlove, and Mos Def who define themselves through spelling and language. In a nation marked by a history of rebellion, challenging the Queen's English becomes a kind of political protest. And misspelling itself becomes a symbol of defiance.

In 1993, Prince took his symbol obsession to the extreme. Following in the steps of Melvil Dewey and Eliza Burnz, Prince legally simplified his name to an unvoiced letter he called "the Love Symbol," which strains the capabilities of our available fonts but looks something like a vertical version of this: O(+>.

If you were a journalist writing about Prince in 1993, you had two options: you could refer to him by the cumbersome label "The Artist Formerly Known as Prince," or you could ask Warner Bros. to mail you a floppy disk containing the font symbol in question. In 1994, a third option opened up: fans could purchase Prince's

---

[*]   Prince would have fit right in with Victorian fashion as well. His signature purple became central to the late-Victorian palette after it was synthesized by a London chemist in 1856. The ensuing nineteenth-century craze over purple clothing was known as the "mauveine measles," and Prince certainly had a bad case of it.

CD-ROM video game *Interactive*, a 3D puzzle quest set in a 16-bit animation of Prince's Paisley Park estate, which came with a downloadable Love Symbol for Macintosh and Windows 3.1.

And so, with a simple name change, Prince nudged the music industry into the technological future, forcing crit-

It's cool to get on the computer, but don't let the computer get on you.

—Prince, 1999

ics to refer to him by what was, essentially, a computer graphic, and forever entwining his artistic persona with the burgeoning digital age.

〰〰〰

In his 1985 appearance on *The Tonight Show*, Gallagher—the comedian known for smashing watermelons as if they'd personally offended him—used a prop to illustrate the nonsense of English spelling. He held up a scoreboard flipper, with four large cards hanging from a spiral coil. On the scoreboard were four letters:

"What's this, gang?" he asks Johnny Carson's audience. A few timid voices respond: "Bomb?" That's right, says Gallagher—"B-O-M-B, *BOMB*." He flips over the first *B* to reveal a *T*.

"*TOM?*" he asks. "No!" the crowd answers. "No!" Gallagher confirms, "that's *TOOM.*" A murmur of epiphany sweeps through the audience. They're catching on. Gallagher flips another card.

The audience smiles with realization. Ten million viewers at home do the same thing. It's the very same "aha!" that once converted Noah Webster and George Bernard Shaw into impassioned reformers. Gallagher continues flipping over cards, hopping from *HOME* to *SOME* to *NUMB* and finally to his applause line: *DUMB.* If there's one word to describe English orthography, that's it.

This now-classic skit caught the attention of at least one spelling reformer: Dr. Edward Rondthaler, vice president of England's Simplified Spelling Society (it had begun styling its name again in the traditional way) and arguably the first simplified speller of the computer age. Rondthaler traveled for years with a scoreboard flipper and a version of Gallagher's bit,* lecturing students on the illogic of English using the timeless pedagogical tool of prop comedy. (There's a video out there of Rondthaler performing this bit in 2007 at the age of 102.) Between Gallagher's orthographic humor and Prince's logographic artistry, the rise of personal computing and the nascent language of coding, the '80s seemed ripe for a new simplified spell-

---

* To be fair, it's unclear whether Gallagher or Rondthaler first originated the bit. There is evidence both ways, and neither man is alive to confirm.

ing push. And Rondthaler knew the best way to go about it: "Until quite recently," he wrote in the *New York Times*, "there was no hope for spelling reform. But today our computers can be programmed to bring it about. They, not we, can lead the way."

Picture it: An author sits at their desk, tapping out a novel in good old-fashioned English. As they type, the letters feed into a system that converts them, condenses them, and spits them onto the page as simplified spelling. It's as easy as autocorrecting *fradge* to *fridge*. "In theory," Rondthaler explained, "virtually all new printed matter, however produced, could be changed to simplified spelling at the flip of a switch—without anybody changing his or her writing or keyboard habits."

If Rondthaler could bring this invention to life, it would mark the first time that words could be simplified through the digital circuits of a machine rather than the neurons of a brain. No relearning. No reschooling. Anyone with a computer could instantly start spelling simply. These days, an app that would do just that could be built in a weekend, but for Edward Rondthaler, working with the primitive PCs of the 1980s, the project took years. When his hardware blueprint proved impractical, he pivoted to software. He teamed up with a computer programmer named Dr. Edward Lias, and by the end of the decade they had a working software prototype (compatible with IBM computers containing at least 256K memory). They put it on the market for $68. They struck deals with distributors in America, Britain, Canada, and Australia.* Then they waited.

"Sound Speler," as they dubbed this simplifying software, followed

---

* In 1972, Australia rebranded one of its government agencies the "Ministry of Helth" by request of Doug Everingham, the "Minister of Helth," a devoted follower of simplified spelling. In jest, Prime Minister Gough Whitlam would start letters to Everingham with "Dear Dug" and sign off with "Yors Gof." *Helth* turned back into *Health* in 1975 when the next administration took over.

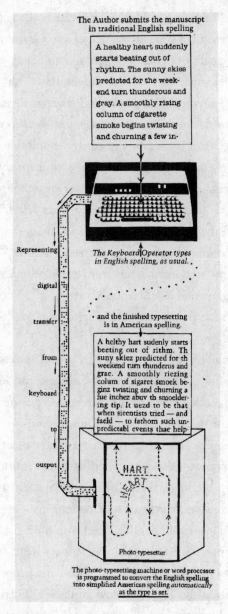

Edward Rondthaler's original design for his
simplified spelling computer, from his 1986 book
A Dictionary of Simplified American Spelling.

a phonetic spelling scheme Rondthaler created called "Sound Spel." Like Ormin's reform of 800 years earlier, which overzealously doubled up letters in pursuit of perfect phonetics, SoundSpel leaned heavily on letter duplication. As an unfortunate result, its "simplified" spellings tend to be anything but. *Jeenius* and *flooid* waste more ink than *genius* and *fluid. Apreeshyaet (appreciate)* and *obichooerry (obituary)* are even worse. And in an effort to convey diphthong vowels—the "gliding" vowels that make two different sounds in the same syllable—an overreliance on *OE*s and *AE*s makes for some arcane-looking *sichuaeshuns*. SoundSpel, consequently, looks less like a modern texting thread than a relic from a medieval manuscript: "We mae nowadaes be chairy about uezing the werd 'jeenius,'" Rondthaler wrote in a sample of translated text from the *London Review of Books,* "but we stil hav a guud iedeea whut is ment bi it." His computerized method may have fit the fast-paced digital age, but his iedeeas for simpler spelling were centuries out of date.

And yet, for all its Ye Olden aesthetics, Sound Speler brought language reform out of the dark days of Carnegie and Roosevelt and into the bright cathode rays of the tech era. As personal computers proceeded with their world domination, Sound Speler aimed to harness the power of machines to achieve what others never could. "Computers do not resist change and have no sentimental attachment to quaint spellings," Rondthaler wrote back in 1982. He was right: the main obstacle for past spelling reforms—the resistance of people to change—could be eliminated with the right combination of zeroes and ones. Spelling logic, meet binary logic.

As a long-term goal, Rondthaler hoped his innovation would help fix the social ills linked to low education and literacy rates: "jooveniel delinqensy, criem-in-th-streets, hard cor unemployment," and other "eevilz that dropouts get mixt up with." It was a worthy cause—but would it succeed? The market answered with a resounding *no*. A year after its 1993 launch, Sound Speler had sold fewer than 100 copies. That April, the *New York Times* ran a feature on Rondthaler depicting him as equal parts computer genius and local oddball: "There seems to be at least one Edward Rondthaler in almost every village in these parts," read the article, "someone obsessed by a mission who will implore, coax or cajole anyone who will listen." By the following year, few people were listening. Fewer were buying.

Sound Speler never landed on school desks like its inventor hoped, never brought down America's criem and delinqensy rates, but it nevertheless signaled a new era—one where the principles of simplified spelling converge with the burgeoning capabilities of digital technology. Sure, Rondthaler's orthography didn't take off. But the other day when I mistakenly typed "lok" instead of "look," my phone autocorrected it to "lol." A machine that favors abbreviation over traditional spelling? That's a legacy Rondthaler might be proud of.

"We have at last the technology to make the dream come true," he wrote presciently in 1973. "Do we have the courage to use it?"

~~~~~

Ever since the Kraze for *K* of the 1920s, reformers had tried to reclaim simplified spelling from the car salesmen, candymakers, and ad men who emblazoned it onto every billboard. And yet, after 70 years, little progress had been made. Simplified spelling still functioned in society primarily as a sales gimmick. Whether it was CDs or cigarettes, Cheez-Its or Froot Loops, a Little Red Corvette or a pre-owned Infiniti, simplified spelling was the language of commerce. It was a commercial adornment, not a conversational convenience. It served no real function in private communication.

That started to change in 1997 with the rise of America Online and its digital chat application, Instant Messenger. "AOL Instant Messenger" for short—"AIM" for even shorter—allowed average Joes and Janes to message each other instantly. (At the brisk speed of dial-up, at least.) In 1999, cell phone providers lifted a restriction that had prevented messaging between different carrier networks, and within five years the text message overtook the phone call as the primary communication technology for adolescents. In 2001, the typical American teenager sent three text messages per day. By 2010, they were sending three texts every waking hour.

Communication was fast-moving and fast-changing, and with it came a need for simplification—a digital shorthand that could handle the hurried demands of the new technology. It so happens that a shorthand had been slowly insinuating itself into the culture since the days of Noah Webster. It had all the appeal of a new slang and grabbed attention like a good sales advertisement. It was fun and playful and even, in a certain way, poetic. Most important, it came wrapped in the coolness of celebrity culture: in fact, none other than Tupac, MC Hammer, Jay-Z, Missy Elliott, and Prince had all given their implied endorsements.

Through the cross-pollination of pop music, advertising, and digital messaging, the practice of abbreviated spelling crept into the daily communications of fast-fingered, orthographically loose teens. *Through* became *thru*. *Great* became *gr8*. *You* became *U*.

Twenty-first-century textspeak was born.

Txtspk

It is quite impossible to stop the progress of language—
it is like the course of the Mississippi . . . it possesses a
momentum quite irresistible. Words and expressions will
be forced into use, in spite of all the exertions of all the
writers in the world.

—Noah Webster

In 2001, the *Guardian* held a poetry contest. Participants were free
to write on any subject, in any style, in any form, with one caveat:
the entries must fit the 160-character limit of a text message.

The winning poem, sent in (texted in, actually) by Hetty Hughes,
read:

txtin iz messin,
mi headn'me englis,
try2rite essays,
they all come out txtis.
Gran not plsed w/letters shes getn,
swears i wrote better
b4 comin2uni.
&she's african.

Textspeak, techspeak, cyber slang, SMS shorthand, the death of
English—it doesn't matter what you call it; we all know it when we

see it. It's the fast-paced rhythm of internet parlance, the condensed communication of acronyms, emoji, and abbreviated spellings. It's there in our texts and our tweets, our product reviews and Yelp rants, and if we're to trust the science-fiction authors, it'll be there with us far, far into the future.

If the internet is a place, then textspeak is its native language. Gretchen McCulloch, in her superb book on digital language, *Because Internet,* recalls a podcaster's introductory remark at a live show in 2014: "You know the internet, right? Many of you are even from there." The residents of this digital territory (McCulloch calls them "Internet People") represent every nationality, religion, and race. Indeed, more than five billion people are "from" the internet today—about two-thirds of the globe—and the rest, it's safe to say, will someday visit.

The language of this digital world developed in the 1990s with the introduction of the mass-market cell phone and a clunky little application called Short Message Service—SMS for short— a.k.a. "texting." Early texting, as you may cringe to remember, was cumbersome and slow. In the days before smartphones and predictive text, each letter would be tediously tapped on an alphanumeric keypad—two taps for *H*, two more for *E*, seven taps all told for a simple "hey" (or eight if you wanted it capitalized). SMS carriers also imposed a per-message character limit (usually 160 characters) and a per-message charge (usually 10 cents). This paragraph alone would've cost 60 cents. Texting could get pricy fast.

To avoid breaking the bank (and the thumbs), users learned to abbreviate. *Though* became *tho. You* became *u.* As entire sentences were stripped to their bare minimum ("sup?"), a briefer, simpler language began revealing itself. "Fine writing," Josh Billings once wrote, "konsists in gitting the most thought into the shortest and simplest form," and the fast-paced, short-spaced dialect of our digital age—call it textspeak, call it anarchy—is but the latest effort by us humans to simplify how we communicate.

"It is bleak, bald, sad shorthand," a British commentator once wrote of textspeak. ". . . It masks dyslexia, poor spelling, and mental laziness." Language purists like this have always been around. They grumble over new slangs, new shortcuts, new technologies, all while sighing nostalgically for the golden age of English when men were men and enough was *enough*. With every advance in our language, from mass printing to social media, these doomsayers stand around decrying its downfall. They haven't been correct once. And while they mourn the good old days and fear the new ones, they miss the creative and artful ways in which the language has changed and continues to change. Let's look at a few of these recent changes.

> As far back as the Roman Empire, purists have decried the falling standards of language. "Spoken Latin has picked up a passel of words considered too casual for written Latin," complained a critic in 63 C.E., "and the grammar people use when speaking has broken down . . . It's gotten to the point that the student of Latin is writing in what is to them an artificial language."
>
> This "too casual" strain of spoken Latin now has a name: French.

Pictorial Simplification

Picture writing is humanity's oldest written expression. It lines the caves of Mesopotamia and the tombs of Ancient Egypt. It adorns highways and street crossings, where rocks fall and moose cross, and it graces the liner notes of Prince albums. And at the very moment you're reading this, it's probably somewhere in space, bouncing off a satellite, beaming down to your phone.

Emoji comes from the Japanese words *e* ("picture") and *moji* ("character").* Those little expressive graphics that we've all come to love and hate were developed in 1997 by SoftBank (formerly J-Phone), a mobile operator based in Japan. Inspired by Japanese manga comics, the initial set of 90 black-and-white emoji served as a rudimentary visual language to bring feeling and tone to digital dialogue, along with other profound concepts like weather and silverware. When other cell providers saw the possibilities in Soft-Bank's pictorial suite, they added bright pops of color (primarily yellow) and expanded its range of emotions, concepts, hairstyles, and skin tones. As of this writing, the Unicode Standard recognizes 3,782 official emoji.

It's fitting that emoji were born in Japan. The Japanese writing system of "kanji" is based on logographs (symbols that stand for an entire word or phrase), which evolved over millennia from pictographs (symbols designed to resemble the actual objects they represent). While some kanji became abstracted over time, many still retain their pictographic essence. The Japanese character for *tree,* for instance, resembles its original pictograph of branches and roots: 木. The kanji for *fire* (火) and *mountain* (山) also recall their ancestral forms. And if you look closely at the kanji for *hand* (手), which some might mistake for a frond or a fern, you'll see rudiments of a modern emoji, waving hello: 🖐.

Before emoji characters became globally available on phones around 2011, texters outside of Japan relied on emoticons to enhance the expressiveness of their text messages. The first emoticon,

---

* Contrary to popular belief, the word *emoji* has no linguistic connection to *emotion* or *emoticon*.

some say, appeared in the transcript of an 1862 Lincoln speech, which records a supposed winking face. Others look at the transcript and see an obvious typo. You be the judge:

> There is no precedent for my appearing before you on this occasion, (applause) but it is also true that there is no precedent for your being here yourselves, (applause and laughter;)

Another candidate for the first emoticon comes from Ambrose Bierce, the American fiction author, who proposed what he called a "snigger point" in his 1887 essay "For Brevity and Clarity":

> It is written thus_and represents, as nearly as may be, a smiling mouth. It is to be appended, with the full stop, to every jocular or ironical sentence.

But the first modern emoticon—that is, the first emoticon used on a computer—occurred at precisely 11:44 AM on September 19, 1982, when Professor Scott Fahlman of Carnegie Mellon University posted the following note to an online message board:

```
I propose that the following character
sequence for joke markers:
:-)
Read it sideways. Actually, it is probably
more economical to mark things that are NOT
jokes, given current trends. For this, use
:-(
```

Emoticons aren't perfect. (Ever tried sticking one between parentheses? It isn't pretty:(). And yet, when it comes to emotional nuance in text conversations, the emoticon is one of our best tools. But what if emotional nuance isn't enough? What if you want to compress an entire sentence into a few simple keystrokes? What if "too long; didn't read"* just takes too damn long to write?

Acronymic Simplification

Some internet acronyms, like *OMG* and *LOL*, have become so entwined in modern life that they now appear in the *OED*. (That's the *Oxford English Dictionary*, BTW.) Others fell out of style and into oblivion. In 2014, the FBI compiled an 83-page glossary of text-speak acronyms (now public via the Freedom of Information Act), which includes some embarrassingly out-of-date doozies:

E2EG: Ear-to-ear grin

SHCOON: Shoot hot coffee out of nose

WWJBD: What would Jack Bauer do?

WYLABOCTGWTR: Would you like a bowl of cream to go with that remark?

PMFJIB: Pardon me for jumping in, but

YKWRGMG: You know what really grinds my gears?

DILLIGAD: Does it look like I give a damn?

IAWTCSM: I agree with this comment so much

---

* *TL;DR* ("too long; didn't read")—the battle cry of the chronically distracted—is a common acronym used to introduce a brief synopsis of a long post or article. Unlike the other acronyms on this page, *TL;DR* says less about linguistic brevity than it does attention deficiency.

Textspeak by State

According to U.S. data collected in 2022 from 18 million geotagged tweets:

- Textspeak is more popular in states with higher populations.
- In West Virginia, the most common acronym is *ily* ("I love you"). In Virginia, the most common acronym is *idc* ("I don't care").
- Among phonetic spellings (abbreviations that match their pronunciation), the most popular simplification in America is *ppl*.
- The acronym for "boyfriend" (*bf*) appears most frequently in Texas. The acronym for "girlfriend" (*gf*) appears most frequently in Montana.
- The most popular textspeak phrase in Milwaukee is *wtf*.

From the moment we began crafting digital acronyms in the 1970s, we've been compiling glossaries to keep track of them. The first was the "Jargon File," a 1975 document that circulated among early computer programmers, cataloging what it called "a special set of jargon words, used to save typing." Expressions like *FYI*, *BTW*, and *R U THERE?* joined the Jargon File in 1977, and as chatroom communities grew in the 1990s, editors added *LOL*, *BRB*, and *WTF*, along with emoticons and other typographical slangs of the early internet.* The print version of the Jargon File—*The Hacker's Dictionary*—became the underground handbook for a generation of computer whizzes.

---

* *OMG* was coined on September 9, 1917, in a letter from an admiral of the British Navy to Winston Churchill: "I hear that a new order of Knighthood is on the tapis— O.M.G. (Oh! My God!) Shower it on the Admiralty!!"

Alphanumeric Simplification

The Hacker's Dictionary also recorded the era's embrace of *B4, CU L8R,* and other faddish number spellings popularized by the music industry—the same logographic style that so enthralled nineteenth-century writers (and befuddled their readers) that an 1865 essay collection by Artemus Ward had to include a disclaimer:

> A few remarks concerning the phraseology in which the following papers are written, seem necessary in this English edition . . . The intermixture of numerals with the text, as in "going 2 see him," or "going 4 2 see him," "be4" for "before," "sow4th" for "soforth," "slam'd the 4dor," "1ce" for "once," "3ten" for "threaten," "2 B or not 2 B," may be looked upon as mere pieces of eccentricity, a sort of rebus fun, or mayhap a notion on Mr Ward's part that it is the correct thing, and shows education to abbreviate one's speech.

In 1991, *The Hacker's Dictionary* gave this shorthand its own name:

> **Hakspek** /hak'speek/ *n.* A shorthand method of spelling [in which] syllables and whole words in a sentence are replaced by single ASCII characters, the names of which are phonetically similar or equivalent, while multiple letters are usually dropped." Hence, "for" becomes "4"; "two," "too," and "to" becomes "2"; "ck" becomes "k." "Before I see you tomorrow" becomes "b4 i c u 2moro."

Outside of the internet, hakspek finds its expression today in the language of the open road, the boundless frontier—or, as linguist Frank H. Nuessel Jr. called it, "License Plate Language":

Phonetic Simplification

Phonetic simplifications are not in *The Hacker's Dictionary*, and don't need to be; most readers can understand *thru, tho, u, ur, msg, thx,* and *pls* just fine without a glossary. While acronyms tend to be cryptic (often deliberately so), and logographs require the occasional disclaimer, phonetic simplification is, well, *simple*. "Al languajs chanje in th corse of time," wrote the reformer Christopher Upward—and if he's right, then perhaps our forthcoming change will be driven by the simple, phonetic spelling of Noah Webster and texters around the globe. Maybe one day, not long from now, this will become the standard. Traditional spelling will fade into history. And reformers and purists alike will join together to proclaim, once and for all, that enough is, quite simply, enuf.

~~~~~

As the millennium approached, the truncated spellings of tech brought a renewed focus on efficiency in communication, and a newfound excitement within the dwindling spelling reform community. The simplifiers—what was left of them—came out of the woodwork.

"Ever sent a text message on a mobile phone?" asked Richard L.

Wade in blinding yellow on his 1999 homepage. ". . . If so, you already know what to do!"

As former editor of the BBC's technology and science program *Tomorrow's World,* Wade fancied himself a tech prophet, capable of predicting the trajectory of technology and society. Here at the cusp of the digital age, he could already see where our language was going. Better to embrace it than fight it, he thought. So, he purchased the domain freespeling.com, drowned it in low-res clip art and auto-play MIDI music, and waged a late-in-life campaign to "chanj the way we spel."

On his website, Wade listed a set of "freespeling guydlines," Websterian in every way (except for the last):

- Drop redundant let(t)ers: de(b)t, (k)nee, favo(u)r, ax(e), definit(e)
- Drop double leters if one wil do: can(n)ot, begin(n)ing, par(r)ot
- Chanj double leters like: (ph)fotograf(ph), (p)syk(ch)ology, sk(ch)ool
- Praktis on your mobile fone: 'I luv u . . . c u 2 moro . . . I o u $5 . . .'

Wade didn't consider himself a spelling reformer, dictating rules from on high. He was a spelling *liberator.* He believed in the wisdom of the crowd and the populism of the internet. And thus, at freespeling.com (now defunct), readers could participate in what he called the "demokratik" duty of the people. Each week, Wade's community would vote on their preferred spellings of 10 words, with the winners joining the "Freespeling Lexicon." (Inaugural inductees included *akomodate, foriner, kaos, frend, nollege,* and *biznis.*)

The simplified spelling movement was now truly online, where the dispersed voices of cyberspace could cast their votes for tomorrow's language without the intervention of a linguistic authority. "I am not a Reformer with a capital R," Wade explained, "because . . . there is no single Authority, with a capital A, which could possibly introduce coherent change."

~~~~~~

Language doesn't evolve from the top down. It doesn't shape to the wills of an elite few. It comes from the bottom, from the people, particularly the younger ones, who walk around with their phones in their fingers and their fingers on the pulse of the culture. Stephen Linstead, the Chairman of the English Spelling Society—formerly the Simplified Speling Soesiety, formerly the Simplified Spelling Society—sees promise in this next generation and their digital lingo. "We're quite sympathetic to the language of texting," he says. "Texting is grassroots. It's bottom-up. And despite the efforts of teachers and others to suppress it, it's certainly here to stay."

In recent years, the English Spelling Society has embraced the idea of textspeak. It sees in its *thru*'s and *2U*'s* an echo of its original goals and a herald, perhaps, of a spelling revolution to come. Today's reform movement not only accepts the language of the internet; it also exists almost entirely *on* the internet. The English Spelling Society, which once boasted the likes of H. G. Wells and George Bernard Shaw and carried out erudite debates in London lecture halls, now deliberates on quarterly Zoom calls and online discussion forums. Under the "Personal Views" tab on its website,

---

* In 2004, the New Zealand branch of the English Spelling Society changed its name to Spell4Literacy.

members are invited to share their own simplified spelling proposals for peer review. (Many worthy schemes have come in over the
years, including Sayspel, Regspel, Lytspel, Lytspel Revised, RichSpel,
RichSpel Revised, Gloebulspel, Lojikl Inglish, Zinglish, Norma-
lyzed Inglish, and Kurrent Spelling.) Under "Media," members post
articles discussing the prospects of simplified spelling in our modern world. ("The Internet is a flexible, inexpensive, global medium
for experimenting," reads one, and "shows popular readiness for
removing impediments in spelling.") And then there is the "Kids
Corner," the Society's brightly colored, child-friendly webpage of
crayon fonts and hand-drawn cartoons that lures in the next crop
of simplified spellers with questions like:

- Why *is* English spelling so mixed up, crazy and irregular?
- Want to find out what is being DONE to end this madness?
- Do YOU want to do something about it?

"We like to think we might find common ground with the
younger generation," says Linstead. "That may be a forlorn hope,
but texting gives us encouragement as to what can happen from
the bottom."

〰〰〰

In a 2013 April Fool's prank, Twitter (now X), the social platform
built upon tight character limits and an ethos of brevity, announced
that all vowels, except *Y*, had been removed from its basic service.
If users wanted access to *A, E, I, O,* and *U,* they would have to pay
$5 a month.

"Y R y00 d0yng thys?" tweeted the comedian Rob Delaney in

Just setting up my twttr.

—Jack Dorsey, first-ever tweet, 2006

playful protest. "We're doing this," explained Twitter, "because we believe that by eliminating vowels, we'll encourage a more efficient and 'dense' form of communication." In keeping with the bit, VP Michael Sippey revealed the inspiration behind the vowel-less service. "I was carpooling home after Twitter's seventh birthday party . . . And then Prince's song 'I Would Die 4 U' came on the radio. I felt like there was something there . . ."

There *is* something there, all right. It's been there for hundreds of years. It was there when Ormin doubbled upp onn connsonnannts and when Auguste Thibaudin d8bled down on n3mbers. It was there for the Artist Formerly Known as Prince and the company formerly known as Twitter. It's there in your pocket. It's our eternal quest to communicate—clearly, swiftly, *simply*. As societies grow and divisions widen, new mavericks emerge, simplifying the language to their own peculiar specifications as they strive, again and again, to find the shortest distance between two points of communication. The quest continues still.

Today, the simplified spelling movement is all around us, calling out from headlines and cereal boxes, winking at us from ads, evolving with our changing world. We encounter it—and participate in it—every day, whether we realize it or not. In fact, you're probably a bit of a simplified speller yourself. Noah Webster was proud of the title. I hope u r 2.

An (Abbreviated) Dictionary of Simplified Spelling

Based on the Writings of Noah Webster

A

abuv (*prep*) • above
abuze (*v*) • abuse
acheev (*v*) • achieve
ahed (*adv*) • ahead
ake (*v, n*) • ache
aker (*n*) • acre
alkemy (*n*) • alchemy
alreddy (*adv*) • already
alternativ (*adj, n*) • alternative
altho (*conj*) • although
amuze (*v*) • amuse
anarky (*n*) • anarchy
ankor (*n*) • anchor
anteek (*n*) • antique
appeer (*v*) • appear
approov (*v*) • approve
argu (*v*) • argue
arize (*v*) • arise
arketype (*n*) • archetype
arkitecture (*n*) • architecture
autograf (*n*) • autograph
autum (*n*) • autumn
az (*prep, conj*) • as

B

bakkanalian (*adj*) • bacchanalian
becauze (*conj*) • because
becum (*v*) • become
beem (*n, v*) • beam
beest (*n*) • beast
behed (*v*) • behead

behoov (*v*) • behoove
beleef (*n*) • belief
beleegur (*v*) • beleaguer
beleev (*v*) • believe
beluv (*v*) • belove
bild (*v*) • build
bin (*v*) • been
biografy (*n*) • biography
bizness (*n*) • business
bizzy (*adj*) • busy
blu (*adj, n*) • blue
blud (*n*) • blood
bouteek (*n*) • boutique
bred (*n*) • bread
breef (*adj, n*) • brief
brest (*n*) • breast
breth (*n*) • breath
burlesk (*n, adj*) • burlesque
butiful (*adj*) • beautiful

C

cartografy (*n*) • cartography
cauze (*n, v*) • cause
ceese (*v*) • cease
cheef (*n, adj*) • chief
cheep (*adj*) • cheap
cheet (*v, n*) • cheat
chooze (*v*) • choose
chozen (*adj, v*) • chosen
cleen (*adj, v*) • clean
cleer (*adj, v*) • clear
cloke (*n*) • cloak

cloze (*v, adj*) • close
clu (*n, v*) • clue
collectiv (*adj, n*) • collective
color (*n, v*) • colour (Br.)
colum (*n*) • column
comparativ (*adj, n*) • comparative
conceel (*v*) • conceal
concizion (*n*) • concision
constru (*v*) • construe
continu (*v*) • continue
criteek (*n, v*) • critique
cumpleet (*adj, v*) • complete
cuver (*v, n*) • cover

D

dawter (*n*) • daughter
deceet (*n*) • deceit
deceev (*v*) • deceive
decizion (*n*) • decision
ded (*n, adj*) • dead
dedly (*adj, adv*) • deadly
deel (*v, n*) • deal
defectiv (*adj*) • defective
defeet (*n, v*) • defeat
definit (*adj*) • definite
desend (*v*) • descend
det (*n*) • debt
determin (*v*) • determine
deth (*n*) • death
detoor (*n, v*) • detour
dettor (*n*) • debtor
devalu (*v*) • devalue
dezerv (*v*) • deserve
dikotomy (*n*) • dichotomy
disapproov (*v*) • disapprove
disbeleef (*n*) • disbelief
disbeleev (*v*) • disbelieve
discurage (*v*) • discourage
discuver (*v*) • discover

diseez (*n*) • disease
dispozition (*n*) • disposition
disproov (*v*) • disprove
divizion (*n*) • division
donkee (*n*) • donkey
dout (*n, v*) • doubt
dred (*v, n*) • dread
du (*adj, prep*) • due

E

edjucation (*n*) • education
eech (*det, pron*) • each
eeger (*adj*) • eager
eer (*n*) • ear
eest (*n, adj*) • east
eestern (*adj*) • eastern
eet (*v*) • eat
eether (*conj, pron, adj, adv*) • either
eezy (*adj*) • easy
electiv (*adj, n*) • elective
encurage (*v*) • encourage
enuf (*n, adj, adv*) • enough
epok (*n*) • epoch
erl (*n*) • earl
erly (*adj, adv*) • early
erozion (*n*) • erosion
erth (*n*) • earth
excessiv (*adj*) • excessive
executiv (*adj, n*) • executive
extensiv (*adj*) • extensive

F

fantom (*n, adj*) • phantom
fasset (*n*) • facet
fateeg (*n*) • fatigue
favorit (*n, adj*) • favorite
feef (*n*) • fief
feer (*n, v*) • fear
feest (*n, v*) • feast

feezable (*adj*) • feasible
fether (*n, v*) • feather
flud (*n, v*) • flood
flurish (*v, n*) • flourish
frend (*n*) • friend
fronteer (*n*) • frontier
fugitiv (*n, adj*) • fugitive
fyzzeek (*n*) • physique
fyzzical (*n, adj*) • physical
fyzzics (*n*) • physics

G

gard (*n, v*) • guard
geografy (*n*) • geography
gilloteen (*n, v*) • guillotine
gilt (*n, v*) • guilt
giv (*v*) • give
gluv (*n*) • glove
goddawter (*n*) • goddaughter
graf (*n, v*) • graph
granddawter (*n*) • granddaughter
greef (*n*) • grief
greev (*v*) • grieve
groop (*n, v*) • group
groov (*n, v*) • groove
grotesk (*adj, n*) • grotesque
guvern (*v*) • govern
guvernment (*n*) • government

H

hanous (*adj*) • heinous
hart (*n*) • heart
hartbeet (*n*) • heartbeat
hav (*v*) • have
haz (*v*) • has
hed (*n, v*) • head
heer (*v, n, adv*) • hear, here
heet (*n, v*) • heat
helth (*n*) • health

hevvy (*n, adj*) • heavy
hierarky (*n*) • hierarchy
hiz (*pron*) • his
homested (*n, v*) • homestead
hu (*n, v*) • hue, hew
huver (*n, v*) • hover

I

iland (*n*) • island
imprizon (*v*) • imprison
improov (*v*) • improve
inactiv (*adj*) • inactive
increese (*v, n*) • increase
incumpleet (*adj*) • incomplete
indeted (*adj*) • indebted
infinit (*adj, n*) • infinite
insted (*adv*) • instead
intreeg (*n, v*) • intrigue
iz (*v*) • is

J

jaundis (*n, adj*) • jaundice
jazmin (*n*) • jasmine
jelousy (*n*) • jealousy
jepardy (*n, v*) • jeopardy
judicativ (*adj*) • judicative
justis (*n*) • justice

K

kaos (*n*) • chaos
karacter (*n*) • character
kasm (*n*) • chasm
kee (*n*) • key
kemistry (*n*) • chemistry
koir (*n*) • choir
kolic (*n*) • cholic
koral (*adj*) • choral
kord (*n, v*) • cord, chord
koreografy (*n*) • choreography

korus (*n, v*) • chorus
kristian (*n, adj*) • Christian
kronic (*adj*) • chronic

L

laf (*v, n*) • laugh
leed (*v, n*) • lead
leeder (*n*) • leader
leef (*n*) • leaf
leeg (*n*) • league
leest (*adj, adv*) • least
leev (*n, v*) • leave
legislativ (*adj*) • legislative
legislatur (*n*) • legislature
lepard (*n*) • leopard
lern (*v*) • learn
lether (*n, adj*) • leather
lifeblud (*n*) • lifeblood
lim (*n*) • limb
liv (*v, adj*) • live
logograf (*n*) • logograph
looz (*v*) • lose
luv (*v, n*) • love
luver (*n*) • lover

M

magazeen (*n*) • magazine
manslawter (*n*) • manslaughter
mareen (*adj, n*) • marine
markee (*n, adj*) • marquee
masheen (*n*) • machine
matriarky (*n*) • matriarchy
meen (*v, adj, n*) • mean
mekanic (*n, adj*) • mechanic
mekanism (*n*) • mechanism
ment (*v, n*) • meant, mint
mezure (*v, n*) • measure
misconstru (*v*) • misconstrue
misdemeenor (*n*) • misdemeanor

mistreet (*v*) • mistreat
monarky (*n*) • monarchy
monograf (*n*) • monograph
moov (*v*) • move
motiv (*n, adj, v*) • motive
munth (*n*) • month
mysteek (*n*) • mystique

N

nabor (*n, v*) • neighbor
naborhood (*n*) • neighborhood
nachural (*adj*) • natural
nachure (*n*) • nature
nativ (*adj, n*) • native
nectareen (*n*) • nectarine
neer (*adj*) • near
neerly (*adv*) • nearly
neet (*adj, adv*) • neat
neether (*conj, pron, adj, adv*) • neither
noize (*n*) • nois
notis (*v, n*) • notice
novis (*n*) • novice
noze (*n, v*) • nose

O

obleek (*adj*) • oblique
obsoleet (*adj*) • obsolete
obzerv (*v*) • observe
opake (*adj*) • opaque
opposit (*adj, n, prep*) • opposite
oppoze (*v*) • oppose
orifis (*n*) • orifice
orkestra (*n*) • orchestra
orkid (*n*) • orchid
orthografy (*n*) • orthography
otherwize (*adv*) • otherwise
overhed (*adv, n, adj*) • overhead

P

paragraf (*n*) • paragraph
parlement (*n*) • parliament
patriarky (*n*) • patriarchy
peece (*n, v*) • piece, peace
peek (*n, v*) • peak, pique
peeple (*n*) • people
pezant (*n*) • peasant
pictograf (*n*) • pictograph
picturesk (*adj*) • picturesque
pleed (*v*) • plead
pleez (*v, interj, n*) • please
plezur (*n, v*) • pleasure
porpess (*n*) • porpoise
preech (*v*) • preach
preecher (*n*) • preacher
preest (*n*) • priest
prerogativ (*n*) • prerogative
prezent (*v, adj, n*) • present
prezerv (*v, n*) • preserve
prezident (*n*) • president
proov (*v*) • prove
provizion (*n*) • provision
pursu (*v*) • pursue

Q

qualitativ (*adj*) • qualitative
quantitativ (*adj*) • quantitative
quaranteen (*n, v*) • quarantine
queezy (*adj*) • queasy
quel (*v*) • quell
quil (*n*) • quill

R

receev (*v*) • receive
recuver (*v, n*) • recover
reddy (*adj, n*) • ready
reder (*n*) • reader
reech (*v, n*) • reach

reed (*v, n*) • read
reezon (*v, n*) • reason
refuze (*v*) • refuse
releef (*n*) • relief
releese (*v, n*) • release
releev (*v*) • relieve
relm (*n*) • realm
remoov (*v*) • remove
repeel (*v, n*) • repeal
repeet (*v, n*) • repeat
repoze (*v, n*) • repose
reserv (*v, n*) • reserve
retreev (*v*) • retrieve
reveel (*n, v*) • reveal
rezide (*v*) • reside
ribin (*n*) • ribbon
rite (*n, v, adj*) • right, write
riter (*n*) • writer
rong (*adj, n, v*) • wrong
ruf (*n, adj*) • rough

S

sed (*v*) • said
seet (*n, v*) • seat
shagrin (*n*) • chagrin
shal (*modal v*) • shall
shandeleer (*n*) • chandelier
shaperone (*n, v*) • chaperone
sharade (*n*) • charade
sharlatan (*n*) • charlatan
shaze (*n*) • chaise
shef (*n*) • chef
shevaleer (*n*) • chevalier
shivalry (*n*) • chivalry
shuv (*n, v*) • shove
sistem (*n*) • system
skedule (*n, v*) • schedule
skolar (*n*) • scholar
skool (*n, v*) • school

slawter (*v, n*) • slaughter
sley (*n, v*) • sleigh
soop (*n*) • soup
speek (*v*) • speak
speer (*n, v*) • spear
speerhed (*n*) • spearhead
spred (*v, n*) • spread
spunge (*n, v*) • sponge
statuesk (*adj*) • statuesque
steddy (*adj, adv, v, n*) • steady
stepdawter (*n*) • stepdaughter
stil (*adv, adj, n*) • still
stile (*n, v*) • style
stomak (*n, v*) • stomach
streem (*n, v*) • stream
subdu (*v*) • subdue
suthern (*adj, n*) • southern
swet (*n, v*) • sweat
sykic (*adj, n*) • psychic

T

teckneek (*n*) • technique
tecknical (*adj, n*) • technical
teech (*v*) • teach
teeze (*v, n*) • tease
theef (*n*) • thief
theze (*det, pron*) • these
tho (*conj, adv*) • though
thoro (*adj, adv*) • thorough
thoroly (*adv*) • thoroughly
thoze (*det, pron*) • those
thred (*n, v*) • thread
thret (*n, v*) • threat
thro (*prep, adv*) • through
thum (*n, v*) • thumb
toor (*n, v*) • tour
tred (*v, n*) • tread
treet (*v, n*) • treat
treezon (*n*) • treason
trezur (*n, v*) • treasure

tru (*adj, adv, n*) • true
trubble (*n, v*) • trouble
tuch (*v, n*) • touch
tuf (*adj, n*) • tough
tung (*n*) • tongue
twelv (*num*) • twelve

U

undu (*v*) • undo
uneek (*adj*) • unique
uneezy (*adj*) • uneasy
unreezonable (*adj*) • unreasonable
unseet (*v*) • unseat
unsteddy (*adj*) • unsteady
unuzual (*adj*) • unusual
upbeet (*adj*) • upbeat
upheeval (*n*) • upheaval
upstreem (*adj, adv*) • upstream
uze (*v, n*) • use
uzual (*adj*) • usual
uzually (*adv*) • usually

V

valu (*n, v*) • value
veel (*n*) • veal
venu (*n*) • venue
verzion (*n, v*) • version
villan (*n*) • villain
vizible (*adj*) • visible
vizion (*n*) • vision
vizit (*n, v*) • visit
volum (*n*) • volume
vu (*n, v*) • view

W

waz (*v*) • was
weery (*adj, v*) • weary
welcum (*adj, n, v*) • welcome
welth (*n*) • wealth
wepon (*n*) • weapon

wether (*conj, n, v*) • whether, weather
wheet (*n*) • wheat
wil (*n, v, modal v*) • will
wimmen (*n*) • women
winsum (*adj*) • winsome
wizdom (*n*) • wisdom
wize (*adj*) • wise
wurd (*n*) • word
wurk (*n, v*) • work

X

xenofobia (*n*) • xenophobia
xenomorfia (*n*) • xenomorphia
xifoforus (*n*) • xiphophorus
xifoid (*adj*) • xiphoid
xylofone (*n*) • xylophone

Y

yeeld (*v, n*) • yield
yeer (*n*) • year
yeest (*n*) • yeast
yel (*n, v*) • yell
yern (*v*) • yearn
yoor (*pron*) • your
yung (*adj*) • young
yuth (*n*) • youth

Z

zeel (*n*) • zeal
zefyr (*n*) • zephyr
zelot (*n*) • zealot
zelotry (*n*) • zealotry
zoforus (*n*) • zophorus
zoografy (*n*) • zoography
zoomorfy (*n*) • zoomorphy

Muzik and Liriks

Music plays a large role in this book and in the lives of many within it. This got me wondering: What if certain songs (specifically ones without copyright risks) had been penned by simplified spellers? How would Ben Franklin handle "Rockin' Robin"? What would Melvil Dewey do with Cole Porter?

Now's the time, dear readers, to lay down your books, pick up yur geetars, and rise up in song, for the spellings they are a-changin'.

"The Star-Spangled Banner"

(In the style of Benjamin Franklin, 1768)

O see, kan iu sii

Bui hi dæn's erlii luit

Wut so præudlii wii heeled

At hi twuiluite's last gliimn?

(Noah Webster, 1789)

Whoze broad stripes and brite stars

Thru the perilus fite

O'er the ramparts we watched

Were so galantly streeming?

(In the style of Auguste Thibaudin, 1842)

8nd th9 r9ckɛt's rɛd gl8r

Th9 b9mbs b1rst6ng 6n 8r

G7v pr2f thr2 th9 n96t

Th9t 92r fl9g w9s st6ll th8r.

(Spelling Reform Association, 1876)

O sa, duz dhat star-spangled banner yet wav,

O'er dhi land əv dhi fri and dhi höm əv dhi brav.

—Francis Scott Key

"Rockin' Robin"

(In the style of Benjamin Franklin, 1768)

Twiidle-lii-dii-dii-dii, twiidle-lii-dii-dii

Twiidle-lii-dii-dii-dii, twiidle-lii-dii-dii

Twiidle-lii-dii-dii-dii, twiidle-lii-dii-dii

Twiit, twiit, twiit, twiit.

Hii rɑks in hi trii tɑps ɑll dee lɑng

Hɑppŋ and a-bɑppŋ and a-singŋ hiz sɑng

ɑll hi litl berdz ɑn Jeeberd Striit

Lyv tu hiir hi rɑbin go twiit, twiit, twiit

Rɑkŋ rɑbin (twiit, twiit, twiit)

Rɑkŋ rɑbin (twiit, twiidle-lii-dii)

Go rɑkŋ rɑbin, 'kɑz wiir riili gyny rɑk tunyit

(Twiit, twiit, twiidle-lii-dii)

—Leon René

"The Twelve Days of Christmas"

(In the style of Ormin, twelfth century)

Onn the twellfth day of Chrisstmass,

My true lovve gave to me

Twellve drummerrs drumminng,

Elevvenn piperrs pipinng,

Tenn lorrds a-leapinng,

Nine ladies danncinng,
Eight maids a-millkinng,
Sevvenn swanns a-swimminng,
Sixx geese a-layinng,
Five goldenn rinngs,
Four callinng birrds,
Three Frennch henns,
Two turrtle dovves,
Annd a parrtriddge inn a pearr tree.
—Traditional

"Old MacDonald Had a Farm"

(In the style of the Anti-Absurd Alphabet, 1844)

əld MʌkDʌ́nəld hʌd ʌ fʌ́rm
ɐ y ɐ y ə!
ʌnd ʌn ʝʌt fʌ́rm hɐ hʌd sʉm chikenz
ɐ y ɐ y ə!
With ʌ klʉk-klʉk hɐr
ʌnd ʌ klʉk-klʉk thar
Hɐr ʌ klʉk, thar ʌ klʉk
Evrɐwar ʌ klʉk-klʉk
əld MʌkDʌ́nəld hʌd ʌ fʌ́rm
ɐ y ɐ y ə!

əld MʌkDʌ́nəld hʌd ʌ fʌ́rm
ɐ y ɐ y ə!
ʌnd ʌn ʝʌt fʌ́rm hɐ hʌd sʉm kowz
ɐ y ɐ y ə!
With ʌ mu-mu hɐr
ʌnd ʌ mu-mu thar

Her ʌ mu, thar ʌ mu
Evrewar ʌ mu-mu
əld MʌkDʌnəld hʌd ʌ fʌrm
ɐ y ɐ y ə!

əld MʌkDʌnəld hʌd ʌ fʌrm
ɐ y ɐ y ə!
ʌnd ʌn ʒʌt fʌrm hɐ hʌd sʌm dɔgz
ɐ y ɐ y ə!
With ʌ wuf-wuf hɐr
ʌnd ʌ wuf-wuf thar
Her ʌ wuf, thar ʌ wuf
Evrewar ʌ wuf-wuf
əld MʌkDʌnəld hʌd ʌ fʌrm
ɐ y ɐ y ə!
—Thomas d'Urfey

"Let's Do It (Let's Fall in Love)"

(In the style of Melvil Dewey)
Burdz du it, beez du it
Eevn ejukayted fleez du it
Let's du it, let's fal in luv.
In Spayn, the best upr sets du it
Lithuwaynianz and Lets du it
Let's du it, let's fal in luv.

The Duch in old Amsturdam du it
Not tu menchin the Finz
Folks in Siyam du it—
Think uv Siyameez twinz.

Sum Arjenteenz, without meenz, du it
Peepul say in Bostun eevn beenz du it
Let's du it, let's fal in luv.

Romantik spunjez, thai sai, du it
Oysturz down in Oystur Bai du it
Let's du it, let's fal in luv.
Kold Kayp Kod klams, 'genst their wish, du it
Eevn lazee jeleefish du it
Let's du it, let's fal in luv.

Eelektrik eelz, I miyt ad, du it
Tho it shoks 'em, I no
Wy ask if shad du it?
Wayter, bring me shad ro!

In shallo sholz, Inglish solz du it
Goldfish in the pryvusi uv bowlz du it
Let's du it, let's fal in luv.
—Cole Porter

"Hello!" (From *The Book of Mormon*)

(In the style of the Deseret Alphabet)
Elder Price:
Ψ𐐼𐐻𐐬!
𐐉𐐿 𐐸𐐯𐐉 𐐻𐐮 𐐼𐐮𐐮𐐼𐐹 𐐉𐐼𐐹𐐬𐐀
𐐾𐐷𐐼 𐐸 𐐹𐐷𐐼 𐐿𐐮𐐩 𐐻𐐰 𐐿𐐷𐐩 𐐮𐐻𐐶 𐐬𐐾𐐼
Ψ 𐐬𐐉𐐻 𐐸𐐷𐐾𐐮𐐼 𐐻𐐰𐐬𐐀 𐐰𐐷𐐬.

Elder Grant:
𐐐𐐯𐑊𐐬!
𐐣𐐴 𐑌𐐩𐑋 𐐮𐑆 𐐇𐑊𐐼𐐲𐑉 𐐘𐑉𐐰𐑌𐐻.
𐐆𐐻𐑅 𐐩 𐐺𐐳𐐿 𐐲𐐺𐐵𐐻 𐐊𐑋𐐯𐑉𐐮𐐿𐐲
𐐁 𐑊𐐫𐑍, 𐑊𐐫𐑍 𐐻𐐴𐑋 𐐲𐑀𐐬.
—Trey Parker, Matt Stone, Robert Lopez

Happy Birthday to You

(In the style of Prince)
Happy birthday 2 U
Happy birthday 2 U
Happy birthday, dear Artist Formerly Known as Prince
Happy birthday 2 U.
—Patty and Mildred Hill

Acknowledgments

First, as always, I want to thank my family: Nora, Danny, and Celina, the bedrock of my existence, who never wavered in their support even during my most questionable life choices; Ruthie, our matriarch, who holds us together even in memory; the Stern-Aschers, who opened their home and provided the space to finish this project; and all the other family members, too many to list, who cooked the meals, stirred the ideas, kept the debates lively, and encouraged me through my years of writing. If I tried to name every one of you, we'd have to raise the price of this book.

For their personal, professional, and occasionally psychiatric support, I owe thanks to the following remarkable humans: Amy Jacobus, Benjamin Levinsohn, Chris Bannon, Martha Mihalick, Chris Willets, Jamie Pietras, Jeremy Levenbach, Julie Kim, Caitlin Gillette, Joe Rivas, Donwill, Fred Firestone, Ophira Eisenberg, Lily Dionne-Jermanovich, Sam Corbin, Erika Ettin, Ally Spier, Hope Morawa, Joylene Ceballos, Charlie Lyman, Camille Cauti, Michael Fine, Kaethe Fine, Antony Fine, Jesse Rosenberg, David Ost, Nick Mullendore, Tia Monahan, Sara Missaoui, Joanne Torres, Annie Salter, Isla Hamblett, Jonathan Metzl, Julian Rhine, Jesse Rhine, Molly Anderson, Lia Seremetis, Tim Rondthaler, Glen Tandberg, Peter Sokolowski at Merriam-Webster, Stephen Linstead at the English Spelling Society, Mariam Touba at the New-York Historical Society, and all my teammates in McCarren, Prospect, Heckscher, and beyond.

For the folks at Dey Street who bet on this book, there aren't enough words in *Webster's* to express my gratitude. Please accept my thunderous, foot-stomping applause instead. Drew Henry, your vision and guidance made this book what it is. An ovation, sir.

A special thank-you to my stellar agent Katherine Hardigan, who believed in this project before anyone else and championed it (and me) every step of the way (with Fenn always lending support in the background). And, of course, Aaron Flores, the man who Makes It Happen.

I am long overdue in thanking John Palencsar—Professor P.—the Hudson Valley legend who introduced me to the simplified spelling movement. John delighted in the quirky, untold relics of history—the marginal doodles, the ancient puns, the lewd letters—and he passed that delight on to me. He lives on in every page of this book.

And lastly, to Claire Lyman, I owe a debt so profound it would make national economies blush. Your capacity for joy and love is a daily inspiration, and your patience for my jokes is nothing short of heroic. Without you, this section of the book would surely be one paragraph shorter.

Notes

Introduction

xi **first told around 1855**: Townshend Mayer, S. R. "Leigh Hunt and Charles Ollier." *St. James's Magazine*, Oct. 1874, p. 406.

xii **According to a study**: Seymour, Philip. "Foundation Literacy Acquisition in European Orthographies." *British Journal of Psychology*, 2003.

xii **English has 44 sounds**: Sethi, J., et al. *A Practical Course in English Pronunciation*. New Delhi, Prentice-Hall of India Pvt. Ltd., 2004, p. 11.

xiii **Of the six signatures**: Bryson, Bill. *Shakespeare*. New York, HarperCollins, 2007, p. 9.

Part I: Washington, D.C., 2010

2 **first Scripps champion**: "Farewell, First Spelling C-h-a-m-p-i-o-n." NPR, 25 Mar. 2011, www.npr.org/sections/talk/2011/03/25/134764423/farewell-first-spelling-c-h-a-m-p-i-o-n.

2 **group of protestors**: "Enuf Is Enuf: DC Spelling Bee Draws Protests." *Christian Science Monitor*, www.csmonitor.com/From-the-news-wires/2010/0604/Enuf-is-enuf-DC-spelling-bee-draws-protests.

Chapter 1: A Man of Letters

6 **Franklin embarked on a campaign**: Stamp, Jimmy. "Benjamin Franklin's Phonetic Alphabet." *Smithsonian*, Smithsonian.com, 10 May 2013, www.smithsonianmag.com/arts-culture/benjamin-franklins-phonetic-alphabet-58078802/.

6 **J joined the alphabet in 1524**: "Meet the Man Responsible for the Letter 'J.'" Dictionary.com, 8 Apr. 2011, www.dictionary.com/e/j/.

7 **his eleventh year**: Isaacson, Walter. *Benjamin Franklin: An American Life*. New York, Simon & Schuster, 2004, p. 47.

7 **Franklin sent his proposal**: "Founders Online: From Benjamin Franklin to Mary Stevenson, 20 July 1768: Phonetic Spelling and Transcription." Founders.archives.gov, founders.archives.gov/documents/Franklin/01–15–02–0095.

8 **"Letter to a Royal Academy"**: Franklin, Benjamin. *Fart Proudly: Writings of Benjamin Franklin You Never Read in School*. Berkeley, California, North Atlantic Books, 2003, p. 13.

8 **Polly sent back her phonetic two cents**: "Founders Online: To Benjamin Franklin from Mary Stevenson, 26 September 1768: Phonetic Spelling and

Transcription." Founders.archives.gov, founders.archives.gov/documents/ Franklin/01–15–02–0122.

Chapter 2: English: A Simplified History

11 "a rich verbal tapestry": Barry, Dave. "Yo! Mr. Language Person!" *The Washington Post*, 27 Jan. 1990.

11 monk known as Ormin: Uckelman, S. L. "Orm." *The Dictionary of Medieval Names from European Sources*, Edition 2023, no. 1.

11 *thowh, thowgh, thoagh*: McIntosh, Angus, et al. *A Linguistic Atlas of Late Medieval English*. United Kingdom, Aberdeen University Press, 1985, p. 143.

12 Ormin proposed doubling: Crystal, David. *Spell It Out: The Singular Story of English Spelling*. London, Profile Books, 2013, p. 53.

12 The average medieval scribe: Lyons, Martyn. *Books: A Living History*. Los Angeles, California, The J. Paul Getty Museum, 2011, pp. 36–41.

13 The earliest documented language in England: Lee, Christopher. *This Sceptred Isle: The Making of the British*. United Kingdom, Little, Brown Book Group, 1997, p. 45.

13 Welsh, Irish, Breton, and Scottish Gaelic: Macaulay, Donald (ed.). *The Celtic Languages*. Cambridge, New York, Cambridge University Press, 1992.

14 Julius Caesar had tried to conquer England twice: Williams, Eifion Wyn. "Julius Caesar's Invasions of Celtic Britain." *Historic UK*, 2019, www. historic-uk.com/HistoryUK/HistoryofWales/Julius-Caesar-Invasions-of-Celtic-Britain/.

14 Celts fled into the outer rural areas: Cunliffe, Barry W. *The Ancient Celts*. United Kingdom, Oxford University Press, 2018, p. 347–378.

14 Rome was sacked by the Visigoths: Cavendish, Richard. "The Visigoths Sack Rome." *History Today*, 2010, www.historytoday.com/archive/months-past/visigoths-sack-rome.

14 Angles, Saxons, Jutes, and Frisians: Myres, John Nowell Linton. *The English Settlements*. United Kingdom, Oxford University Press, 1989, p. 46.

15 Words were spelled as they sounded: Crystal, David. "The Story of English Spelling." *The Guardian*, 23 Aug. 2012, www.theguardian.com/books/2012/aug/23/david-crystal-story-english-spelling.

15 their preference for *SK* sounds: Stroud, Kevin. *The History of English Podcast*. 8 June 2018, ep. 112.

15 They came from Denmark: Weiss, Daniel. "The Viking Great Army." *Archaeology*, Apr. 2018.

16 These invaders hailed from Normandy: Cartwright, Mark. "The Impact of the Norman Conquest of England." *World History Encyclopedia*,

23 Jan. 2019, www.worldhistory.org/article/1323/the-impact-of-the-norman-conquest-of-england/.

16 **The English courts adopted French words:** Bryson, Bill. *The Mother Tongue: English & How It Got That Way.* New York, Bard, 1998, pp. 53–55.

16 **five major English dialects:** Jewell, Helen M. *The North-South Divide.* Manchester, Manchester University Press, 1994, p. 198.

17 **axed for mete:** Mugglestone, Lynda. *The Oxford History of English.* Oxford, Oxford University Press, 2012, p. 150.

17 **For reasons historians don't fully understand:** Crystal, pp. 147–148.

17 **Great Vowel Shift:** Bryson, pp. 92–93.

18 *Meat* and *great*: Kottmeyer, William. *Except After C: The Story of English Spelling.* United States, McGraw-Hill, 1988, p. 39.

18 **On a trading trip to Cologne:** "William Caxton: The 15th-Century Influencer." *Great British Life*, 21 June 2023, www.greatbritishlife.co.uk/people/23528618.william-caxton-15th-century-influencer-printer/.

18 **"broad and rude":** Knight, Charles. *William Caxton, the First English Printer.* Legare Street Press, 27 Oct. 2022, p. 9.

19 **"Chancery Standard":** Baddeley, Susan, and Anja Voeste. *Orthographies in Early Modern Europe.* Berlin, De Gruyter, 2012, p. 148.

19 **justified margins:** Crystal, p. 137.

20 **"marginal hyphens":** "Hyphen | Definition, History, Dash, Symbol, & Facts | Britannica." *Britannica*, www.britannica.com/topic/hyphen.

20 *pity*, *pitty*, and *pittye*: Crystal, pp. 137–138.

20 **Wynkyn de Worde:** Crystal, pp. 136, 139.

21 **our modern word *sneeze*:** Merriam-Webster, Inc. *The Merriam-Webster New Book of Word Histories.* Merriam-Webster, 1991, p. 436.

Chapter 3: The Faẏer, Sun, and Holi Ghoost

22 **"An intelligent child":** "Books: G.B.S. On a Joy Ride." *Time*, 1 Nov. 1948.

22 **Copernicus's heliocentric theory:** Kowalczyk, Ernest. "How Copernicus Put the Sun at the Center of the Cosmos." *History*, 9 Apr. 2019, www.nationalgeographic.com/history/history-magazine/article/astronomy-theories-nicolaus-copernicus.

22 **Europeans are tasting chocolate for the first time:** Hart, Hugh. "July 7, 1550: Europeans Discover Chocolate." *Wired*, 7 July 2010, www.wired.com/2010/07/0707chocolate-introduced-europe/.

22 **tutor to the twelve-year-old King:** "Sir John Cheke." The Tudor Society, 16 June 2016, www.tudorsociety.com/john-cheke/.

22 **seven-point plan:** Strype, John. *The Life of the Learned Sir John Cheke, Kt., first instructor, afterwards secretary of state, to King Edward VI.: a Work*

wherein many remarkable Points of History . . . are brought to light. Oxford, Clarendon Press, 1821, p. 161.

22 **Remove the silent *E*:** Strype, John. *The Life of the Learned Sir John Cheke, Kt.* 1705, p. 211.

23 **"of toungues, of the scripture, of philosophie and all liberal sciences":** Howitt, William. *John Cassell's Illustrated History of England.* Cassell, Petter and Galpin, 1857, p. 298.

23 **"If English spelling was a mess":** Crystal, p. 156.

24 **The word *sissors* received:** Crystal, pp. 159–160.

24 **"Our own tung should be written cleane and pure":** Shariatmadari, David. "Why It's Time to Stop Worrying about the Decline of the English Language." *The Guardian*, 15 Aug. 2019, www.theguardian.com/science/2019/aug/15/why-its-time-to-stop-worrying-about-the-decline-of-the-english-language.

25 **"Enter in bi a narrow gaat":** Cheke, John. *The Gospel According to Saint Matthew and Part of the First Chapter of the Gospel According to Saint Mark.* Cambridge, J. and J. J. Deighton, 1843, p. 39.

25 **landed behind bars:** Strype, p. 94.

25 **officer of arms:** Hart, John. *John Hart's Works on English Orthography and Pronunciation* [1551, 1569, 1570]. Uppsala, Almqvist & Wiksell, 1963.

25 **"To use as many letters":** Wesley, John. "Rhetorical Delivery for Renaissance English: Voice, Gesture, Emotion, and the Sixteenth-Century Vernacular Turn." *Renaissance Quarterly*, vol. 68, no. 4, 2015, pp. 1265–96.

26 **"Hierbei iu mę persęv":** Carey, Stan. "A Brief History of English Spelling Reform." *History Today*, www.historytoday.com/brief-history-english-spelling-reform.

26 **he wrote *moond*:** Marsh, George Perkins. *The Origin and History of the English Language.* C. Scribner, 1862, p. 521.

28 **"nothing but the traditional spelling":** Jespersen, Otto. *John Hart's Pronunciation of English.* Heidelberg, 1907, pp. 19–20.

28 **"whipping fits":** Lewalski, Barbara K. *The Life of John Milton.* John Wiley & Sons, 15 Apr. 2008, p. 8.

28 **"cant speech":** Hitchings, Henry. *The Language Wars.* Farrar, Straus and Giroux, 25 Oct. 2011, p. 128.

29 **slicing and dicing:** Frazier, Walt. New York Knicks, MSG Network.

29 **A trained musicologist:** Pruett, James. "Charles Butler—Musician, Grammarian, Apiarist." *The Musical Quarterly*, vol. 49, no. 4, 1963, pp. 498–509.

29 **the buzz of a beehive:** Butler, Charls. *Đe Feminin' Monarķi', or Đe histori of bee's.* Oxford, William Turner, 1634.

31 ***canoe* and *maize*:** Mencken, H. L. *The American Language.* New York, Alfred A. Knopf, 1936, p. 3.

Chapter 4: O Spare, We Beseech You, Our Mother-Tongue!

32 "I am willing to love all mankind": Martin, Peter. "Escaping Samuel Johnson." *The Paris Review*, 30 May 2019, www.theparisreview.org/blog/2019/05/30/escaping-samuel-johnson/.

32 "Belittle! What an expression!": Keyes, Ralph. "Word Wars." *The Hidden History of Coined Words*. New York, 2021; online edition, Oxford Academic, 22 July 2021.

32 *eggnog*: Dias, Elizabeth. "A Brief History of Eggnog." *Time*, 21 December 2011, time.com/3957265/history-of-eggnog/.

33 culinary treats like *cookies*: Kurlansky, Mark. *The Big Oyster: History on the Half Shell*. United Kingdom, Random House Publishing Group, 2007, p. 66.

33 the needs of a new land and new people: Mencken, pp. 104–110.

33 "a race of convicts": Boswell, James. *The Life of Samuel Johnson, LL.D.* United Kingdom, J. Richardson, 1823, p. 316.

33 townhouse overlooking Gough Square: "Dr Johnson's House Home Page." www.drjohnsonshouse.org/.

34 "The books he used for this purpose": Newton, A. Edward. "The Ghosts of Gough Square." *The Atlantic*, June 1925.

34 Carl Linnaeus in Sweden: Beil, Karen Magnuson. *What Linnaeus Saw: A Scientist's Quest to Name Every Living Thing*. United States, Norton, 2019.

34 doubled the *L* in *uphill*: *Handbook of Simplified Spelling*. United States, Simplified Spelling Board, 1920, p. 7.

34 Most scientific plant names: Linnaeus, Carl, *Species Plantarum*. Stockholm, Laurentius Salvius, 1753.

35 He declared that a word: Wolman, David. "There's Never a Last Word on Spelling." *Los Angeles Times*, 27 May 2009, www.latimes.com/archives/la-xpm-2009-may-27-oe-wolman27-story.html.

36 ten-by-eighteen-inch folio ones: Christianson, Scott and Colin Salter. *100 Books That Changed the World*. New York, Universe Publishing, 2018.

36 as much as a car tire: *Weight and Density of Tires*. Global Recycling Equipment, globalrecyclingequipment.com/weight-and-density-of-tires/.

36 Samuel Johnson suffered from Tourette's syndrome: Lynch, Jack. *The Oxford Handbook of Samuel Johnson*. Oxford University Press, 22 Sept. 2022, pp. 14–15.

36 Five pages alone: Hitchings, Henry. "An A-Z of English (without the X)." *The Guardian*, 1 Apr. 2005, theguardian.com/books/2005/apr/02/classics.wordsandlanguage1.

37 It was now 1786 . . . hall in Philadelphia: Kornfeld, Eve. *Creating an American Culture, 1775–1800: A Brief History with Documents*. Boston, Bedford/St. Martin's, 2001, p. 21.

37 "squeaky": Micklethwait, David. *Noah Webster and the American Dictionary*. Jefferson, North Carolina, McFarland & Company, 2005, p. 97.

37 "language, as well as government": Kornfeld, p. 23.

38 a former reserve militiaman: Kendall, Joshua. *The Forgotten Founding Father*. Penguin, 2010, p. 2.

38 25 million copies in his lifetime: Jones, Keith Marshall. *The Farms of Farmingville*. 2001, p. 405.

38 a penny royalty on each: Kendall, p. 227.

38 to teach his granddaughter how to read: Landrigan, Leslie. "Noah Webster Cures the Blues with a Spelling Book." *New England Historical Society*, 16 Oct. 2015, newenglandhistoricalsociety.com/noah-webster-cures-the-blues-with-a-spelling-book/.

38 "There seems to be an inclination": Logan, Conrad T. "Noah Webster's Influence on American Spelling." *The Elementary English Review*, vol. 14, no. 1, 1937, pp. 18–21. *JSTOR*, http://www.jstor.org/stable/41380997.

39 Marquis de Chastellux: Dillard, Joey L. *Perspectives on American English*. Paris, Mouton Publishers, 1980, p. 19.

39 "Hebrew substituted to the English": Lepore, Jill. *A Is for American: Letters and Other Characters in the Newly United States*. New York, Vintage Books, 2003, p. 22.

40 "Our ideas are so nearly similar": Lepore, p. 35.

40 "as few new characters": Mencken, p. 381.

40 "It has been observed by all writers": Webster, Noah. *Dissertations on the English Language*. Boston, I. Thomas and Company, 1789, pp. 393–394.

41 "Noah Cobweb": Micklethwait, p. 121.

41 the Friendly Club: Walker Read, Allen. "The Philological Society of New York, 1788." *American Speech*, April 1934.

42 "Thus *greef*": Webster, p. 395.

43 four hundred of his own dollars: Kendall, p. 163.

43 "I suspect . . . pruning Knife": Skeel, Emily Ellsworth Ford (ed.). *Notes on the Life of Noah Webster*. United States, Priv. Print., 1912, p. 288.

43 "I join with you . . . mode of spelling": Skeel, p. 297.

43 "proposal for reformation": Lepore, p. 39.

44 "peculiar and unsightly": Lepore, p. 39.

44 "There iz no alternativ": Micklethwait, p. 103.

44 "must strike every reflecting mind with a sense of the mildness": Lepore, p. 39.

44 "I ain't yet quite ripe": Lepore, p. 6.

44 nearly outsold the Bible: Adams, Michael. "The Making of American English Dictionaries" in Ogilvie, S. (ed.). *The Cambridge Companion to English Dictionaries*. Cambridge Companions to Literature. Cambridge University Press, 2020, pp. 157–169.

44 local schoolmasters for jobs: Kendall, p. 139.

44 "sold for wrapping paper": Skeel, p. 309.

45 "a pusillanimous, half-begotten, self-dubbed patriot": Lepore, p. 58.

45 "a toad in the service of sans-culottism," "a great fool, and a barefaced liar," "a spiteful viper," "a prostitute wretch": Mencken, H. L. *The American Language: An Inquiry Into the Development of English in the United States.* New York, Alfred A. Knopf, 1945, p. 22.

45 "a maniacal pedant": Doll, Jen. "Noah Webster, Father of the American Dictionary, Was Unemployable." *The Atlantic*, 16 Oct. 2012, www.theatlantic.com/culture/archive/2012/10/noah-webster-father-american-dictionary-was-unemployable/322508/.

45 "a dunghill cock of faction": Lepore, p. 58.

45 "an incurable lunatic": Ellis, Joseph J. *After the Revolution: Profiles of Early American Culture.* W. W. Norton & Company, 17 Mar. 2002, p. 199.

45 proposed to resurrect George Washington's corpse: Klein, Christopher. "The Bizarre Plan to Bring George Washington back to Life." *History*, 13 Feb. 2024, www.history.com/news/george-washington-death-revival-plan.

45 1792 essay competition: Lepore, p. 44.

Chapter 5: A Nue Merrykin Dikshunary

47 "Avoid the fashionable impropriety": Wesley, John. *The Works of the Late Reverend John Wesley, A.M. (Volume V).* United States, Waugh and Mason, 1835, p. 225.

47 Roget would count his steps: Kendall, p. 106.

47 That June: Kendall, p. 231.

48 *The Gazette of the United States*: Lepore, p. 113.

49 first six years of his project on the letters *A* and *B*: Kendall, pp. 285–298.

49 "When I had come to the last word": Kendall, p. 298.

49 *psychology, phophorescent*) . . . {*savings-bank, re-organize*: Kendall, p. 304.

49 an early abridged edition: Webster, Noah. *A Compendious Dictionary of the English Language.* New Haven, Sidney's Press, 1806.

49 cost $1.50: Kendall, p. 245.

51 Henry Alford: Beal, Joan C. *English in Modern Times.* London, Taylor & Francis, 2014, p. 118.

51 "To the Last of the Vowels": Kendall, p. 283.

52 mortgage his home to finance a new edition: "The History of Webster's Dictionary." *Websters Dictionary 1828*, webstersdictionary1828.com/NoahWebster.

52 "I desire . . .": Snyder, K. Alan. *Defining Noah Webster: A Spiritual Biography.* Fairfax, VA, Allegiance Press, 2002, p. 278.

52 "the age of dictionaries": Crystal, p. 201.

53 James Ruggles: Ruggles, James. *A Universal Language.* Cincinnati, M'Calla and Davis, 1829.

53 "Something New": Barton, Michael. *Something New: Comprising a New and Perfect Alphabet Containing 40 Distinct Characters . . . .* United States, 1830–1833.

53 *Esperanto*: Patterson, Robert, et al. "The Decline and Fall of Esperanto: Lessons for Standards Committees." *Journal of the American Medical Informatics Association,* Nov.–Dec. 1999.

54 **Auguste Thibaudin**: Thibaudin, Auguste. *A. Thibaudin's Proposed Original System for a Radical, Universal and Philosophical Reform in the Spelling of Languages.* United Kingdom, 1842.

55 **"phrenotypics"**: Beniowski, Bartłomiej. *Phrenotypics; or, a New Method of Studying and Committing to Memory Languages, Sciences, and Arts.* United Kingdom, 1842.

56 an **"ABOMINABLE ABSURDITY"**: Beniowski, Bartłomiej. *The Anti-Absurd Or Phrenotypic English Pronouncing & Orthographical Dictionary.* London, T. Hatton, 1844.

57 **"The piece of furniture usually called table"**: Beniowski, *The Anti-Absurd,* p. 6.

58 **"Every man short of an idiot"**: Beniowski, *The Anti-Absurd,* p. 10.

58 **"Sailaid"**: Beniowski, *The Anti-Absurd,* p. 16.

60 **"Thus: the word *man*"**: Beniowski, *The Anti-Absurd,* p. 8.

60 record for **"most pi places memorized"**: *Guinness World Records 2018.* Macmillan, 2017, p. 84.

Part II: Illinois, 1859

61 **a peculiar envelope**: Baron, Dennis. "A Spelling Reformer Writes to Mr. Lincoln." June 2009, https://blogs.illinois.edu/view/25/6643.

62 **Lincoln reads aloud**: Leacock, Stephen. "The Humorist Who Made Lincoln Laugh." *The New York Times,* 22 Apr. 1934.

Chapter 6: The Phunny Phellows

63 **"Essa on the Muel bi Josh Billings"**: *The Literature of America and Our Favorite Authors.* United States, Irving, 1898, p. 352.

64 **"Dont be diskouraged"**: Billings, Josh. *Old Farmer's Allminax, 1870–1879.* United States, G. W. Dillingham Company, 1902, p. 29.

64 **"The yung female"**: Billings, p. 16.

65 **critics began grouping another author with them**: *Phunny Phellows: Mark Twain, Josh Billings, Robt. Burdette, Artemus Ward, and Others.* United States, Rhodes & McClure, 1885.

66 **"Affurisms"**: Billings, Josh. *Josh Billings: His Book of Sayings.* London, John Camden Hotten, 1869.

66 **"OK"**: "Ok | Etymology, Origin and Meaning of the Name Ok by Etymonline." www.etymonline.com/word/OK.

66   "What is't that ails the people, Joe?": Metcalf, Allan. *OK: The Improbable Story of America's Greatest Word*. Oxford University Press, 2010, p. 50.

68   first stand-up comedians: Federman, Wayne. *The History of Stand-Up: From Mark Twain to Dave Chappelle*. 2021, pp. 14–16.

69   "Shood it be my fate 2 perish": *Yankee Drolleries: The Most Celebrated Works of the Best American Humourists*. United Kingdom, Chatto and Windus, 1876, p. 15.

Chapter 7: The Deseret Alphabet

70   "The incarnations of the Hindoo gods": Falzone, Catherine. "The Mormon Alphabet Experiment | New-York Historical Society." 21 May 2014, www.nyhistory.org/blogs/mormon-alphabet-experiment.

70   digging irrigation ditches: Turner, John. *Brigham Young: Pioneer Prophet*. Cambridge, MA, The Belknap Press of Harvard University Press, 2012, p. 168.

70   "The English language": Stucki, Beau. "The Deseret Alphabet, a 38-Letter Writing System Developed by Mormons." *Atlas Obscura*, 21 June 2017, www.atlasobscura.com/articles/deseret-alphabet-mormon.

71   *Plea for Phonotypy and Phonography*: Zimmer, Ben. "Ghoti." *The New York Times*, 25 June 2010.

71   "The child is perplexed": Pugh, Jeremy. "The Deseret Alphabet: Brigham Young's Linguistic Experiment." *Salt Lake Magazine*, 18 Apr. 2024, www.saltlakemagazine.com/the-deseret-alphabet/.

71   56 wives and 57 children: Babington, Charles. "Relative Unknowns Also Stand Tall at U.S. Capitol." *Arkansas Democrat-Gazette*. 22 Sept. 2013.

72   as he saw the steam engine: Morgan, Dale. *Dale Morgan on the Mormons*. University of Oklahoma Press, 2012, p. 169.

72   "We want a new kind of alphabet": Beesley, Kenneth. *Typesetting the Deseret Alphabet with L a T E X and METAFONT*. TeX, XML, and Digital Typography. *Lecture Notes in Computer Science*. Vol. 25, 2004.

73   "These characters are much more simple": Christensen, Danielle. "Deseret Alphabet Created by Mormon Pioneers is Over 150 Years Old." *Deseret News*, 22 Jun. 2017, www.deseret.com/2017/6/22/20614613/deseret-alphabet-created-by-mormon-pioneers-is-over-150-years-old/.

74   to make Deseret the 31st state: Dorn, Nathan. "The State of What?? U.S. States That Never Made the Cut." In Custodia Legis: Law Librarians of Congress. 10 May 2012, blogs.loc.gov/law/2012/05/the-state-of-what-u-s-states-that-never-made-the-cut/.

74   "It will be the means of introducing uniformity": Weeks, Andy. *Forgotten Tales of Utah*. Arcadia Publishing, 2017, p. 28.

74   The word *bee* in *spelling bee*: Devlin, Thomas Moore. "The Buzzy History of Spelling Bees." *Babbel Magazine*, 6 July 2021, www.babbel.com/en/magazine/history-of-spelling-bees.

75 chased by pitchfork mobs: Bitton, Davis and Thomas G. Alexander. *The A to Z of Mormonism.* Scarecrow Press, 2009, p. xxxi.

75 first official British convert to Mormonism: Watt, Ronald G. *Mormon Passage of George D. Watt.* Utah State University Press, 2009.

76 lop off all "ascenders" and "descenders": Beesley, p. 81.

76 $20,000 on its first sets: Bray, Alyssa. "The Deseret Alphabet—Brigham Young's Most Expensive Failed Experiment." *Utah Stories,* 13 Dec. 2017, utahstories.com/2017/12/the-deseret-alphabet-brigham-youngs-most-expensive-failed-experiment/.

76 custom ordered from St. Louis: Beesley, pp. 81–90.

76 $5 million over the next several years: Bray, "The Deseret Alphabet."

77 the war remained (mostly) cold: Roberts, David. "The Brink of War." *Smithsonian Magazine,* June 2008.

77 In 1869, the Union Pacific railroad: "Union Pacific in Utah, 1868–1899." 2019, utahrails.net/up/up-in-ut-1868–1899.php.

77 Watt joined Godbe's sectarian offshoot: Watt, p. 7.

77 "On ascertaining the locality or route of the troops": Linn, William Alexander. *The Story of the Mormons.* United States, Macmillan, 1902, p. 835.

77 By polygamous entanglement: "Isaac Decker's Families." freepages.rootsweb.com/~timbaloo/history/IsaacDecker/pages/families.htm.

Chapter 8: The Charge of Suffragist Shorthanders

79 "I attribiut mei helth": Baker, Alfred. *The Life of Sir Isaac Pitman.* London, I. Pitman & Sons, 1909, p. 312.

79 Britain's Vegetarian Society: Baker, p. 311.

79 After quitting alcohol and meat: Baker, pp. 28–29.

79 Swedenborgian mysticism: Baker, p. 301.

80 Pitman quit school at 13: Reed, Thomas Allen. *A Biography of Isaac Pitman (Inventor of Phonography).* London and Sydney, Griffith, Farran, Okeden and Welsh, 1890, p. 2.

80 12-hour clerking shift: Baker, p. 8.

81 His childhood music teacher: Baker, p. 9.

81 "two loves": Reed, p. 6.

81 house organist in the Conigree Chapel: Reed, p. 97.

81 "By means of the principle of writing words in position": Pitman, Isaac. *Shorthand Instructor: A Complete Exposition of Isaac Pitman's System of Phonography.* New York, I. Pitman & Sons, 1909, p. 179.

82 "Pitman's phonographic alphabet looks rather like": Bryson, p. 121.

82 Tironian shorthand: Daniels, Peter T. *The World's Writing Systems.* New York, Oxford University Press, 1996, pp. 807–808.

82 Gurney shorthand: Vice, John. "Charles Dickens and Gurney's Shorthand: 'That Savage Stenographic Mystery.'" *Language & History,* 2018, pp. 77–93.

82 **Gregg shorthand:** Hollier, Dennis. "How to Write 225 Words per Minute with a Pen." *The Atlantic*, 24 June 2014, www.theatlantic. com/technology/archive/2014/06/yeah-i-still-use-shorthand-and-a-smartpen/373281/.

83 **Until the 1860s:** "Stenography in the Late 19th Century." *History of Sound Recording Technology*, recordinghistory.org/the-history-of-sound-recording/culture/men-women-and-sound-recording/stenography-in-the-late-19th-century/.

83 **Maud Slater's Shorthand and Typing School:** "Blue Plaque to Commemorate 100 Years of Women's Suffrage." *Arts University Plymouth*, 8 Jan. 2019, www.aup.ac.uk/posts/blue-plaque-to-commemorate-100-years-of-womens-suffrage. Accessed 7 June 2024.

84 **"freedom dress":** Chrisman-Campbell, Kimberly. "When American Suffragists Tried to 'Wear the Pants.'" *The Atlantic*, 12 June 2019, www. theatlantic.com/entertainment/archive/2019/06/american-suffragists-bloomers-pants-history/591484/.

84 **"the whole plan in its wonderful simplicity":** *The Phonographic World*, Vol. 10. New York, E.N. Miner, 1895, p. 119.

84 **Burnz, with a Z:** *The Phonographic World*, p. 123.

84 **Foneta:** Burnz, Channing. *In Memoriam, Eliza Boardman Burnz*. New York, Burnz & Company, 1906, p. 29.

85 **a genuine spelling rampage:** *The Phonographic World*, p. 119.

85 **Burnz School of Shorthand:** *Democrat and Chronicle*. Rochester, New York, 12 May 1889, p. 4.

85 **one memorable publicity stunt:** *School: Devoted to the Public Schools and Educational Interests*. Vol. 31. United States, School News Company, 1919, p. 470.

85 **"The Association for the Total Suppression of White Hats!":** Durbach, Nadja. *Bodily Matters: The Anti-Vaccination Movement in England, 1853–1907*. Durham, Duke University Press, 2005, p. 42.

86 **"And shall not we the railroad-writing scheme":** *Comstock's Phonetic Magazine*, Vol. 1. United States, A. Comstock, 1846, p. 34.

Chapter 9: Frĕdum Speling

88 **"Dianism":** Nickell, William. "The Twain Shall Be of One Mind: Tolstoy in 'Leag' with Eliza Burnz and Henry Parkhurst." *Tolstoy Studies Journal*, New York, 1 Jan 1993, p. 123.

88 **"man needs fyzical relief from a continūus secretion":** Parkhurst, Henry M. *Diana: A Psycho-Fyziological Essay on Sexual Relations, for Married Men and Women*. New York, Burnz & Company, 1882, p. 26.

88 **the "ferst fonetik pêper publisht in America":** "Our Language: Devoted to Speling-Riform Niuz and Dhi Diskushun ov Kweschunz in Alfabetiks." Vol. 2, No. 11. New York, Feb. 1893.

89 "freedom of the affections": "The Free Lovers: Practical Operation of the Free-Love League in the City of New-York." *The New-York Daily Times*, 10 Oct. 1855, pp. 1–2.

89 "the implicit following of every freak of fancy": "Free Love and Spiritualism" (Letter to the Editor). *The New-York Daily Times*, 12 Oct. 1855.

89 Taylor's Saloon: "A Rich Development. Free Love Nowhere. The 'Club' Broken Up by the Police . . ." *The New-York Daily Times*, 19 Oct. 1855.

90 series of educational classes: "'The Club' Described by One of its Members" (Letter to the Editor). *The New-York Daily Tribune*, 13 Oct. 1855.

90 a plan to liberate Texas's slaves: Sussman, Mark. "The Plan to Sell Texas to Great Britain." *JSTOR Daily*, 7 Nov. 2018, daily.jstor.org/plan-sell-texas-great-britain/.

90 "Examine them": *The Phonographic Magazine*, Vol. 7. Cincinnati, The Phonographic Institute Co., 1893, p. 26.

91 postbellum years teaching: *The Phonographic World*, p. 120.

93 collecting and preserving spirituals, plantation songs: "'Wishing I Were There'—Time Travel to Hampton Institute Graduation, 1875." *American Realities with Bill Youngs*, 28 Sept. 2013, www.americanrealities.com/home-page/wishing-i-were-there-time-travel-to-hampton-institute-graduation-1875.

93 founded a primary school: Washington, Booker T., and Louis R. Harlan (ed.). *The Booker T. Washington Papers. Vol. 2, 1860–89.* Chicago, University of Illinois Press, 1972, p. 55.

93 "Mr. Towe spoke for his rase": Ackermann, Marsha E. *How Do You Spell Ruzevelt? A History of Spelling in America Today and Yesterday.* Archway Publishing, 2014, p. 91.

94 the leading pro-Lincoln newspaper: Tucker, Spencer C. *American Civil War: The Definitive Encyclopedia and Document Collection.* United States, Bloomsbury Publishing, 2013.

94 Angelina and Thomas Grimké: Lerner, Gerda. *The Grimké Sisters from South Carolina: Pioneers for Women's Rights and Abolition.* New York, Oxford University Press, 1998, p. 83.

94 Cornelius Larison: "Dr. C. W. Larison and His 'Fonic Publishing House.'" *The History of the Book.* 4 Mar. 2020. https://web.colby.edu/bookhistory2020/2020/03/04/dr-c-w-larison-and-his-fonic-publishing-house-a-19th-century-kickstarter/.

96 sad legacy of the whimsical *K*: Pound, Louise. "The Kraze for 'K.'" *American Speech: A Quarterly of Linguistic Usage*, Oct. 1925, pp. 43–44.

Chapter 10: The Sentenial Ekspozishun

97 "The greatest obstacl to reform": March, Francis. *The Spelling Reform.* Washington, Government Printing Office, 1893, p. 15.

97   **the latest in gadgetry and innovation:** Olson, Emily. "America's First Tradeshow: The Centennial Exposition of 1876." *Exhibit City News*, 29 Sept. 2022, exhibitcitynews.com/americas-first-tradeshow-the-centennial-exposition-of-1876/.

97   **"International Convention for the Amendment of English Orthografy":** Spelling Reform Association. *Proceedings of the International Convention for the Amendment of the English Orthography*, 1876.

99   **"Takigrafy":** Lindsley, David. *The Hand-Book of Takigrafy: Giving Briefly the Principles of the Contracted Style, and Designed for the Use of Amanuenses and Verbatim Reporter—with an Introductory Chapter on the Simple Style* Chicago, D. Kimball, 1879.

99   **"Analytic Orthography":** Haldeman, Samuel Stehman. *Analytic Orthography: An Investigation of the Sounds of the Voice, and Their Alphabetic Notation.* United States, American Philosophical Society, 1859.

99   **influenced Charles Darwin:** "Samuel Haldeman." Haldeman Mansion Preservation Society. www.haldeman-mansion.org/samuel-haldeman.

99   **"I never pursue one branch of science":** "Sketch of Professor S. S. Haldeman." *Popular Science Monthly*, Vol. 21, July 1882.

100 **living with the Creek Indians of Florida:** Spelling Reform Association, p. 11.

100 **rain poured and temperatures approached 90 degrees:** "Historical Weather Data for Philadelphia." The Franklin Institute. fi.edu/en/science-and-education/collection/historical-weather-data-philadelphia.

100 **The Alfabet ov Least Rezistanç:** *Proceedings of the International Convention for the Amendment of the English Orthography*, p. 4.

102 **"Never before in the history of the language":** "Buletin ov the Speling Reform Asoshiashun." No. 1. Boston, April 1877.

102 **Dewey invented the book classification method:** Glazer, Gwen. "Which Dewey Decimal Number Are You?" *The New York Public Library*, 10 Dec. 2018, www.nypl.org/blog/2018/12/10/dewey-quiz.

102 **Dewey became a simplified speller at age 12:** *The Journal of Library History, Philosophy and Comparative Librarianship*, Vol. 3. United States, School of Library Science, 1968, p. 331.

102 **the Library Bureau:** Jacobs, Frank. "Dewey Decimal: The Sorting System That Revolutionized Libraries." *Big Think*, 8 Apr. 2024, bigthink.com/strange-maps/dewey-decimal/.

103 **"Speling Skolars agree":** *Melvil Dewey, His Enduring Presence in Librarianship*. Colorado, Libraries Unlimited Incorporated, 1978, p. 225.

103 **shortened his name from Melville Dewey:** Jacobs, Frank. "Dewey Decimal: The Sorting System That Revolutionized Libraries." *Big Think*, 8 Apr. 2024, bigthink.com/strange-maps/dewey-decimal/.

103 **"Sum day, dear Amherst":** "Melvil Dewey, the Womanizing OCD Librarian Who Organized the Olympics." *New England Historical*

Society, 11 Apr. 2021, newenglandhistoricalsociety.com/melvil-dewey-the-womanizing-ocd-librarian-who-organized-the-olympics/.

104 **Dewey tried to do everything in tens:** Kendall, Joshua. "Melvil Dewey, Compulsive Innovator." *American Libraries Magazine*, 24 Mar. 2014, americanlibrariesmagazine.org/2014/03/24/melvil-dewey-compulsive-innovator/.

104 **proud to share a birthday with the metric system:** López, Vladimir. "How the French Revolution Created the Metric System." *National Geographic*, 10 Sept. 2020.

104 **"The air is ful of hope":** "Bulletin of the Spelling Reform Association." No. 14. Boston, Sept. 1879.

104 **"Last yīr wī tōct ov hop":** "Buletin ov dhi Speling Reform Asoshiēshun." No. 16. Boston, July 1880.

104 **Charles Darwin and Alfred, Lord Tennyson:** *The Athenaeum: A Journal of Literature, Science, the Fine Arts, Music, and the Drama.* London, J. Francis, 1880, p. 69.

106 **its founding in 1857:** Holcomb, Sabrina. "History of NEA." National Education Association, 26 May 2021, www.nea.org/about-nea/mission-vision-values/history-nea.

106 **"Twelv Words":** Simplified Spelling Board. *Handbook of Simplified Spelling.* New York, 1920, p. 14.

106 **a "feeler":** Simplified Spelling Board, *Simplified Spelling.* Washington, D.C., Government Printing Office, 1906, p. 25.

107 **two separate transcripts:** American Association of School Administrators. *Proceedings of the Annual Meeting.* University of Chicago Press, 1899, p. 40. *Journal of Education,* Vol. 53, No. 11. Boston and Chicago, 1901, p. 164.

108 **the NEA voted:** *Proceedings of the Annual Meeting,* p. 5.

108 **"The Spelling Reform Association had in its ranks":** *Handbook of Simplified Spelling,* p. 14.

Part III: Washington, D.C., 1906

109 **Gridiron Dinner:** Dunn, Arthur Wallace. *Gridiron Nights: Humorous and Satirical Views of Politics and Statesmen as Presented by the Famous Dining Club.* New York, Frederick A. Stokes Company, 1915, p. 171.

109 **filet mignon and cherrystone oysters:** *The Simpler Speller and Gridiron Dikshunary.* Washington, D.C., W. F. Roberts Company, 1906.

Chapter 11: Ruzevelt Speling

111 **"The chief obstacle":** Wiegand, Wayne. *Irrepressible Reformer: A Biography of Melvil Dewey.* Chicago and London, American Library Association, 1990, p. 247.

111   **Florence Woodworth and May Seymour:** Kendall, "Melvil Dewey, Compulsive Innovator."

111   **Adelaide Hasse:** Beck, Clare. *The New Woman as Librarian.* Scarecrow Press, 31 Aug. 2006, p. 103.

112   **during a 10-day Alaska cruise:** Katz, Brigit. "Melvil Dewey's Name Stripped from Top Library Award." *Smithsonian Magazine,* 28 June 2019.

112   **for his open anti-Semitism:** Wiegand, Wayne. "'Jew Attack': The Story behind Melvil Dewey's Resignation as New York State Librarian in 1905." *American Jewish History,* Vol. 83, No. 3, 1995, pp. 359–79.

112   **$15,000 annual endowment:** Mencken, p. 400.

112   **offices on Madison Avenue:** *Handbook of Simplified Spelling,* p. 40.

114   **"I am here to make an appeal":** "Address at the Annual Dinner of the Associated Press, at the Waldorf-Astoria." 18 Sept. 1906.

115   **freshman class of the Simplified Spelling Board:** "Carnegie Assaults the Spelling Book." *The New York Times,* 12 Mar. 1906.

115   **"Simplification by omission":** Lang, Ossian (ed.). *The School Journal,* Vol. 72, No. 18. New York and New Jersey, 5 May 1906.

116   **"I will use in my correspondence":** *School and Home Education,* Vol. 25, No. 10, June 1906.

116   **The Board of Superintendents recommended:** *Handbook of Simplified Spelling,* p. 21.

117   **"Fonetic Speling Assosiashun of Kolumbia University":** *The New York Times,* 23 Mar. 1906, p. 9.

117   **directed his stenographer to recast the voice of the president:** Wolman, David. *Firsthand: A Decade of Reporting.* Firsthand Publishing Group, 2014.

118   **"My dear Mr. Stillings":** Brands, H. W. *The Selected Letters of Theodore Roosevelt.* Rowman & Littlefield Publishers, 1951, pp. 433–444.

119   **"laughing stock":** Daugherty, Greg. "Teddy Roosevelt's Bold (but Doomed) Battle to Change American Spelling." *History,* 9 Mar. 2018, www.history.com/news/theodore-roosevelt-spelling-controversy.

119   **"not in 'Karnegi,' [or] 'Ruzvelt'":** "The Gazette Will Be Printed in English." *The Worcester Evening Gazette,* 27 Aug. 1906.

119   **"Mr. Andru Karnegi":** Horobin, Simon. *Does Spelling Matter?* Oxford, United Kingdom, Oxford University Press, 2013, p. 203.

123   **approved the resolution, 142 to 24:** *The Independent,* Vol. 61, No. 3029. New York, 20 Dec. 1906.

125   **"look at his pestiferous simple spelling":** Ackermann, p. 82.

Chapter 12: Ye Olde or the Nu?

126   **the streets were decorated:** "Colored Girl Wins Big Spelling Bee." *The New York Times,* 30 June 1908, p. 7.

126 Spelling bees have existed in America: Sealfon, Rebecca. "The History of the Spelling Bee." *Smithsonian Magazine.* May 2019, www.smithsonianmag. com/arts-culture/history-spelling-bee-180971916/.

127 Were Carnegie and his Board pulling the strings?: Harbaugh, William Henry. *Power and Responsibility: The Life and Times of Theodore Roosevelt.* New York, Farrar, Straus, and Cudahy, 1961, p. 246.

128 "It would probably make [the contest] more exciting": *The Mansfield News,* 7 July 1908, p. 4.

128 the "freakish idea": *Pittsburgh Post-Gazette,* 19 Apr. 1908, p. 12.

128 refused to spell *honest* with an *H*: *The Indiana Weekly Messenger,* 25 Mar. 1908, p. 8.

128 refusing her first-place prize: *The Evansville Journal,* 24 Jan. 1908, p. 8.

129 tricky English words like *umbrella*: *American Journal of Education,* Vol. 17, No. 1. St. Louis and Milwaukee, Sept. 1908.

130 Marie Bolden: Albeck-Ripka, Livia. "A Black Girl Won the 1908 Spelling Bee. Her Family Is Searching for Her Medal." *The New York Times,* 1 June 2023.

131 "Several of the New Orleans children": "Put Aside Race Prejudice." *The Cincinnati Enquirer,* 30 June 1908, p. 3.

131 school board would later censure him: Karst, James. "P-R-E-J-U-D-I-C-E and S-C-A-N-D-A-L at the 1908 National Spelling Bee." *The Times-Picayune,* 23 Apr. 2017.

131 *Restaurant* turned out to be a stumbling block: "Negro Girls Wins Spelling Bee." *The South Bend Tribune,* 30 June 1908, p. 3.

132 Erie finished fourth: *American Journal of Education,* Vol. 17, No. 1. St. Louis and Milwaukee, Sept. 1908.

132 "The convention was swept with a storm of applause": "Our Colored Society." *The Oskaloosa Herald,* 9 July 1908, p. 6.

132 first Black person invited to dine at the White House: Davis, Deborah. *Guest of Honor: Booker T. Washington, Theodore Roosevelt, and the White House Dinner That Shocked a Nation.* United Kingdom, Atria Books, 2012, p. 1.

Chapter 13: Our Drunken Alphabet

134 "The da ma ov koars kum": Twain, Mark. *What is Man? and Other Essays.* London, Chatto & Windus, 1919, p. 262.

134 "a uniform and arbitrary way of spelling words": "Ours Is a Mongrel Language." *PRINT Magazine,* 3 Jan. 2012, www.printmag.com/daily-heller/ours-is-a-mongrel-language/.

135 "I disrespect our orthography most heartily": Twain, Mark. *Autobiography of Mark Twain: Volume 2: Complete and Authoritative Edition.* Berkeley, California, University of California Press, 2013, p. 274.

135 "Maybe it is wrong for me": Mancini, Mark. "11 Historical Figures Who Were Really Bad at Spelling." Mental Floss, 30 Aug. 2018, www.mentalfloss. com/article/51224/11-historical-figures-who-were-really-bad-spelling.

135 to write 10 magazine pages: Twain, Mark. *Great Speeches by Mark Twain*. New York, Dover Publications, 2013, pp. 133–134.

136 "I never write 'metropolis'": *Great Speeches by Mark Twain*, pp. 133–134.

136 "a kindly feeling, a friendly feeling": *What is Man?* p. 256.

137 "drunken old alphabet": *What is Man?* p. 262.

137 "invented by a drunken thief": *Great Speeches by Mark Twain*, p. 163.

137 "For I do love revolutions and violence": Twain, Mark and Paul Fatout (ed.). *Mark Twain Speaks for Himself*. Indiana, Purdue University Press, 1997, p. 212.

137 "Simplified spelling is all right": "Ours Is a Mongrel Language," 2012.

138 "There's not a vowel in [our alphabet] with a definite value": *Great Speeches by Mark Twain*, p. 163.

138 satirized his own Simplified Spelling Board: Twain, Mark. *Letters From the Earth*. Harper & Row, 1962, pp. 159–164.

Chapter 14: Hi Soesiety

141 raised his annual endowment to $25,000: Mencken, p. 400.

141 "Please note, not one Eastern paper": "Carnegie General Donations, Gifts and Grants to Simplified Spelling Board, New York, N.Y." Carnegie Corporation Oral History Project, dlc.library.columbia.edu/carnegie/cul:vmcvdncmfr.

142 ten Londoners gathered at the Holborn Restaurant: Wolman, David. *Righting the Mother Tongue*. HarperCollins, 2008, p. 121.

142 a membership of luminaries: Yule, Valerie. *The Book of Spells & Misspells*. Book Guild, 2005, p. 105.

143 "In consideraishon ov yur paiing our checs": Simplified Spelling Society. "Minits of Comiti Meeting held at 44, Great Russell Street, London, W.C.," March 13, 1913.

144 "neer enuf tu acyurasy and consistensy": Simplified Speling Soesiety. *The Pioneer Ov Simplified Speling*, Vol. 1, No. 1. London, Mar. 1912, p. 1.

144 "The Indianz wer enthyuziastic": "Minits of Comiti Meeting held at 44, Great Russell Street, London, W.C.," April, 1913.

144 "I am delieted at [the spelling's] amaizing simplicity": *The Pioneer Ov Simplified Speling*, Vol. 1, No. 1, p. 11.

145 a 1915 letter to Henry Holt: "Carnegie General Donations, Gifts and Grants . . ." dlc.library.columbia.edu/carnegie/cul:vmcvdncmfr.

145 "Words, like women's skirts": "Useless Letters Dropt While We Slept." *South Bend News-Times,* 11 Apr. 1916, p. 6.

146 "answer only to the name Brandr Mathus": "Suggest Changes in Our Spelling." *The Bryan Democrat,* 21 Apr. 1916, p. 3.

147 **"brekfast" menu:** Adirondack Almanac, 2010.

148 **"One of the hardships":** *The Brooklyn Daily Eagle,* 18 Jul. 1923, p. 21.

148 **"Simplified Spelling Leag":** *Spelling,* Vol. 2, No. 5, Mar. 1931, p. 18.

149 **"Adirondak Loj":** "The History of the Adirondak Loj in the High Peaks Area." www.adirondack.net/history/adirondack-loj/.

149 **America's Switzerland:** "Golf at Lake Placid—An American Switzerland." *Golf Illustrated,* 5 Dec. 1902, p. 187.

149 **After a visit to the Lake Placid Club:** Mackin, Tom. *Making Other Plans.* Author House, 2009, p. 97.

Part IV: Washington, D.C., 1962

151 **three crayoned pages:** "Archives Staff Picks: Children's Letters to the President: An Inside Look." The JFK Library Archives, 1 Mar. 2023, jfk.blogs.archives.gov/2023/03/01/archives-staff-picks-childrens-letters-to-the-president/.

151 **summer vacation nine months long:** Dorre, Howard. "Kids' Letters to President Kennedy." *Plodding through the Presidents,* 29 May 2018, www.ploddingthroughthepresidents.com/2018/05/kids-letters-to-president-kennedy.html.

152 **"a subject of vast importance":** Tune, Newell (ed.). *Spelling Reform Anthology.* www.spellingsociety.org/uploaded_books/a2arguments.pdf.

153 **a poor speller himself:** Anderson, Catherine Corley. *John F. Kennedy.* Minneapolis, Lerner Publishing Group, 2004, p. 9.

Chapter 15: Mad Men

156 **the top tennis player in the U.S.:** Cochran, Robert. *Louise Pound: Scholar, Athlete, Feminist Pioneer.* University of Nebraska Press, 2009.

157 **"Kraze for *K*":** Pound, Louise. "The Kraze for 'K.'" *American Speech: A Quarterly of Linguistic Usage.* Oct. 1925, pp. 43–44.

159 **"Fifty-seven years in this business":** Helitzer, Melvin, and Mark Shatz. *Comedy Writing Secrets.* Cincinnati, Ohio, F+W Media, 2016, p. 65.

159 **Charles and George Merriam:** "Are All 'Webster's' Dictionaries Published by Merriam-Webster?" Merriam-Webster. www.merriam-webster.com/help/faq-websters-dictionaries.

160 **The *Coca-Cola Webster's* arrived in 1924:** "1924 Websters Little Gem Dictionary - Compliments of the Coca-Cola Bottling Co | #425033383." WorthPoint, www.worthpoint.com/worthopedia/1924-websters-little-gem-dictionary-425033383.

160 **the *Standard Oil Webster's*:** "The Dictionary Does Not Exist." Word Matters, Episode 29. Merriam-Webster. www.merriam-webster.com/word-matters-podcast/episode-29-the-dictionary.

160 **genericized trademark:** Martin, Peter. *The Dictionary Wars: The American*

Fight Over the English Language. New Jersey, Princeton University Press, 2019, p. 291.

161 **Donald M. Alexander notes:** Alexander, Donald M. "Why Not 'U' for 'You'?" *American Speech*, Vol. 5, No. 1, 1929, pp. 24–26.

161 **The first-person singular:** Wełna, Jerzy. "The Rise of Standard I (< Me Ich): A Contribution to the Study of Functional Change in English." *Studia Anglica Posnaniensia*, vol. 49, no. 3, Apr. 2015, pp. 29–41.

162 **These four letters—"U.P.: up":** Simpson, John. "U.P: Up and Away." www.jjon.org/joyce-s-allusions/up-up.

163 **"the language of advertising may":** Pound, Louise. "Spelling-Manipulation and Present-Day Advertising." *Dialect Notes,* No. 5, 1923, pp. 226–232.

Chapter 16: Cn U Rd Ths?

164 **"I never will need shorthand":** Rankovic, Catherine. *"I Never Will Need Shorthand": Sylvia Plath and Speedwriting.* Plath Profiles, Vol. 11, 2019.

164 **Crafted by Emma Dearborn:** Dearborn, Emma. *Speedwriting, the Natural Shorthand.* Brief English Systems, Inc. 1925.

165 **glamorous full-page color ads:** *Woman's Home Companion,* Vol. 56, 1929, p. 97. *Good Housekeeping,* Vol. 87, July 1928, p. 230.

165 **more than 100,000 students:** Rankovic, *"I Never Will Need Shorthand."*

165 **In preparation for an antarctic expedition:** "Byrd Fetes Scouts Ere Choosing Aide." *Buffalo Evening News,*10 Aug. 1928, p. 6.

166 **Franklin's New Deal:** U.S. Office of Education. *Bulletin,* No. 18, 1936, p. 61.

166 **letters to her mother:** *The Letters of Sylvia Plath: Volume 2: 1956–1963.* HarperCollins, 2018.

167 **"I wanted to dictate my own thrilling letters":** Plath, Sylvia. *The Bell Jar.* Heinemann. 1963.

168 **"There is no literary merit":** "Brief English Systems v. Owen," 48 F.2d 555 (2d Cir. 1931). U.S. Court of Appeals for the Second Circuit. 6 Apr. 1931.

168 **eight people plunged:** "Eight Killed in Falls from N.Y. Windows." *Ottawa Evening Journal*, 30 July 1937.

169 **Robert McCormick:** Simon, Scott. "'America First,' Invoked by Trump, Has a Complicated History." NPR, 23 July 2016, www.npr.org/2016/07/23/487097111/america-first-invoked-by-trump-has-a-complicated-history.

170 **"The response was vehement":** Bennett, James O'Donnell. "Tribune Saner Spelling Draws Praise, Abuse." *Chicago Tribune,* 25 Feb. 1934, p. 1.

172 **along the Arctic Circle:** "From Chicago to Berlin and Back in the 'Untin Bowler.'" *Chicago Tribune,* 30 June 1929, p. 67.

172 **Major League Baseball All-Star Game:** Rumore, Kori and Mather, Marianne. "Vintage Chicago Tribune: We Started Baseball's First All-Star Game—90 Years Ago." *Chicago Tribune*, 6 July 2023, www.chicagotribune.

com/2023/07/06/vintage-chicago-tribune-we-started-baseballs-first-all-star-game-90-years-ago/.

172 **"Briefer Spelling":** "The Briefer Spelling." *Chicago Tribune,* 25 Apr. 1880, p. 20.

172 **an abolitionist and a teetotaler:** Sawyers, June Skinner. *Chicago Portraits.* Illinois, Northwestern University Press, 2012, p. 214.

172 **"millions of English-speaking people in lifelong bondage":** Sides, W. Hampton. "Killer Bees." *The Washington Post,* 29 May 1993.

172 **"lerning tu spel and red":** Ackermann, p. 97.

172 **He named his radio station WGN:** "Robert R. McCormick's Biography." First Division Museum, www.fdmuseum.org/researchers/robert-r-mccormick-biography/.

173 **"a congress of newspapermen":** "Spelling Reform." *Chicago Tribune,* 9 Sep. 1879, p. 3.

173 **became known as the White Sox:** Dickson, Paul. *The New Dickson Baseball Dictionary.* United States, Harcourt Brace & Company, 1999, p. 113.

173 **became the "Red Sox":** Nowlin, Bill. *Boston Red Sox Firsts: The Players, Moments, and Records That Were First in Team History.* United States, Lyons Press, 2023, p. 48.

Chapter 17: Shaw(t)hand

176 **"My specialty is being right":** Shaw, George Bernard. *The Collected Works of George Bernard Shaw: Plays, Novels, Articles, Letters and Essays.* Good Press, 2024.

176 **George Bernard Shaw wrote some 60 plays:** "George Bernard Shaw 1856–1950." Tate Britain. www.tate.org.uk/art/artists/george-bernard-shaw-19472.

176 **Shakespeare only wrote 38:** "Frequently Asked Questions about Shakespeare's Works." Folger Shakespeare Library. www.folger.edu/explore/shakespeares-works/frequently-asked-questions/.

176 **"[It] is entirely senseless":** "Education: Gungs & Boms." *TIME,* 7 Jan. 1946, time.com/archive/6600107/education-gungs-boms/.

177 **"an advertisement of the science of phonetics":** Shaw, George Bernard. *On Language.* Philosophical Library, 1963, p. 39.

177 **Henry Sweet:** Gawne, Lauren. "The Real Phoneticians of My Fair Lady." Superlinguo, 2 May 2016, www.superlinguo.com/post/143705139037/the-real-phoneticians-of-my-fair-lady.

177 **a devout Pitmanite:** Intelligent Education. *Study Guide to Pygmalion by George Bernard Shaw.* Influence Publishers, 2020.

178 **a drizzly Friday morning in 1949:** "March 11, 1949 Weather History in London." Weather Spark. weatherspark.com/h/d/45062/1949/3/11/Historical-Weather-on-Friday-March-11–1949-in-London-United-Kingdom#Figures-Temperature.

178 "I do not think that a Bill of this kind": "Spelling Reform Bill, Volume 462: Debated on Friday 11 March 1949." UK Parliament. hansard. parliament.uk/Commons/1949–03–11/debates/78cbc532-f537–4a1a-b80f-e5946c4b788f/SpellingReformBill.

179 "Churchill, who was reading the *Daily Worker*": Follick, Mont. *The Case for Spelling Reform*. London, Isaac Pitman & Sons, 1965, pp. 249–250.

179 a vote of 84 to 87: "Foreign News: No Ghoti Today." *TIME*, 21 Mar. 1949, time.com/archive/6866901/foreign-news-no-ghoti-today/.

179 "That evening it was the first item": Follick, p. 278.

180 the parliamentary exchanges that unfolded: "Simplified English Spelling, Volume 497: Debated on 6 March 1952." UK Parliament. api. parliament.uk/historic-hansard/commons/1952/mar/06/simplified-english-spelling.

180 the bill passed the Commons: Reed, William. "Spelling and Parliament." *Spelling Progress Bulletin*, 1975, p. 5.

182 a significant portion of his estate: Haas, William. *Alphabets for English*. Manchester University Press, 1969, pp. 34–35.

182 a lengthy court battle: Carney, Edward. *A Survey of English Spelling*. Routledge, 1994, p. 483.

182 "WANTED: A new alphabet": Pitman, I. J. *Star Weekly*, 12 July 1958, p. 29.

183 467 alphabets: Pitman, James and St. John, John. *Alphabets and Reading: The Initial Teaching Alphabet*. New York, Sir Isaac Pitman & Sons, 1969, p. 104.

183 "Shaw's interest in speech": *On Language*, p. 179.

184 "I have in mind the possibility": Philp, Leo. "Shavian (3/3): Typographic Implementation." CAST, 18 Jan. 2022, articles.c-a-s-t.com/shavian-3-3-typographic-implementation-3a43d3bbb8b8.

184 "EVERYONE MAY SOON BE DOING SHAW(T)HAND": *Leicester Evening Mail*, 28 Aug. 1963, p. 4.

185 which sold for £29: Read, Ronald Kingsley. *Sound-writing 1892–1972: George Bernard Shaw and a Modern Alphabet*. University of Reading, 1972.

185 "Doolittle Garamond": "Shavian Alphabet Info—Fonts." Shavian: An Alternative Alphabet for English. www.shavian.info/shavian_fonts/.

Chapter 18: Kool Kidz

186 "'I' before 'C'": Barry, Dave. "Yo! Mr. Language Person!" *The Washington Post*, 27 Jan. 1990.

186 Bar-B-Q: *The Buffalo Daily Republic*, 30 Oct. 1956, p. 3.

186 ToysЯUs: Biron, Bethany, and McDowell, Erin. "Inside the Wild and Tumultuous History of Toys R Us. *Business Insider*, 2 Feb. 2021, www.businessinsider.com/the-tumultuous-history-of-toys-r-us-photos-2020–8.

186 Dunkin' Donuts: Taylor, Kate. "Dunkin' Donuts Convinced the World

to Spell 'Doughnut' All Wrong." *Yahoo News*, 2 June 2017, finance.yahoo. com/news/dunkin-donuts-convinced-america-spell-145804674.html.

186   **trained canines in World War II:** Hutton, Robin. *War Animals: The Unsung Heroes of World War II.* Skyhorse, 2018, p. 32.

187   **Saf-Tee-Belt:** "Auto Centers Push Use of Safety Belts." *Corpus Christi Caller-Times*, 27 Feb. 1961, p. 15.

187   **won't become mandatory:** "Seat Belts | GHSA." Governors Highway Safety Association. www.ghsa.org/issues/seat-belts.

187   **"Live Burlesk":** Globe Theatre, 1482 Broadway, in Times Square, 18 May 1960. www.nydailynews.com/2021/08/23/peep-shows-porn-theaters-and-sex-workers-of-1970s-and-1980s-times-square/.

187   **"Nearly everything I have ever read":** *The Collected Letters of C.S. Lewis, Volume 3*. New York, HarperCollins, 2004, p. 1120.

189   **"Now r is correct":** Chomsky, Carol. "Write First, Read Later." *Childhood Education*, Mar. 1971.

190   **"[Her] spelling is frequently desperate":** Smith, Harriet Elinor (ed.). *Autobiography of Mark Twain, Volume 1*. Lulu Press, 2010, p. 338.

191   **"You can't help respecting anybody":** Milne, A. A. *The House at Pooh Corner*. New York, E. P. Dutton & Co., 1928, p. 75.

193   **"But the immediate thing was the sign":** Bradbury, Ray. *The Golden Apples of the Sun*. New York, Doubleday & Company, 1953, p. 203–215.

193   **Alfred Bester visualizes a twenty-fourth century:** Bester, Alfred. *The Demolished Man*. Shasta Publishers, 1953.

193   **"Isolayshun Ward":** *Doctor Who*. Season 15, Episode 5: "The Invisible Enemy." BBC1, 1 Oct. 1977.

193   **Even *The Simpsons* played on the trope:** Collins, Adrian. "The Newest Couch Gag from the Simpsons Is Their Weirdest Yet." Entertainment. ie, 30 Sept. 2014, entertainment.ie/tv/tv-news/watch-the-newest-couch-gag-from-the-simpsons-is-their-weirdest-yet-217793/.

194   **"Yurs veri sinsjrli":** Smith, David C. (ed.). *The Correspondence of H.G. Wells: Volume 1, 1880–1903*. Routledge, 1998, p. 36.

195   **more than 500 published books:** Rothstein, Mervyn. "Isaac Asimov, Whose Thoughts and Books Traveled the Universe, Is Dead at 72." *New York Times*, 7 Apr. 1992.

195   **"If you don't know in advance":** Asimov, Isaac. "A Question of Spelling." *The Roving Mind*. New York, Prometheus Books, 1983, p. 340.

195   **mistranslated their Cyrillic surname:** Asimov, Isaac. *I, Asimov: A Memoir*. New York, Bantam Books, 1994, p. 521.

195   **"the spelling of the future":** Mencken, p. 406.

Chapter 19: Εεzy Rεεding

197   **"Gwen Stefani has done more":** Birbiglia, Mike. @birbigs. X, 25 May 2014, x.com/birbigs/status/470754960905621505.

198 **one fateful evening in 1958:** Malone, John. "My Fair Language: Do We Need a New Alphabet?" *Chicago Sunday Sun-Times,* 29 May 1960.

198 **For three weeks, television cameras:** Anderson, Kenneth C. "Why Unifon?" Unifon.org. July 2006. www.unifon.org/docs/why-unifon.pdf.

198 **weaving Unifon into its first-grade curriculum:** *Illinois Education,* Vol. 55. Illinois Education Association, 1966.

199 **"Your child will discover":** Ratz, Margaret S. and John Malone. "Presentation to Parents and Teachers." 1960. www.unifon.org/docs/presentation-to-parents-and-teachers.pdf.

199 **"Words in Colour":** Gattegno, Caleb. *Teaching Reading with Words in Color.* New York, Educational Solutions Worldwide Inc., 1967.

199 **notably in dyslexia classrooms:** Stringer, Ronald, et al. "Jacob, a Case Study of Dyslexia in Canada." *International Case Studies of Dyslexia.* Routledge, 2011.

200 **"Initial Teaching Alphabet":** Hall, Jeremy. "The Initial Teaching Alphabet." *Eye Magazine,* 2005, www.eyemagazine.com/feature/article/the-initial-teaching-alphabet.

200 **joined England's Simplified Spelling Soesiety in 1936:** Harrison, Maurice. "A Short Account of Simplified Spelling and the Simplified Spelling Society." *Simplified Spelling Society Pamphlet No. 11.* 1971.

202 **ITA program in 20 select English schools:** Alcantara, Rebecca D., et al. *Technical Writing.* Goodwill Trading Co., Inc., 2003, p. 110.

202 **Queen Elizabeth's five-year-old son:** Tune, Newell W. *Spelling Progress Bulletin,* Volume 6, No. 2. Summer 1966, p. 1.

202 **began touring schools and conferences:** "Conferences, Visits and Meetings 1960–1982." *Pitman Collection: Initial Teaching Alphabet.* University of Bath, 2023, p. 67.

203 **traumatic orthographic memories:** "Anybody Else Taught How to Read Using ITA?" *College Confidential Forums,* 30 Aug. 2013, talk.collegeconfidential.com/t/anybody-else-taught-how-to-read-using-ita-initial-teaching-alphabet/1254234/21?page=2.

Chapter 20: Nothing Compares 2 U

204 **"You should never/write words using numbers":** Yankovic, "Weird Al." "Word Crimes." *Mandatory Fun,* RCA Records, 2014.

204 **The Turtles objected:** Patton, Alli. "Behind the Band Name: The Turtles." *American Songwriter,* June 2023, americansongwriter.com/behind-the-band-name-the-turtles/.

205 *17 consecutive misspelled Top 20 hits:* "Slade." *TeachRock,* teachrock.org/people/slade/.

207 **reminiscent of a writing system known as *logography*:** Crystal, David. "2b or Not 2b: David Crystal on Why Texting Is Good for Language."

The Guardian, 4 July 2008, www.theguardian.com/books/2008/jul/05/saturdayreviewsfeatres.guardianreview.

208 **The beef spanned thirty years:** Ducker, Jesse. "Revisiting K-Solo's Debut Album 'Tell the World My Name' (1990) | Retrospective Tribute." *Albumism*, 20 May 2020, albumism.com/features/k-solo-debut-album-tell-the-world-my-name-turns-30-anniversary-retrospective.

208 **Prince idolized Joni Mitchell:** Coffman, Tim. "Why Joni Mitchell's Office Intercepted Letters from Prince." *Far Out Magazine*, 27 May 2023, faroutmagazine.co.uk/joni-mitchell-office-intercepted-letters-from-prince/.

208 **raised on Cap'n Crunch:** Clerc, Benoît. *Prince: All the Songs: The Story Behind Every Track.* Mitchell Beazley, 2022.

208 **Sly and the Family Stone:** Kielty, Martin. "The Sly Stone and Prince Collaboration That Nearly but Never Was." *Ultimate Classic Rock*, 15 Oct. 2023, ultimateclassicrock.com/sly-stone-prince-collaboration/.

208 **Cap'n Crunch instead of alcohol:** D'Angelo, Chris. "Once upon a Time, Prince Served His Favorite Cereal in Lieu of Booze." *HuffPost*, 30 Apr. 2016, www.huffpost.com/entry/prince-served-capn-crunch-instead-of-cocktails_n_5723de16e4b0f309baf0f707.

208 **"the attention of a 10-year-old":** *New York Magazine*, Vol. 27, No. 45, 14 Nov 1994, p. 18.

209 **"From virt U nev R D V 8":** Bombaugh, Charles (ed.). *Gleanings for the Curious from the Harvest Fields of Literature.* Philadelphia, J.B. Lippincott Company, 1867, p. 69.

209 **"TO THE MEMORY OF MISS ELLEN GEE, OF KEW":** *The New Monthly Magazine.* London, H. Colburn, 1828, p. 360.

210 **Abey Isaacs:** Wells, Carolyn (ed.). *The Book of Humorous Verse.* New York, George H. Doran Company, 1920, p. 788.

210 **Emily Kay:** *The Atheneum; or Spirit of the English Magazines.* Boston, John Cotton, 1828, p. 283.

210 **"He says he loves U 2 X S":** Bombaugh, p. 69.

213 **Six of Prince's eight great-grandparents:** "Did You Know about Prince's Louisiana Roots?" *The Daily Advertiser*, 21 Apr. 2016, www.theadvertiser.com/story/news/local/louisiana/2016/04/21/did-you-know-princes-louisiana-roots/83341568/.

213 **ask Warner Bros. to mail you a floppy disk:** "Prince's Dispute with Warner Brothers Records." *Goldies Parade*, goldiesparade.co.uk/new-power-generation/.

213 **"mauveine measles":** Cummings, Joanna. "Purple's Reign." *The Analytical Scientist*, 25 Jan. 2017, theanalyticalscientist.com/fields-applications/purples-reign.

214 **CD-ROM video game *Interactive*:** Obias, Rudie. "Prince Released an Interactive Video Game in 1994." *Mental Floss*, 25 Apr. 2016, www.mentalfloss.com/article/79007/prince-released-interactive-video-game-1994.

214   "It's cool to get on the computer": Alleyne, Mike, and Kirsty Fairclough. *Prince and Popular Music: Critical Perspectives on an Interdisciplinary Life.* Bloomsbury Publishing USA, 2020, p. 180.

214   appearance on *The Tonight Show*: *The Tonight Show Starring Johnny Carson.* Episode 5405, NBC, 10 Sept. 1985.

216   "computers can be programmed": Rondthaler, Edward. "Opinion: Literacy for All, With a Computer's Help." *The New York Times*, 27 Aug. 1982, p. 22.

216   working software prototype: Radcliffe, Donnie. "A Sound Idea for Barbara Bush's Favorite Cause?" *The Washington Post*, 15 Jan. 1990.

216   "Ministry of Helth": Baker, Andrew. "'Helth' under Whitlam." *The Centre for Independent Studies*, 13 July 2012, www.cis.org.au/commentary/opinion/helth-under-whitlam/.

218   "We mae nowadaes be chairy": Rondthaler, Edward. "SoundSpel." *English Spelling Society.* 1999, p. 7.

218   "jooveniel delinqensy, criem-in-th-streets, hard cor unemployment": Shenker, Israel. "Lurn to Reed Eezy Wae Soundspel." *The New York Times*, 12 July 1977, p. 27.

219   "There seems to be at least one Edward Rondthaler": Berger, Joseph. "Struggling to Put the 'Ortho' Back in Orthography." *The New York Times*, 23 Apr. 1994, p. 30.

220   In 1999, cellphone providers lifted a restriction: "Hppy Bthdy Txt!" BBC News. 3 Dec. 2002. news.bbc.co.uk/2/hi/uk_news/2538083.stm.

220   In 2001, the typical teenager: Grinter, Rebecca, and Margery Eldridge. "y do tngrs luv 2 txt msg?" Proceedings of the Seventh European Conference on Computer Supported Cooperative Work ECSCW '01. Kluwer Academic Publishers, 2001, pp. 219–238.

220   three texts every waking hour: "U.S. Teen Mobile Report Calling Yesterday, Texting Today, Using Apps Tomorrow." *Nielsen*, Oct. 2010, www.nielsen.com/insights/2010/u-s-teen-mobile-report-calling-yesterday-texting-today-using-apps-tomorrow/.

Chapter 21: Txtspk

221   "impossible to stop the progress of language": Burk, Kathleen. *Old World, New World: Great Britain and America from the Beginning.* New York, Grove Press, 2009, p. 285.

221   *Guardian* held a poetry contest: Keegan, Victor. "Hitting the Jackpot." *The Guardian*, 2 May 2001, www.theguardian.com/technology/2001/may/03/internetnews.onlinesupplement3.

222   "You know the internet, right?": McCulloch, Gretchen. *Because Internet: Understanding the New Rules of Language.* New York, Riverhead Books, 2019, p. 64.

222 **five billion people:** Pelchen, Lexie. "Internet Usage Statistics in 2024." *Forbes Home*, 1 Mar. 2024, www.forbes.com/home-improvement/internet/internet-statistics/.

222 **per-message character limit:** Dunne, Danielle. "What Is SMS?" CNN. 27 Sept. 2001, www.cnn.com/2001/TECH/ptech/09/27/sms.catching.on.idg/. Accessed 11 June 2024.

222 **per-message charge:** Foderaro, Lisa W. "Young Cell Users Rack up Debt, a Message at a Time." *The New York Times*, 9 Jan. 2005, www.nytimes.com/2005/01/09/technology/young-cell-users-rack-up-debt-a-message-at-a-time.html. Accessed 11 June 2024.

222 **"Fine writing konsists in gitting":** Billings, Josh. *Josh Billings' Wit and Humor.* London, George Routledge and Sons, 1874, p. 414.

223 **"bleak, bald, sad shorthand":** "Cn U Txt?" *The Guardian*, 11 Nov. 2002, www.theguardian.com/technology/2002/nov/11/rnobilephones2.

223 **"Spoken Latin has picked up":** Schmitt, Norbert. *Language Power: 100 Things You Need to Know to Make Language Work for You.* United States, Wayzgoose Press, 2023.

224 *Emoji* **comes from the Japanese words:** "Emoji & Pictographs." Unicode. unicode.org/faq/emoji_dingbats.html.

224 **1997 by SoftBank:** Ariola, Katrina. "If Shigetaka Kurita Did Not Invent the World's First Emoji, Who Did?" *International Business Times*, 17 July 2020, www.ibtimes.com/world-emoji-day-if-shigetaka-kurita-did-not-create-first-emoji-who-did-3013062.

224 **Inspired by Japanese manga:** Danesi, Marcel. *The Semiotics of Emoji: The Rise of Visual Language in the Age of the Internet.* New York, Bloomsbury Publishing, 2016, p. 2.

224 **the Unicode Standard:** "Emoji Counts, V13.1." Unicode. unicode.org/emoji/charts/emoji-counts.html.

225 **an 1862 Lincoln speech:** Lee, Jennifer 8. "Is That an Emoticon in 1862?" *New York Times.* 19 Jan. 2009, archive.nytimes.com/cityroom.blogs.nytimes.com/2009/01/19/hfo-emoticon/.

225 **a "snigger point":** Bierce, Ambrose. *The Collected Works of Ambrose Bierce.* Vol. 11, New York and Washington, Neale Publishing Company, 1912, p. 387.

225 **the first modern emoticon:** Golijan, Rosa. "29 Years Ago, a Smiley Was Born:-)." NBC News. 19 Sept. 2011, www.nbcnews.com/news/world/29-years-ago-smiley-was-born-flna120616.

226 **an 83-page glossary of textspeak:** Dewey, Caitlin. "The FBI Maintains an 83-Page Glossary of Internet Slang. And It Is Hilariously, Frighteningly out of Touch." *Washington Post*, 17 June 2014, www.washingtonpost.com/news/the-intersect/wp/2014/06/17/the-fbi-maintains-an-83-page-glossary-of-internet-slang-and-it-is-hilariously-frighteningly-out-of-touch/.

227 **"Jargon File":** McCulloch, p. 71.

227 *OMG* **was coined:** Madrigal, Alexis C. "Winston Churchill Was the Recipient of the First OMG." *The Atlantic*, 25 Mar. 2011, www.theatlantic.com/technology/archive/2011/03/winston-churchill-was-the-recipient-of-the-first-omg/73054/.

227 **Textspeak by State:** Kaplan, Jessica. "These Are the Most Uniquely Popular Texting Acronyms in Every State." *Reader's Digest*, 20 Mar. 2023, www.rd.com/article/most-popular-texting-acronyms-every-state/.

228 **"A few remarks concerning the phraseology":** Hotten, John Camden (ed.). *Artemus Ward, His Book.* London, John Camden Hotten, 1865, p. 15.

228 **Hakspek:** Raymond, Eric S. *The New Hacker's Dictionary.* Cambridge and London, MIT Press, 1991, p. 238.

229 **"License Plate Language":** Nuessel, Frank H. "License Plate Language." *American Speech*, vol. 57, no. 4, 1982, pp. 256–59.

229 **"Al languajs chanje in th corse of time":** "Failed Attempts to Reform English Spelling." Merriam-Webster. www.merriam-webster.com/grammar/spelling-suggestions-that-didnt-stick.

229 **"Ever sent a text message":** Wade, Richard L. "Freespeling.com | Wayback Machine." 31 Mar. 2001, web.archive.org/web/20010331213729/www.freespeling.com/.

230 **former editor of the BBC's technology and science program** *Tomorrow's World*: "This Rticl Is Very Ezi to Reed." BBC News. 12 Apr. 2001, news.bbc.co.uk/2/hi/uk_news/1268771.stm.

231 **"I am not a Reformer with a capital R":** Bett, Steve (ed.). "What's Freespeling and the World Vote Really About?" *Journal of the Simplified Spelling Society J30, 2002/1.* www.spellingsociety.org/uploaded_journals/j30-journal.pdf.

232 **"global medium for experimenting":** Yule, Valerie. "The International Costs of English Spelling, and the Comparative Costs of Improvement." OzIdeas. www.valerieyule.com.au/spellcosts.htm.

232 **In a 2013 April Fool's prank:** "Annncng: Twttr." *Blog.x.com*, 1 Apr. 2013, blog.x.com/en_us/a/2013/annncng-twttr.

Index

Index page references in italics refer to graphics.

Adventures of Huckleberry Finn (Twain), 65
advertising industry/simplified spelling
    example/on drive (1960s), 186–87
    K use, 95–96, 157–59, *158*, 164, 219
    marketing to children, 191–92
    mass media/examples (1920s), 155–58, *156*, *158*, 160, 162–63, 219–20
    Pound on, 155, 156–57, 159, 163, 164
    U use, 160–61, 164, 186
Aesop's Fables, 27–28, *28*
Alexander, Donald M., 161
Alford, Henry, 51
Alvin Ailey Dance Theater, 93n
American Dictionary of the English Language, An (Webster)
    brands/coauthored dictionaries and, 159–60, 160n
    Merriams/copyright and, 159
    Webster status and, 49, 52
    See also Webster, Noah/American dictionary
American English
    development, 31
    England's response, 31, 32–33, 48, 51
    identity/pride, 33
    Jefferson's using *belittle*, 32
    non-Anglo language proposals, 39
    push back against British, 36, 39, 40
    See also specific individuals
Americanisms/examples, 31, 32–33, 48, 49
American Library Association (ALA), 102, 112
American Metric Bureau, 104
American Philosophical Society, 45–46
American Revolution/Independence, 37, 38, 39
American Speech (Alexander), 161
American Spelling Book, The/Blue-Backed Speller (Webster), 38, 38n, 39
America's first World Fair/Centennial Exposition (1876), 97

Anderson, Marian, 93n
Andrew, Prince, 202
Andrews, Julie, 183
Andrews, Stephen Pearl
    abolition and, 90–91
    free love and, 88–90
    Pitman and, 91
    simplified spelling and, 88, 91
    See also New York Free Love League/The Club
Androcles and the Lion, 184, 185
Angles, 14
Anglo-Norse dialect, 15–16
Anglo-Sacsun, 88, 91
Anglo-Saxons in England/language consequences, 14–15
AOL/Instant Messenger, 220
Aristotle, 30
Asimov, Isaac
    background, 195
    spelling reform, 196
Augustine, St., 14
Australian government/simplified spelling, 216n

Barry, Dave, 11, 186
Barton, Michael
    Lord's Prayer, *53*
    simplified spelling, 53
baseball
    Chicago teams/name shortenings, 173, *173*, 173n
    first All-Star Game, 172
Because Internet (McCulloch), 222
bees
    Butler and, 29–31, 29n, *30*, 31n
    Feminin' Monarķi', Đe/Histori of Bee's, Đe (Butler), 29–31, 29n, *30*, 31n
Belknap, Jeremy, 43
Bell, Alexander Graham, 97
Bendix Corporation, 197–98
Beniowski, Bartomiej
    background/personality traits, 55–56
    on English language absurdity, 56, *57*, 58

Lord's Prayer versions, *56, 60*
spelling reform/ "Anti-Absurd
    Alphabet," 56, 58–60, *59*
Bester, Alfred, 193
Bibles/medieval scribes, 12n
Bierce, Ambrose, 225
Biggs Weekly Argus, 120
Billboard, 205
Billings, Josh
    "affurisms," *66*
    "Farmer's Allminax" of, 64, *64*
    Phunny Phellows and, 63–65
    simplifying communication and,
        222–23
    success and, 63–64
binomial nomenclature, 34
Birbiglia, Mike, 197
Bloomer dress, 84
*Blue-Backed Speller/American Spelling
    Book, The* (Webster), 38, 38n, 39
Bolden, Marie
    background, 130
    first national spelling bee and,
        130–31, 132, 142
    photo, *132*
Bombaugh, Charles, 210–11
Booke at large (Bullokar), 27, *27*
Boston Daily Times, 66–68
Boston Red Sox, 173
Bradbury, Ray, 192
Brewer, David, 115
British Journal of Psychology, xii
British Museum, 182
Brooklyn Daily Eagle, 148
Bryson, Bill, 82, 170, 171
Bullokar, William
    Aesop's Fables and, 27–28, *28*
    spelling reform, 27–28
    subtitling and, 27, *27*
Burnz, Eliza
    businesses, 85, 99
    counterculture movements and,
        88, 91
    Dianism and, 88
    Foneta (daughter), 84
    given name/background, 84–85
    as mother of women stenographers,
        84, 99
    Pitman shorthand/phonetic spelling
        and, 84, 85, 86
    slavery/former slaves and, 91
    spelling reform convention/SRA,
        99, 101, 108

women's rights and, 84, 85–86
Burnz School of Shorthand, 85, 99
Butler, Charls
    bees and, 29–31, 29n, *30,* 31n
    spelling reform, 29–31, 31n
Butler, Nicholas, 115
Byrd, Richard E./crew, 165–66

Caesar, Julius, 14, 22
Cap'n Crunch cereal, 208, 208n
Carnegie, Andrew
    death, 146
    Dewey and, 111
    philanthropy of, 111
    Simplified Spelling Society
        (Simplified Speling Soesiety),
        England and, 142
Carnegie, Andrew/simplified spelling
    as advocate, 111, 112–17, 133, 156
    Columbia University and, 117
    press mocking of, 112–14, 116
    Roosevelt harming, 123, 141
    support for, 115, 116–17
    See also Simplified Spelling Board
        (Carnegie)
Carroll, Lewis, 109, 209n, 211–12
Carson, Johnny, 214
Caxton, William
    depiction, *21*
    printing press/language
        standardization and, 18–21
    Wynkyn and, 20–21
Celtic language
    description, 13
    Romans and, 13, 14
Celts, 13, 14
Centennial Exposition/America's first
    World Fair (1876), 97
Chastellux, Marquis de, 39
Chattanooga Daily Times, 115
Cheke, John
    Latin letters/words and, 23, 24–25,
        26
    spelling reform and, 22–23, 24–25,
        26
    treason charge and, 25
    as tutor, 22, 23
Chesterton, G. K., 181
Chicago Times-Herald, 107
Chicago Tribune, 94, 173
Chicago Tribune/Briefer Spelling, 172–73
Chicago Tribune/"Saner Spelling"
    descriptions, 169, 170–72

responses, 170, *171*, 174
reversing, 174–75
See also McCormick, Robert
Childhood Education (Carol Chomsky),
    188–89
Chomsky, Carol/inventive spelling,
    188–89, 190
Chomsky, Harry/spelling, 189
Chomsky, Noam, 190
Chronicles of Narnia, The (Lewis), 187
Churchill, Winston
    background, 178
    OMG and, 227n
    spelling reform and, 178–79
Church of Jesus Christ of Latter-day
    Saints/Mormon Church
    Deseret News, 72–73, 74, 76
    leader of, 71
    Union Pacific railroad and, 77
    war/Utah War and, 76–77, 77n
    western settlement/background,
        70, 75
    See also Deseret Alphabet; *specific
        individuals*
Cicero, 82n
Cincinnati Enquirer, 131
Civil War (US), 83, 91, 93n
Clarke, S. H., 130, 131
classification during Enlightenment, 34
Claudius, Emperor, 14
Club, The. *See* New York Free Love
    League/The Club
College Confidential, 203
Collier's Weekly, 121, 122
Columbia University, 117
Coolidge, Calvin, 2
countercultural movements
    crank term and, *85*
    names of organizations/parodies of
        names, *85*
    simplified spelling movement and,
        79
    See also specific individuals/movements
Creek Indians, Florida, 100
Critical Pronouncing Dictionary (Walker),
    80
Crystal, David, 23, 52
Current Shorthand, 177
cyber slang. *See* textspeak

Daily News, 173
Daily Picayune, 133
Daily Worker, 179

Darwin, Charles
    On the Origin of Species, 99
    spelling reform/convention and
        SRA, 99, 104, 106, 107–8
Darwin, Charles Galton, 142
Dearborn, Emma
    depression/death, 168
    Great Depression and, 168
    position, 164
    Speedwriting and, 164, 165–67,
        168
Delaney, Rob, 232–33
Demolished Man, The (Bester), 193
Deseret Alphabet
    descriptions/examples, *73*, 76
    finances and, 76–77
    Mormon benefits and, 74–75,
        76–77
    People's Party of Utah campaign
        ticket and, 78, *78*
    using/fall of, 75–76, 77
    Watt and, 72, 72n, *75*, 76, 78
    Young and, 70–72, 74–75
Deseret First Book, 74
Detroit News, 124
Dewey, Melvil(le)
    anti-Semitism of, 112
    background, 102–3
    Carnegie and, 111, 115
    death, 149
    description/traits, 102, 111–12
    Lake Placid Club/simplified
        spelling, 146–49
    letter to Amherst, *103*
    libraries and, 102, 102n, 111–12
    number ten and, *104*
    simplified spelling and, 102–3, 111,
        112, 146–49, 156
    SRA and, 102, 108
    womanizing, 111–12
Dewey Decimal System, 102
de Worde, Wynkyn
    Caxton and, 20–21
    depiction, *21*
    Flemish and, 20, 20n
dialect writing vs. simplified spelling
    humor, 65
*Diana: A Psycho-Fyziological Essay on
    Sexual Relations, for Married Men and
    Women* (Parkhurst), 88
Diana, goddess of chastity, 88
Dianism, 88
Dickens, Charles, 82n

dictionaries
    age of dictionaries, 52, 52n
    first American dictionary, 47–48
    See also specific dictionaries/individuals
Dictionary of the English Language, A
    (Johnson), 35–36
*Dissertations with A Collection of Essays
    and Fugitiv Writings* (Webster), 44, 48
Dissertations on the English Language
    (Webster), 43–44, 48
Doctor Who, 193, 193n
Doolittle Garamond font, 185
Dorsey, Jack, 233
doubt origins/evolution, 23–24
Douglas, Stephen, 61
Dubois, Silvia, 94–95, 95, 95n
Dunlap, William, 41

Early Modern English, 21
Easton, Warren, 131
Educational Review, The, 106–7
Edward IV, King, 21
Edward VI, King, 22, 23
Elgin Review, 127
Elizabeth I, Queen, 23, 26n, 30n
Elizabeth II, Queen, 202
Ellington, Duke, 93n
Ellis, Alexander J./spelling absurdity, 71
Emancipation Proclamation, 62
emoji, 224, 224n
emoticons, 224–26
English language
    class and, 16
    regional differences, 15n, 16–17,
        17n
    See also specific individuals/groups
English language/spelling
    difficulties (summary), xi, xii–xiii
    history, 13–21
    reform/reformers and (summary),
        xi–xii, xiii–xv, *xiv*
    as social gatekeeping, 94
English Spelling Society/activities,
    231–32, 231n
Enlightenment, 34
Esperanto, 53n

Fahlman, Scott, 225–26
FBI textspeak glossary, 226
feminine monarchy, 29–31, 29n, 30, 30n
Feminin' Monarki', Đe/Histori of Bee's, Đe
    (Butler), 29–31, 29n, 30, 31n
flexible spelling. *See* inventive spelling

Follick, Montefiore
    background/Shaw and, 178
    Spelling Reform Bill/spelling reform
        and, 178–80, *179,* 182, 200
Forgotten Founding Father, The
    (Kendall), 40
Franklin, Benjamin
    abandoning ideas for spelling
        reform, 36–37
    American Philosophical Society,
        45–46
    inventions, 7, 37
    simplified spelling/method, 2, 5–6,
        6, 11
    spelling reform correspondence,
        7–10, 8n, 9n, 36
    Webster and, 37–38, 40
free divorce, 89
free love, 88–90
freespeling.com, 230
free spelling. *See* inventive spelling
Frisians, 14
Fugitive Slave Act (1850), 61–62

Gage, Lyman J., 115
Gallagher/scoreboard flipper, 214–15,
    215n
Gattegno, Caleb, 199
Gazette of the United States, 48
genericized trademark meaning, 160
Gil, Alexander (Gil the Elder)
    language passion, 28–29
    personality traits, 28–29
    St. Paul's School, London and, 28
Godbe, William S., 77
Godbeites, 77
Good Housekeeping, 165
*Grammatical Institute of the English
    Language, A* (Webster), 38
Great Chicago Fire (1871), 172
Great Depression, 168–69
    See also specific individuals
Great Vowel Shift/pronunciations, 17–18,
    18n
Gregg shorthand, 82n, 167
Grey, Jane, Lady, 25, 30n
Grimké, Angelina, 94
Grimké, Thomas, 94
Guardian, 221
Gurney, Thomas, 82n
Gurney shorthand, 82n
Gutenberg, Johannes, 18

Hacker's Dictionary, The, 227–28
hakspek, 228–29
Haldeman, Samuel, 99, 99n, 101
Hare, Julius, Archdeacon of Lewes, 51
Harris, William T., 115
Hart, John
    books/Lord's Prayer, 26, *26*
    simplifying spelling/method, 25–26,
        26, 26n
Hasse, Adelaide, 111
Hazard, Ebenezer, 43
Hepburn, Audrey, 185
Histori of Bee's, Ðe/Feminin' Monarķi', Ðe
    (Butler), 29–31, 29n, 30, 31n
history of English spelling, 13–21
Holt, Henry, 115, 145
Howells, William Dean, 108
Hughes, Emrys, 190
Hughes, Hetty, 221

Initial Teaching Alphabet (ITA)
    descriptions, 201–2, *201*
    Ladybird publisher/children's books
        and, 201–2
    origins, 182, 200
    users unlearning and, 202–3
Intelligence, The, 106–7
International Convention for the
    Amendment of English Orthografy
    Anglo-American alphabet/rules,
        100–101
    description/location, 97
    goal, 97–98
    participants, 99, 100, 101
    patience and, 99–100
    proceedings, 100–101
    See also Spelling Reform Association
        (SRA)
International Phonetic Alphabet (IPA),
    26n
inventive spelling
    backlash against, 189–90
    Carol Chomsky and, 188–89, 190
    childhood learning theory and,
        188–90
    descriptions, 119, 135, 187, 188,
        188
    Lewis and, 187, 188
    Twain and, 135, 190–91
Iola Daily Record, 111
I origins/evolution, 161

James, William, 115
Jargon File, 227
Jefferson, Thomas, 32
Jespersen, Otto, 18n, 28
Johnson, Samuel
    background/language and, 33
    compulsion/counting, 47
    feelings toward Americans/American
        English, 32, 33, *33*, 48
    Tourette's syndrome and, 36n
Johnson, Samuel/dictionary
    definitions in, *35*
    descriptions, 36, 49
    spellings in, 34–35, 38
    writing, 33–36
Johnson, Samuel, Jr., 47–48
Jones, Daniel, 144
Jordan, David, 115
Joyce, James, 182
Jungle, The (Sinclair), 151, 152
Jutes, 14

kanji, 224
Kansas City Star, 113
Kendall, Joshua, 40
Kennedy, John F.
    Sinclair letter to, 151–53
    unsolicited political advice
        examples, 151–53
klan/Ku Klux Klan
    descriptions/origins, 96
    K sounds, 96, 159n
klan origins, 96
Krapp, George Philip, 195–96
Ku Klux Klan. *See* klan/Ku Klux Klan
K use/sounds
    advertising industry, 95–96,
        157–59, *158*, 164, 219
    as funny, 158–59

Lake Placid Club
    Anglic orthography, *148*
    descriptions, 147, 148, 149
    Dewey and, 146–49
    menus, *147*, 148, 149
    simplified spelling, 146–49
    Winter Olympics, 149
Larison, Cornelius, 94–95, 95, 95n
Latin
    Cheke and, 23, 24–25, *26*
    language/falling standards, 14, *223*
Leicester Evening Mail, 184

Lewis, C. S., 187, 188
lexicographers
    compulsive trait and, 47
    definition, 47
    See also specific individuals
Lexington Herald, 113
Lias, Edward, 216, 217, 218
"License Plate Language", 229, 229
Lincoln, Abraham
    elections and, 61
    Pikard letter to, 61, 62, 62n
    transcript of speech/emoticon and,
        224–25
    Ward and, 61, 62
Lincoln Journal Star, 113
Lindsley, David, 99, 101
Linnaeus, Carl
    cataloging plants (binomial
        nomenclature), 34
    Species Plantarum, 34, 34n
Linstead, Stephen, 231, 232
Little, Feramorz, 77–78, 77n, 78
logography
    definition, 207
    kanji and, 224
    pictographs vs., 211n
London Review of Books, 218
London Times, 17
Lord's Prayer
    Barton, *53*
    Beniowski, *56, 60*
    Hart, 26, *26*
    Thibaudin, *55*

McCormick, Joseph Medill, 173
McCormick, Robert
    background, 169
    *Chicago Tribune/*innovations and,
        172
    death and *Chicago Tribune* "Saner
        Spelling," 174–75
    description/traits, 169–70, 172
    radio station and, 172, 172n
    "Saner Spelling" biases/arbitrary
        rationale, 170, 171
    "Saner Spelling"/*Chicago Tribune*
        and, 169, 170–72, 173
    See also Chicago Tribune/"Saner
        Spelling"
McCulloch, Gretchen, 222
Malone, John, 197–98
Mansfield News, 127–28
March, Francis, 101

Mary I, Queen, 25
Matthews, Brander
    background, 115
    Carnegie funding and, 141, 146
    Roosevelt and, 117
    Simplified Spelling Board, 115, 117,
        141, 146
Maud Slater's Shorthand and Typing
    School, Scotland, 83–84
MC Hammer, 205, 211, 220
Meat Inspection Act, 152
medieval scribes/Bibles, 12n
Medill, Joseph
    as Chicago Mayor, 172
    Chicago Tribune/"Briefer Spelling,"
        172–73, *173*
    death, 173
    grandchildren of, 173
    racial equality, 94, 172
    simplified spelling, 94, 172–73, *173*
memory athletes, 55
Methode, A (Hart), 26, *26*
Methodism, 47
Middle English, 15, 16–17
Milne, A. A., 191
Milton, John, 28
Minneapolis Journal, 120, 122
Mitchell, Joni, 208
Mormon Church. *See* Church of Jesus
    Christ of Latter-day Saints/Mormon
    Church
Mother Tongue, The, 170
musical notation, 81, 81
My Fair Lady (film), 176, 185
My Fair Lady (play), 183, 198

Nabokov, Vladimir, 162
Nasby, Petroleum Vesuvius, 63, 64–65,
    69
    See also Phunny Phellows
National Education Association (NEA)
    SRA and, 106–7, 108
    union and, 106n
National Gallery of Ireland, 182
NEA. *See* National Education Association
    (NEA)
Nelson, Rogers. *See* Prince
New Monthly Magazine, The, 209–10
newspapers
    misspellings/abbreviations (1830s),
        66–68
    spelling norms and, 68
    See also specific newspapers

New-York Daily Times, The, 89
New York Free Love League/The Club
    abolition and, 90–91
    descriptions, 89–90
    social reform and, 90–91
    See also Andrews, Stephen Pearl
New York Globe, 122, 124
New York Philological Society/Friendly
    Club, 40–42
New York Times, 115, 119, 216, 219
1960s
    descriptions, 187, 190
    drive/simplified spelling examples,
        186–87
    inventive spelling, 187–91, *188*
    spelling and, 186–87
Norman-French dialect, 16
Nuessel, Frank H., Jr., 229

obsessive-compulsive disorder, 47n
O'Connor, Sinéad, 205, 207, 211
Oil! (Sinclair), 151
OK origins/use, 66–68
Old English (Anglo-Saxon), 15, 16
OMG (textspeak), 226, 227, 227n
On the Origin of Species (Darwin), 99
Ormin
    background/position, 11
    Middle English, 15
    name meaning, 11
    spelling/modifications and, xiii,
        11–12, 17, 218, 233
"ormography," 12
Ormulum (Ormin), 12
Oskaloosa Herald, 132
Oxford English Dictionary (OED), 226

Paine, Henry G., 108
Palencsar, Professor, xiii
Parkhurst, Henry M., 88
Patterson, Eleanor Medill, 173
Patterson, Joseph Medill, 173
Patterson, Robert Wilson, 173
Philadelphia Item, 121, 122
Philadelphia Press, 123, 123n
phonetic spelling
    Old English and, 15
    See also Phunny Phellows; simplified
        spelling/movements
Phrenological Journal, 84
"phrenotypics," 55
Phunny Phellows
    backgrounds, 68

"performing" and, 68
    simplified spelling movement and,
        69
    those included/descriptions, 64–65
    See also specific individuals
Pickering, Timothy, 44
pictographs
    definition, 211
    logographs vs., 211n
    pictorial simplification overview,
        223–26
Pikard, A. B., 61, 62, 62n
Pitman, Benjamin, 83
Pitman, Isaac
    Andrews and, 91
    brothers of, *83*
    Burnz and, 84, 85, 86
    childhood/background, 80–81
    descriptions/countercultural
        movements, 79–80, 88, 91
    music and, 81
    Sound-hand, 81–82, *82*
    spelling reform/simplified writing
        system, 79–80, 80n, 200–201
Pitman, Jacob, 83
Pitman, James
    background/activities, 202
    ITA and, 201–2
    My Fair Lady and, 183
    Read/"Shar Typewriter," 184
    "Shaw Alphabet" and, 182–85, *184*
    simplified spelling and, 182–85,
        183, 200–201
Pitman shorthand
    descriptions/use, 82–83, *82*, 82n,
        91–92
    as "Railroad Writing," 86–87
    Speedwriting comparisons, 167
    stenographers and, 83
    Sweet and, 177, 177n
    Twain and, 136–37
Pittsburgh Post-Gazette, 128
Plain Dealer, 122
Plath, Sylvia
    depression, 168
    on sound-hand, 82
    Speedwriting/book, 164, 166–68
Plea for Phonotypy and Phonography
    (Ellis), 71
pop stars and spelling/misspellings
    background/as children, 204–5
    communication simplification/speed
        and, 220

examples, 204, 204n, 205–7, 205n, 208n
rap rivalry, 208n
selling records and, 204
See also Prince
Popular Science Monthly, 165
Pound, Louise
on advertising industry/simplified spelling and, 155, 156–57, 158, 159, 163, 164
on Ku Klux Klan, 159n
position/sports, 155, 156
Prince
ancestors/slavery, 213
fashion, 213, 213n
Joni Mitchell and, 208
minimalism/simplified spelling, 206–7, 208–9, 211, 213, 220, 233
name changes, 204, 206, 213–14
pictorial simplification, 211, 213–14, 223
printing press
beginnings, 18
England, 18–20
Germany/Gutenberg, 18
Pursey, Harry, 180
Pygmalion (play/Shaw), 176, 177

Read, Ronald Kingsley
"Shaw Alphabet" and, 183
"Shaw Typewriter," 184
rebus poetry, xiv, 209–11
Richmond Times-Dispatch, 185
Robertson, William S., 100
Rochester Post Express, 127
Roget, Peter Mark, 47
Romans
England and, 14
Latin language/falling standards, 14, *223*
Rondthaler, Edward
computers/software and, 216, *217,* 218–19
scoreboard flipper and, 215, 215n
simplified spelling and, 215–16, *217,* 218–19
Roosevelt, Edith, 119n
Roosevelt, Franklin Delano
New Deal, 166
Speedwriting and, 166
Roosevelt, Theodore
description/traits, 117, 119

Gridiron Dinner, 109–10, 123
harming simplified spelling movement, 123, 141
Jungle, The and, 152
leaving office, 125
Loeb (stenographer) and, 117
mocking simplified spelling of, 109–10, 119–20, *120–22,* 123, 124, *124,* 125
simplified spelling and, 109–10, 117–19, 128–29, 155, 156–57
Roosevelt, Theodore, Jr., 166
Royal Academy of Dramatic Art, 182
Ruggles, James/"Universal Language," 53

Sanborn, Irving, 173
Saner Spelling. *See Chicago Tribune*/"Saner Spelling," McCormick, Robert
Saxons, 14
Scandinavian words/English language, 15–16
"Scheme for a New Alphabet and Reformed Mode of Spelling, A" (Franklin), 7, 11
science fiction
simplified spelling and, 192–96
See also specific examples
scissors, 71
scoreboard flipper use, 214–15, 215n
Scripps National Spelling Bee
description, 1–3
first winner, 2
gladiolus and, 2
simplified spelling protestors, 2–3
Seymour, May, 111
Shakespeare, William, xiii
Shaw, George Bernard
death/estate, 182–85
description/traits, 176
Isacc Pitman and, 177
play writing, 176–77
simplified spelling/legacy and, 22, 65, 142, 176–78, 181, 182–85, *183,* 215, 231
spelling of *bomb* and, 176
"Shaw Alphabet"
competition and, 182–83
descriptions, *183,* 184, *184*
uses, 183–84, *183*
Shaw Typewriter, 184–85, 185
shorthand
comparisons to Speedwriting, 167

examples, 82n, 99
ideology, 86–87
See also specific shorthands
Short Message service (SMS), 222
See also textspeak
Silvia Dubois (Now 116 Yers Old): A Biografy of the Slav who Whipt Her Mistres and Gand Her Fredom (Larison), 94–95, 95, 95n
Simon, Neil, 158–59
Simplified Spelling Board (Carnegie)
   beginnings, 112
   Carnegie rules and, 115–16, 116n, 123
   Carnegie's impatience with/funding and, 141, 145, 146
   Dewey and, 115
   end, 146
   members, 114, 115
   motto, 164
   pledges, 116–17
   Pound on, 156
   recommendations/respellings, 116
   revamping and, 146–47
   Theodore Roosevelt, 117
   Twain, 112, 114, 137, 138–40
simplified spelling/movements
   abolitionist alliance, 91–95
   fragmentation/factions and, 97, 98
   Latinizing/mistakes and, 23–24
   making fun of/humor and, 63
   other countercultural movements and, 79, 88
   reformer arc, 10
   regional accents and, 199–200, 199n
   successes (1800s), 98
   today, 2, 229–31, 233
   See also Phunny Phellows; specific individuals/organizations
Simplified Spelling Society (Simplified Speling Soesiety), England
   access to empire and, 144–45
   banks/checks and, 143
   benefits, *144*
   Carnegie and, 142
   comparisons to simplified Spelling Board (Carnegie), 142, 143
   as English Spelling Society/activities, 231–32, 231n
   formation/members, 142, 194, 200, 215, 231
   new spellings and, 143–44

Pioneer ov Simplified Speling, 141, 142–43, *143*
Simpsons, The, 193–94
Sinclair, Upton
   as muckraker, 151–52
   simplified spelling/Kennedy and, 151–53
   See also specific works
Sippey, Michael, 233
slavery/former slaves
   literacy/education and, 91–95, 93n
   voter suppression, 93
   See also specific individuals/groups
Sly and the Family Stone, 206, 208
sneeze origins/evolution, 21
Sokolowski, Peter, 34
"Something New," 53
Sound-hand, 81–82, 82
Sound Speler software, 218–19
"Sound of Thunder, A," 192–93
Species Plantarum (Linnaeus), 34, 34n
Speedwriting
   advertising of, 165, 167, *167*
   copycats, 168
   Dearborn and, 164, 165–67, 168
   descriptions, 164–65, *165*, 167–68
   Great Depression and, 168
   Plath and, 164, 166–68
   users, 164, 165–68
spelling bees
   bee origins, 74n
   early contests descriptions, 126–27
   Follick on, *179*
   locations and, xi, *179*
   modern format, 132n
   Scripps National Spelling Bee, 1–3
spelling bees, first national
   descriptions, 129–32
   location/date, 126, 127
   officiant/issues, 130, 131
   racism and, 130–31
   simplified spelling and, 126, 127–29, *127*
   team/individual winners, 132
   teams defeated excuses, 133
Spelling Reform Association (SRA)
   American/Britain offices, 104, 106
   communications/bulletins, 102, *105*
   finances and, 107–8, 111
   name versions, 104
   NEA endorsement and, 106–7
   NEA funding/debate and, 107–8
   rules/revisions, 101, 103

See also International Convention for the Amendment of English Orthografy; *specific individuals*
"Spell My Name with an S" (Asimov), 196
Sprague, Charles E., 115, 116n
"Star, The" (Wells), 194
Star Weekly, 182
Stefani, Gwen, 197
Stenographic Sound-Hand (Pitman), 81
stenography
    male to female change, 83
    Pitman shorthand and, 83
    suffragists and, 83–84
Stevenson, Mary ("Polly")
    depiction, *9*
    Franklin/spelling reform correspondence, 7–10, 8n, 9n, 36
Stillings, Charles, 118–19
suffragists, 83–84
    See also specific individuals
Sun, London, 119
Sun, The, 125
Sunshine Boys, The (Simon), 158–59
Swedenborg, Emanuel, 79n
Swedenborgian mysticism, 79, 79n
Sweet, Henry, 177, 177n

techspeak *See* textspeak
temperance meaning, 80
Tennyson, Alfred, Lord, 104, 106, 107, 108
text messages
    popularity, 220
    See also textspeak
textspeak
    abbreviations/acronyms, 222, 226–27
    alphanumeric simplification, 228–29
    beginnings/development, 220, 222
    criticism, 223
    descriptions, 222–23, 233
    English Spelling Society and, 231–32
    glossaries/dictionaries, 226–28
    Guardian poetry contest/winner, 221
    OMG, 226, 227, 227n
    phonetic simplification, 229
    TL;DR, 226, 226n
    use by location, *227*
    See also specific components

There Will Be Blood, 151
Thibaudin, Auguste
    Lord's Prayer, *55*
    simplified spelling, xiii, 54–55, *54*, 233
Thompson, Slosson, 107–8
Thornton, William
    background, 45n
    spelling reform/methods, 45–46, *46*
Thursby, Mae, 132
Time Machine, The (Wells), 194
Tiro, Marcus Tullius, 82n
Tironian shorthand, 82n
Tonight Show, The, 214
Tourette's syndrome, 36n
Towe, Joseph B.
    background, 93
    music and, 93, 93n
    simplified spelling/educating former slaves, 93–94
    spelling reform convention, 100
    training wheel alphabets use description, 197
    See also specific types
Trumbull, James Hammond, 97, 98
Twain, Mark
    Associated Press dinner and, 114
    death, 140
    description/traits, 135
    drunken use, 137
    Olivia's spelling (wife), 135
    Phunny Phellows and, 65
    Pitman shorthand and, 136–37
    seven cents per word payment/consequences, 135–36
    Simplified Spelling Board (Carnegie), 112, 114, 137, 138–40
    simplified spelling justifications, 114, 134, 136–37
    speech at Hartford spelling bee, 134
    spelling/wavering and, 65, 114, 125, 134, 136–37, 156, 190–91
    story on hieroglyphics-Phoenician alphabet, 138–40
    Suzy's spelling (daughter), 190–91
Twitter (X)
    April Fool's prank (2013), 232–33
    brevity and, 232

Ulysses (Joyce), 162
Unicode Standard, 224
Unifon
    beginnings, 197–98

description, 197, 198–99
United States Telegraph, 51
"Universal Language" proposals, 53, 53n
University of Deseret/University of Utah, 74
Upward, Christopher, 229

Vaile, Edwin, 107–8
Vikings
    French influence/English language, 16
    from Denmark/English language consequences, 15–16, 17n
    Normans/English language consequences, 16–17, 17n
Visigoths, 14

Wade, Richard L., 229–31
Walker, John, 89
Ward, Artemus
    Lincoln and, 61, 62
    logographic style/disclaimer and, 228
    See also Phunny Phellows
War of the Worlds, The (Wells), 194
Washington, Booker T., 132–33
Washington, George, 39, 45n
Washington Times, 119
Washington Times-Herald, 173
Watt, George
    as first English convert/Mormon, 75
    Godbeites/Mormon excommunication, 77
    spelling/Deseret alphabet, 70, 72, 72n, 75, 76, 78
Webster, Noah
    American national language, 37, 39–41, 98
    background, 38
    backlash/criticism of spelling reform, 43–44, 45, 46
    description/traits, 37, 40, 41, 45
    "Essay on a Reformed Mode of Spelling," 42, 43, 47, 47n
    Franklin and, 37–38, 40
    New York Philological Society, 40–41
    on progress of language, 221
    spelling reform/writings, 37–38, 39–41, 42–44, 215, 229, 233
Webster, Noah/American dictionary
    abridged edition, 49n
    announcement/expectations, 47–48

descriptions, 49–50
mocking of, 48–49
plagiarism of, 52n
publishing, 49, 49n
reception/use, 49, 51, 103
revisions/new edition, 51–52
spelling simplifications in, xiv, 48, 50–51, 50, 51n
Webster's Dictionary. See American Dictionary of the English Language, An (Webster)
Wells, H. G.
    London's Simplified Speling Soesity, 142, 194
    simplified spelling and, 142, 194, 231
Wesley, John, 47
Winter Olympics (1932), 149
Wister, Owen, 126
Woman's Home Companion, 165
Woodville, Elizabeth, Queen, 21
Woodworth, Florence, 111
Worcester, Joseph, 52n
Worcester Evening Gazette, The, 119
Words in Colour, 199–200, 199n
Works Progress Administration, 166
World Anti-Slavery Convention, London, 90–91
World Memory Championships, 55, 60

Yellow Journalism, 113
Young, Brigham
    Deseret Alphabet and, 70–72, 74–75
    Deseret territory/symbolism, 73–74
    English language/spellings and, 70–72
    Mormons and, 70–71, 73–74
    the West/Salt Lake Valley, 70
    wives/children and, 71, 71n

Zamenhoff, L.L.
    Esperanto, 53n
    "Universal Language," 53n
Zorn, Eric, 174

Gabe Henry is the author of three books, including the poetry anthology *Eating Salad Drunk*, a humor collaboration with Jerry Seinfeld, Bob Odenkirk, Margaret Cho, Mike Birbiglia, Janeane Garofalo, Roy Wood Jr., and other titans of comedy. He has spent more than a decade exploring the strange and forgotten history of simplified spelling, which, by his own admission, has only made him a worse speller. He lives in New York.